TECH TALLY

APPROACHES TO
ASSESSING
TECHNOLOGICAL
LITERACY

Committee on Assessing Technological Literacy

Elsa Garmire and Greg Pearson, Editors

NATIONAL ACADEMY OF ENGINEERING *AND*
NATIONAL RESEARCH COUNCIL
OF THE NATIONAL ACADEMIES

THE NATIONAL ACADEMIES PRESS
Washington, D.C.
www.nap.edu

NATIONAL ACADEMIES PRESS • **500 Fifth Street, N.W.** • **Washington, DC 20001**

NOTICE: The project that is the subject of this report was approved by the Governing Board of the National Research Council, whose members are drawn from the councils of the National Academy of Sciences, the National Academy of Engineering, and the Institute of Medicine. The members of the committee responsible for the report were chosen for their special competences and with regard for appropriate balance.

This study was supported by Contract/Grant No. ESI-0138715 between the National Academy of Sciences and the National Science Foundation. Any opinions, findings, conclusions, or recommendations expressed in this publication are those of the author(s) and do not necessarily reflect the views of the organizations or agencies that provided support for the project.

Library of Congress Cataloging-in-Publication Data

Tech tally : approaches to assessing technological literacy / Committee on Assessing
Technological Literacy in the United States ; Elsa Garmire and Greg Pearson, editors.
   p. cm.
  Includes bibliographical references and index.
  ISBN 0-309-10183-2 (hardcover) — ISBN 0-309-66003-3 (pdf) 1. Technical education—
United States—Evaluation. 2. Technological literacy—United States. I. Garmire, E.
II. Pearson, Greg. III. National Academy of Engineering. Committee on Assessing
Technological Literacy in the United States. IV. Title.

  T73.T4165 2006
  609.73—dc22
                    2006019673

Additional copies of this report are available from National Academy Press, 2101 Constitution Avenue, N.W., Lockbox 285, Washington, DC 20055; (800) 624-6242 or (202) 334-3313 (in the Washington metropolitan area); Internet, http://www.nap.edu.

Printed in the United States of America

THE NATIONAL ACADEMIES
Advisers to the Nation on Science, Engineering, and Medicine

The **National Academy of Sciences** is a private, nonprofit, self-perpetuating society of distinguished scholars engaged in scientific and engineering research, dedicated to the furtherance of science and technology and to their use for the general welfare. Upon the authority of the charter granted to it by the Congress in 1863, the Academy has a mandate that requires it to advise the federal government on scientific and technical matters. Dr. Ralph J. Cicerone is president of the National Academy of Sciences.

The **National Academy of Engineering** was established in 1964, under the charter of the National Academy of Sciences, as a parallel organization of outstanding engineers. It is autonomous in its administration and in the selection of its members, sharing with the National Academy of Sciences the responsibility for advising the federal government. The National Academy of Engineering also sponsors engineering programs aimed at meeting national needs, encourages education and research, and recognizes the superior achievements of engineers. Dr. Wm. A. Wulf is president of the National Academy of Engineering.

The **Institute of Medicine** was established in 1970 by the National Academy of Sciences to secure the services of eminent members of appropriate professions in the examination of policy matters pertaining to the health of the public. The Institute acts under the responsibility given to the National Academy of Sciences by its congressional charter to be an adviser to the federal government and, upon its own initiative, to identify issues of medical care, research, and education. Dr. Harvey V. Fineberg is president of the Institute of Medicine.

The **National Research Council** was organized by the National Academy of Sciences in 1916 to associate the broad community of science and technology with the Academy's purposes of furthering knowledge and advising the federal government. Functioning in accordance with general policies determined by the Academy, the Council has become the principal operating agency of both the National Academy of Sciences and the National Academy of Engineering in providing services to the government, the public, and the scientific and engineering communities. The Council is administered jointly by both Academies and the Institute of Medicine. Dr. Ralph J. Cicerone and Dr. Wm. A. Wulf are chair and vice chair, respectively, of the National Research Council.

www.national-academies.org

Committee on Assessing Technological Literacy

ELSA GARMIRE, *chair*, Dartmouth College, Hanover, New Hampshire
RODGER BYBEE, Biological Sciences Curriculum Study, Colorado
Springs, Colorado
RODNEY L. CUSTER, Illinois State University, Normal
MARTHA N. CYR, Worcester Polytechnic Institute, Worcester,
Massachusetts
MARC J. de VRIES, Eindhoven University of Technology, Eindhoven,
The Netherlands
WILLIAM E. DUGGER JR., International Technology Education
Association, Blacksburg, Virginia
ARTHUR EISENKRAFT, University of Massachusetts Boston
J. DEXTER FLETCHER, Institute for Defense Analyses, Alexandria,
Virginia
ALAN J. FRIEDMAN, New York Hall of Science, Queens
RICHARD KIMBELL, University of London, New Cross, London,
United Kingdom
JOSÉ P. MESTRE, University of Illinois, Champagne-Urbana
JON D. MILLER, Northwestern University Medical School,
Chicago, Illinois
SUSANNA HORNIG PRIEST, University of South Carolina,
Columbia
SHARIF SHAKRANI, National Assessment Governing Board,
Washington, D.C.
JOHN D. STUART, PTC, Needham, Massachusetts
MARY YAKIMOWSKI-SREBNICK, Yakimowski and Associates and
Council of Chief State School Officers, Suffolk, Virginia

Project Staff

GREG PEARSON, Study Director and Program Officer, National
Academy of Engineering
STUART ELLIOTT, Director, Board on Testing and Assessment,
National Research Council *(June 2003 to project end)*
PASQUALE DEVITO, Director, Board on Testing and Assessment,
National Research Council *(October 2002 to May 2003)*

CAROL R. ARENBERG, Senior Editor, National Academy
of Engineering
MARIBETH KEITZ, Senior Public Understanding of Engineering
Associate, National Academy of Engineering *(April 2003 to
project end)*
MATTHEW CAIA, Senior Project Assistant *(October 2002 to
March 2003)*
EILEEN GENTLEMAN, Christine Mirzayan Science and
Technology Policy Graduate Fellow *(January 2005 to March 2005)*
STEVE MEYER, Christine Mirzayan Science and Technology Policy
Intern *(September 2002 to November 2002)*
ROBERT POOL, Freelance Writer

NAE Council Committee on Programs

LAWRENCE PAPAY, *chair*, Science Applications International Corporation (retired), La Jolla, California

RAY BEEBE, Homestake Mining Company (retired), Tucson Arizona

W. DALE COMPTON, Purdue University, West Lafayette, Indiana

RUTH DAVIS, Pymatuning Group Inc., Alexandria, Virginia

ELSA GARMIRE, Dartmouth College, Hanover, New Hampshire

ELISABETH PATÉ-CORNELL, Stanford University, Stanford, California

JOHN SLAUGHTER, National Action Council for Minorities in Engineering, White Plains, New York

WM. A. WULF,* National Academy of Engineering, Washington, D.C.

Staff

PROCTOR REID, Director, NAE Program Office

---

*Ex Officio.

Preface

This report is the final product of a two-year study by the Committee on Assessing Technological Literacy, a group of experts on diverse subjects under the auspices of the National Academy of Engineering (NAE) and the Board on Testing and Assessment at the Center for Education, part of the National Research Council (NRC). The committee's charge was to determine the most viable approach or approaches to assessing technological literacy in U.S. K–12 students, K–12 teachers, and out-of-school adults. To fulfill that charge, the committee considered opportunities and obstacles to developing one or more scientifically valid and broadly applicable assessment instruments for technological literacy in the three target populations and specified subtest areas and sample test items for such assessments.

This report is based on *Technically Speaking: Why All Americans Need to Know More About Technology*, a 2002 publication by the National Academies, in which technological literacy was defined and a case was made for its importance. A key finding of that report was that few data are available about what Americans—children or adults—know and can do with respect to technology. The general feeling, then as now, was that people in this country are poorly prepared to think critically about many important technological issues—from the safety of genetically modified foods to privacy concerns raised by post-9/11 data gathering to the value and risks of a new manned mission to the moon. But without valid and reliable data from assessments, developing an effective strategy for improving the situation is all but impossible. The present report is intended to provide a road map for organizations and individuals to begin to fill this data gap.

The Committee on Assessing Technological Literacy adopted the broad definition of technology used in *Technically Speaking*. Technology includes not only the tangible artifacts of the human-designed world and the systems of which these artifacts are a part, but also the people, infrastructure, and processes required to design, manufacture, operate, and repair the artifacts. This comprehensive definition differs markedly from the more common, narrower public view, in which technology is almost exclusively associated with computers and other electronics.

This report will be of special interest to individuals and groups promoting technological literacy in the United States or developing or using the results of assessments in the domain of technology. Education and government policy makers in federal and state agencies, as well as the education research community, will also find much to think about. At the policy level, growing concerns about the competitiveness of the U.S. science and engineering workforce have highlighted the need for putting more emphasis on what people—particularly K–12 students—know and can do with respect to technology. For researchers, efforts to investigate the dimensions of technological literacy have revealed a largely unexplored territory related to how children and adults learn technological concepts and how computer-based simulation might be used as an assessment tool.

The committee met seven times, sponsored one stakeholders' workshop, and talked informally with a number of nationally recognized experts on assessment, cognition, and related areas. The workshop, held September 2004, brought together more than 20 individuals representing public and private assessment organizations; technology-based industries; classrooms, schools, and school systems; and researchers interested in workforce and employment. The committee also received critical input from workshop participants.

Two reviews of the literature were commissioned, one on how people learn technology-related concepts and the other on how people learn engineering-related concepts. The committee also commissioned an analysis of data from the long-term science assessment conducted as part of the National Assessment of Educational Progress. The panel collected and reviewed some 30 assessment instruments on various aspects of technological literacy. Finally, beyond this data gathering, the report also reflects the personal and professional experiences and judgments of committee members.

For better or worse, we live in a numbers-oriented world, in education as well as other sectors. Many people can only be convinced of the need for greater technological literacy if the argument can be backed by hard data. For a variety of reasons, gathering such data will not be easy, but it is important that we do so. This report provides a solid platform from which to launch the effort.

Elsa M. Garmire, *chair*
Committee on Assessing Technological Literacy

Acknowledgments

This report has been reviewed in draft form by individuals chosen for their diverse perspectives and technical expertise, in accordance with procedures approved by the NRC's Report Review Committee. The purpose of this independent review is to provide candid and critical comments that will assist the institution in making its published report as sound as possible and to ensure that the report meets institutional standards for objectivity, evidence, and responsiveness to the study charge. The review comments and draft manuscript remain confidential to protect the integrity of the deliberative process. We wish to thank the following individuals for their review of this report:

Philip Bell, Cognitive Studies in Education, University
of Washington
Christopher T. Cross, Chairman's Office, Cross & Joftus, LLC
Sharon Dunwoody, School of Journalism and Mass
Communication, University of Wisconsin-Madison
Paul Fleury, School of Engineering, Yale University
Joan Herman, Center for Research on Evaluation, Standards,
and Student Testing, University of California, Los Angeles
Marie Hoepfl, Department of Technology, Appalachian
State University
Brett D. Moulding, Science Education and Curriculum, Utah
Office of Education
Nancy S. Petersen, Measurement and Statistical Research,
ACT Inc.

John M. Rauschenberger, Personnel Research and
Development, Ford Motor Company
Larry Snyder, Department of Computer Science, University
of Washington
Mark Wilson, Graduate School of Education, University
of California, Berkeley

Although the reviewers listed above have provided many constructive comments and suggestions, they were not asked to endorse the conclusions or recommendations nor did they see the final draft of the report before its release. The review of this report was overseen by Lauress Wise, President's Office, Human Resources Research Organization (HumRRO) and William G. Agnew, Retired Director, Programs and Plans, General Motors Corporation. Appointed by the National Research Council, they were responsible for making certain that an independent examination of this report was carried out in accordance with institutional procedures and that all review comments were carefully considered. Responsibility for the final content of this report rests entirely with the authoring committee and the institution.

In addition to the reviewers, many other individuals assisted in the development of this report. Stephen Petrina, at the University of British Columbia, and Alisha Waller, at Georgia State University, conducted extensive reviews of the literature reviews on behalf of the committee. Larry O. Hatch, at Bowling Green State University, performed a detailed analysis of data on long-term trends from the National Assessment of Educational Progress science assessment. Project evaluators Patricia Bourexis and Senta Raizen, at The Study Group Inc., provided a valuable analysis of input from the workshop. Dan Householder, at the National Science Foundation, provided patient and wise guidance throughout the project. And participants in the committee's workshop and other, informal information-gathering activities supplied much-needed perspectives on the topics under consideration.

Thanks are also due to the project staff. Matthew Caia provided administrative support during the early phases of the project. Maribeth Keitz ably managed the bulk of the logistical and administrative needs, making sure meetings and workshops ran efficiently and smoothly. Christine Mirzayan Science and Technology Policy Intern Steve Meyer helped create a Web-based system for recording information about the assessment instruments the committee collected, and Christine Mirzayan Science and Technology Policy Graduate Fellow Eileen Gentleman prepared summaries of those documents. Freelance writer Robert Pool helped write the introductory chapters. NAE Senior Editor Carol R. Arenberg substantially improved the readability of the report. Special thanks are due to Pasquale Devito, head of the NRC Board on Testing and Assessment, who helped guide the project at its inception, and to his successor, Stuart Elliott, who provided insights and advice throughout the study process. Greg Pearson, at NAE, played a key role in conceptualizing the study and managed the project from start to finish.

Contents

APPENDIXES

Executive Summary

In a broad sense, technology is any modification of the natural world made to fulfill human needs or desires. Although people tend to focus on the most recent technological inventions, such as computers, cell phones, and the Internet, technology also includes automobiles, frozen food, irrigation systems, manufacturing robots, and a myriad of other devices and systems that profoundly affect everyone in a modern society.

Because of the pervasiveness of technology, an understanding of what technology is, how it works, how it is created, how it shapes society, and how society influences technological development is critical to informed citizenship. Technological choices influence our health and economic well-being, the types of jobs and recreation available, even our means of self-expression. How well citizens are prepared to make those choices depends in large part on their level of technological literacy.

The National Science Foundation (NSF) has been involved in raising public awareness of the need for an understanding of technology since the 1980s (Bloch, 1986). More recently, the American Association for the Advancement of Science (AAAS, 1990), the International Technology Education Association (ITEA, 1996), and other organizations have also called for Americans to become more savvy about technology. A case for technological literacy has been spelled out in *Technically Speaking: Why All Americans Need to Know More About Technology* (NAE and NRC, 2002) and in detailed requirements for the development of understanding and capabilities related to technology among K–12 students (ITEA, 2000).

No one really knows the level of technological literacy among people in this country—or for that matter, in other countries. Although many concerns have been raised that Americans are not as technologically literate as they should be (e.g., Rutherford, 2004), these statements are based on general impressions with little hard data to back them up. Therefore, the starting point for improving technological literacy must be to determine the current level of technological understanding and capability, which areas require improvement first, and how technological literacy varies among different populations—children and adults, for instance.

The goal of the Committee on Assessing Technological Literacy was "to determine the most viable approach or approaches for assessing technological literacy in three distinct populations in the United States: K–12 students, K–12 teachers, and out-of-school adults."[1] The committee was not asked to develop assessment tools but to point the way toward their development.

Assessing Technological Literacy

To assess technological literacy, one must have not only a clear idea of what it is, but also a good deal of knowledge about assessment. Basically, technological literacy is an understanding of technology at a level that enables effective functioning in a modern technological society. For the purposes of this report, the committee defined technological literacy as having three major components, or dimensions: knowledge, capabilities, and critical thinking and decision making (Figure ES-1). A similar three-part model of literacy has been proposed for information technology (IT) (NRC, 1999).

The "knowledge dimension" of technological literacy includes both factual knowledge and conceptual understanding. The "capabilities dimension" relates to how well a person can use technology (defined in its broadest sense) and carry out a design process to solve a problem. A technologically literate person should, for example, be able to use an automobile, a VCR, a microwave, a computer, and other technologies commonly found in the home or office and should be able to do basic troubleshooting when necessary. The final dimension—the "critical thinking and decision-making dimension"—has to do with one's approach to technological issues. For example, when a person with highly developed critical-thinking and decision-making skills is confronted with a new

> Technological literacy is an understanding of technology at a level that enables effective functioning in a modern technological society.

---

[1]The original charge, which included K–16 students and teachers, was modified because the committee was unable to identify opportunities for assessing college students and faculty (with the exception of pre-service teachers).

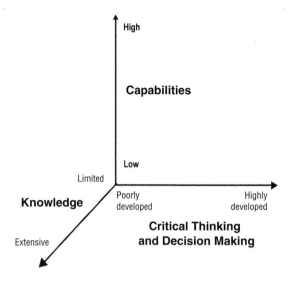

FIGURE ES-1 The three dimensions of technological literacy. Source: Adapted from NAE and NRC, 2002.

technology, he or she asks questions about risks and benefits and can participate in discussions and debates about the uses of that technology.

The committee does not consider attitude to be a cognitive dimension in the same way knowledge, capability, and critical thinking and decision making are. However, a person's attitude toward technology can provide a context for interpreting the results of an assessment. In other words, what a person knows—or does not know—about a subject can sometimes be correlated with his or her attitude toward that subject.

Although few assessments have been developed for technological literacy, many good assessment tools have been developed for other subjects, from reading and writing to science and mathematics. Indeed, the field of assessment is mature in many other domains.

Benefits

Of the many groups that would benefit from the development of assessments of technological literacy, the most obvious is the formal-education community. As more and more states move toward adopting technology-education standards for K–12 students (Meade and Dugger, 2004), schools will have to measure how well they are implementing those standards. Assessments will provide a gauge of how effectively schools promote technological literacy and an indication of where improvements can be made.

For K–12 students to become technologically literate, their teachers must also become technologically literate. To this end, colleges of education will need assessment tools to gauge the level of technological literacy of teachers-in-training. Even teachers of nontechnical subjects must be technologically literate to make connections between their subject areas and technology. Many other institutions and organizations—such as media outlets, museums, government agencies, and associations that represent industries—would benefit from knowing the level of technological literacy of their customers, patrons, or target audiences.

Levels and types of technological literacy are bound to differ among people from different social, cultural, educational, and work backgrounds. To the extent that these differences put particular people or groups at a disadvantage (e.g., related to educational or employment opportunities), technological literacy can be considered a social-justice issue. Assessment can identify these differences, thus creating opportunities for lessening them.

However, to make a case for raising the level of technological literacy, one must first be able to show that the present level is low, which is difficult to do without a good measure of technological literacy. Until technological literacy is assessed in a rigorous, systematic way, it is not likely to be considered a priority by policy makers, educators, or average citizens.

Existing Assessment Instruments

As a context for discussion, the committee collected examples of assessments that can measure an aspect of technological literacy, even if they were not developed for that purpose. Altogether, the committee identified 28 such instruments, including several developed outside the United States. About two-thirds target K–12 students, nearly one-third focus on out-of-school adults, and two are intended for teachers. Most existing assessments for out-of-school adults tend to focus on awareness, attitudes, and opinions, rather than on knowledge or capabilities.

The committee concluded that none of these instruments is completely adequate to the task of assessing technological literacy, because none of them fully covers the three dimensions spelled out in *Technically Speaking*. Most of them emphasize the knowledge dimension, although a number include items that explore technological capabilities, and a handful even focus solely on the capability dimension. But very few include the

> Levels and types of technological literacy are bound to differ among people from different social, cultural, educational, and work backgrounds.

critical-thinking and decision-making dimension. Assessing technology-related capability, which includes the ability to use a design process, is more difficult than gauging knowledge, and only a few methods have been tried for assessing it, partly because this tends to be very expensive, at least for large-scale application. Nevertheless, assessing the capability dimension is crucial. Only a few instruments encourage higher order thinking (critical thinking and decision making), although a goal of all types of learning is to encourage thinking that considers uncertainty and requires nuanced judgment, rather than just factual recall.

Developing a Conceptual Framework

One step common to the design of assessments is the development of a framework that describes the cognitive and content components of the proposed assessment. The framework often suggests the relative emphasis on each area of content, depending on the age of the test population and other factors. The conceptual underpinnings of the framework can be represented visually as a two-dimensional matrix, which serves as a blueprint for the more detailed phases of assessment design, the development of test specifications, and, ultimately, the development of test items.

> One step common to the design of assessments is the development of a framework.

The committee developed a sample assessment matrix (Figure ES-2) modeled after conceptual frameworks developed for the National Assessment of Educational Progress (NAEP) for closely related subjects (e.g., science and mathematics) (NAGB, 2002, 2004). With one modification, the matrix includes the three dimensions of technological literacy described in *Technically Speaking*—knowledge, capabilities, and

COGNITIVE DIMENSIONS

	KNOWLEDGE	CAPABILITIES	CRITICALTHINKING AND DECISION MAKING
TECHNOLOGY AND SOCIETY			
DESIGN			
PRODUCTS AND SYSTEMS			
CHARACTERISTICS, CORE CONCEPTS, AND CONNECTIONS			

CONTENT AREAS

FIGURE ES-2 Proposed assessment matrix for technological literacy.

ways of thinking and acting (renamed "critical thinking and decision making")—as the cognitive levels, that is, the three column heads. For each cognitive level, there are four content areas, the row heads: technology and society; design; products and systems; and characteristics, core concepts, and connections.

The proposed matrix is intended to be a starting point for designers of assessment frameworks for technological literacy. The committee recognizes that a number of other arrangements of content are possible.

General Principles

After reviewing existing assessment instruments and the literature on assessment, cognition, and technological literacy; consulting with a variety of stakeholders; and drawing upon the expertise of committee members, the committee developed the following general principles to guide the development of assessments of technological literacy for students, teachers, and out-of-school adults:

1. **Assessments should be designed with a clear purpose in mind.**
2. **Assessment developers should take into account research findings related to how children and adults learn, including how they learn about technology.**
3. **The content of an assessment should be based on rigorously developed learning standards.**
4. **Assessments should provide information about all three dimensions of technological literacy—knowledge, capabilities, and critical thinking and decision making.**
5. **Assessments should not reflect gender, culture, or socioeconomic bias.**
6. **Assessments should be accessible to people with mental or physical disabilities.**

Findings and Recommendations

In addition to these general principles, the committee developed findings and 12 related recommendations that address five critical areas (Table ES-1): instrument development; research on learning; computer-based assessment methods; framework development; and public perceptions of technology.

TABLE ES-1 Recommendations by Category and Target Population

	Opportunities for Assessment					
	Integrating Items into Existing Instruments	Developing New Instruments	Leveraging Research on Learning	Exploiting Innovative Measurement Techniques	Developing Frameworks	Broadening the Definition of Technology
K–12 Students	1, 2	3	7, 8	10	11	12
Teachers	4	5	8	10	11	12
Out-of-School Adults	6, 9	6	9	10	11	12

The committee's overarching finding, based on the review of assessment instruments described above and the results of a committee-sponsored workshop, is that assessment of technological literacy in the United States is in its infancy. This is not surprising given that most students do not take (or have access to) courses in technology, the number of teachers involved in teaching about technology is relatively small, and little effort has been made to determine the nature and extent of adult knowledge of, or attitudes toward, technology.

On a more positive note, the committee finds no reason why valid, reliable assessments cannot be developed that address one or more of the cognitive dimensions and all of the content domains of technological literacy. Items related to ways of critical thinking and decision making may be the most challenging for assessment developers, and items intended to measure design-related capability pose special challenges related to time and resource constraints. But both types of items can and should be developed.

Assessment of technological literacy in the United States is in its infancy.

Opportunities for Assessment

There are two significant opportunities for expanding and improving the assessment of technological literacy in all three populations of interest. The first is to integrate technology-related items into existing instruments focused on related topics; the second is to create new assessments specifically for the measurement of technological literacy. These strategies are not mutually exclusive, and the committee believes that they should be pursued simultaneously.

K–12 Students

Technology-related items might be added to a handful of national and international assessments for K–12 students. These assessments are designed to measure levels of knowledge, capability, and reasoning related to mathematics, science, and history.

Recommendation 1. The National Assessment Governing Board, which oversees the National Assessment of Educational Progress (NAEP), should authorize special studies of the assessment of technological literacy as part of the 2009 NAEP mathematics and science assessments and the 2010 NAEP U.S. history assessment. The studies should explore the content connections between technology, science, mathematics, and U.S. history to determine the feasibility of adding technology-related items to future NAEP assessments in these subjects.

Recommendation 2. The U.S. Department of Education and National Science Foundation should send a recommendation to the International Association for the Evaluation of Educational Achievement and the Trends in Mathematics and Science Study (TIMSS) governing board encouraging them to include technological literacy items in TIMSS assessments as a context for assessments of science and mathematics. The U.S. Department of Education and National Science Foundation should send a recommendation to the Organization for Economic Cooperation and Development and the governing board for the Programme for International Student Assessment (PISA) supporting the inclusion of technological literacy items as a cross-curricular competency.

The second area of opportunity for the K–12 population, the creation of new instruments for assessing technological literacy, would break new ground. The challenges to this ambitious approach would be great, but so would the potential benefits, especially the realization of a comprehensive picture of what young people know and can do with relation to technology.

Recommendation 3. The National Science Foundation should fund a number of sample-based studies of technological literacy in K–12 students. The studies should have different assessment designs and should assess different population subsets, based on geography, population density, socioeconomic status, and other factors. Decisions about the content of test items, the distribution of items among the three dimensions of technological literacy, and performance levels should be based on a detailed assessment framework.

K–12 Teachers

Although many students have sophisticated technological capabilities, they cannot be expected to be fully technologically literate unless their teachers are. Technology is integral to all educational disciplines, from history to art to science, and teachers should be able to discuss technology-related issues in one form or another. However, very little information is available on the technological literacy of teachers. Although teachers and teachers' unions may resist the idea of assessing technological literacy, the teacher-quality provisions of the No Child Left Behind Act (NCLB) may provide an opportunity to introduce technology-related test items into existing test instruments. New, stand-alone assessments would require protections of teachers' privacy and limited uses of test data to encourage participation.

Recommendation 4. When states determine whether teachers are "highly qualified" under the provisions of the No Child Left Behind Act (NCLB), they should ensure—to the extent possible—that assessments used for this purpose include items that measure technological literacy. This is especially important for science, mathematics, history, and social studies teachers, but it should also be considered for teachers of other subjects. In the review of state plans for compliance with NCLB, the U.S. Department of Education should consider the extent to which states have fulfilled this objective.

Recommendation 5. The National Science Foundation and U.S. Department of Education should fund the development and pilot testing of sample-based assessments of technological literacy among pre-service and in-service teachers of science, technology, English, social studies, and mathematics. These assessments should be informed by carefully developed assessment frameworks. The results should be disseminated to schools of education, curriculum developers, state boards of education, and other groups involved in teacher preparation and teacher quality.

Out-of-School Adults

Very little is known about the technological literacy of out-of-school adults, although a few instruments, such as the 2001 and 2004 ITEA/Gallup polls (ITEA, 2001, 2004) and the NSF's now-discontinued biannual surveys of public understanding of science and technology (e.g., NSB, 2004) have focused on the understanding, attitudes, and opinions of adults related to technology. Recently, the United States and several other countries have developed and administered a revamped international literacy assessment, the Adult Literacy and Lifeskills Survey (ALL), that focuses on prose and document literacy but redefines quantitative literacy as numeracy, implying a broad range of content items, some of which could be relevant to the assessment of technological literacy (Lemke, 2004). In addition, ALL measures a cross-curricular area of competency related to problem solving, which is a distinguishing feature of the technological design process.

> Very little is known about the technological literacy of out-of-school adults.

Recommendation 6. The International Technology Education Association should continue to conduct a poll on technological literacy every several years, adding items that address the three dimensions of technological literacy, in order to build a database that reflects changes over time in adult knowledge of and attitudes toward technology. In addition, the U.S. Department of Education, working with its international partners, should expand the problem-solving component of the Adult Literacy and Lifeskills Survey to include items relevant to the assessment of technological literacy. These items should be designed to gauge participants' general problem-solving capabilities in the context of familiar, relevant situations. Agencies that could benefit by knowing more about adult understanding of technology, such as the National Science Foundation, U.S. Department of Education, U.S. Department of Defense, and National Institutes of Health, should consider funding projects to develop and conduct studies of technological literacy. Finally, opportunities for integrating relevant knowledge and attitude measures into existing studies, such as the General Social Survey, the National Household Education Survey, and Surveys of Consumers, should be pursued.

Research on Learning

Because the assessment of technological literacy is in its infancy, many questions related to the nature of technological learning remain unanswered—in some cases, unasked. Therefore, the first step must be to collect and analyze work that has already been done that might suggest promising avenues for further investigation. The committee commissioned two reviews of the literature—one on learning related to technology (Petrina et al., 2004) and one on learning related to engineering (Waller, 2004). The reviews provided background information on cognitive issues related to technological literacy. In retrospect, however, the committee—and those interested in assessment in the domain of technology—would also have benefited from an analysis of studies in other areas, such as learning in science and mathematics, spatial reasoning, design thinking, and problem solving.

Recommendation 7. The National Science Foundation or U.S. Department of Education should fund a synthesis study focused on how children learn technological concepts. The study should draw on the findings of multidisciplinary research in mathematics learning, spatial reasoning, design thinking, and problem solving. The study should provide guidance on pedagogical, assessment, teacher education, and curricular issues of interest to educators at all levels, teacher-education providers and licensing bodies, education researchers, and federal and state education agencies.

An understanding of how people learn is critical to designing valid, meaningful assessment instruments. However, the research base on how people learn about technology, engineering, design, and related ideas is relatively immature compared with the state of knowledge in the general science of learning. Most of the information—particularly for engineering—is focused on what people know and how this varies by population, rather than on how information is acquired, processed, and represented. As the research base on learning about technology grows, assessments of technological literacy will also improve. However, real progress will require a decade or more of sustained effort, including the training of a cadre of researchers.

> An understanding of how people learn is critical to designing valid, meaningful assessment instruments.

Recommendation 8. The National Science Foundation (NSF) and U.S. Department of Education should support a research-capacity-building initiative related to the assessment of technological literacy. The initiative should focus on supporting graduate and postgraduate research related to how students and teachers learn technology and engineering concepts. Funding should be directed to academic centers of excellence in education research—including, but not limited to, NSF-funded centers for learning and teaching—whose missions and capabilities are aligned with the goal of this recommendation.

To the committee's knowledge, no rigorous efforts have been made to ascertain how adults acquire and use technological knowledge. School and work experience could affect their performance, but adults who are no longer in the formal education system are also influenced by a variety of free-choice learning opportunities, including popular culture, the news media, and museums and science centers.

Recommendation 9. The National Science Foundation should take the lead in organizing an interagency federal research initiative to investigate technological learning in adults. Because adult learning is continuous, longitudinal studies should be encouraged. Informal-learning institutions that engage broad populations, such as museums and science centers, should be considered important venues for research on adult learning, particularly related to technological capability. To ensure that the perspectives of adults from a variety of cultural and socioeconomic backgrounds are included, studies should also involve community colleges, nonprofit community outreach programs, and other programs that engage diverse populations.

Exploiting Innovative Measurement Techniques

The increasing speed, power, and ubiquity of computers in various configurations (e.g., desktops, laptops, personal digital assistants, e-tablets, and cell phones), combined with increasing access to the Internet, suggest a variety of innovative approaches to assessment in many domains, but particularly for assessment of technological literacy. Computer-adaptive testing, for example, has the potential to assess student knowledge of technology quickly, reliably, and inexpensively. Simulation could be a safe and economical approach to assessing procedural, analytical, and abstract capabilities and skills. Internet-based, massive, multiplayer online games could be an inexpensive way of engaging very large numbers of individuals for extended periods of time.

However, more research and development will be necessary before computer-based assessments of technological literacy can be used with full confidence. For one thing, the formal, psychometric properties of simulation must be better understood. For another, the costs of developing simulations *de novo* may be prohibitive.

Recommendation 10. The National Institute of Standards and Technology, which has a broad mandate to promote technology development and an extensive track record in organizing research conferences, should convene a major national meeting to explore the potential of innovative, computer-based techniques for assessing technological literacy in students, teachers, and out-of-school adults. The conference should be informed by research related to assessments of science inquiry and scientific reasoning and should consider how innovative assessment techniques compare with traditional methods.

Framework Development

A necessary first step in the development of assessments for technological literacy is the creation of a conceptual framework. Although a number of frameworks exist in other subjects, such as mathematics, science, and history, the committee found none in the domain of technology. The committee believes that existing content standards for K–12 students and, by inference, for pre-service teachers and out-of-school adults, are overly ambitious. Criteria similar to the ones used by AAAS Project 2061 (AAAS, 1990) to identify the most important ideas in science could be developed to help specify appropriate expectations in technology. In general, framework designers will have to narrow and prioritize the content to be assessed.

Recommendation 11. Assessments of technological literacy in K–12 students, K–12 teachers, and out-of-school adults should be guided by rigorously developed assessment frameworks, as described in this report.

- **For K–12 students,** the National Assessment Governing Board, which has considerable experience in the development of assessment frameworks in other subjects, should commission the development of a framework to guide the development of national and state-level assessments of technological literacy.

- **For K–12 teachers,** the National Science Foundation and U.S. Department of Education, which both have programmatic interests in improving teacher quality, should fund research to develop a framework for an assessment of technological literacy in this population. The research should focus on (1) determining how the technological literacy needs of teachers differ from those of student populations and (2) strategies for implementing teacher assessments in a way that would provide useful information for both teachers and policy makers. The resulting framework would be a prerequisite for assessments of all teachers, including generalists and middle- and high-school subject-matter specialists.

- **For out-of-school adults,** the National Science Foundation and U.S. Department of Education, which both have programmatic activities that address adult literacy, should fund research to develop a framework for the assessment of technological literacy in this population. The research should focus on determining thresholds of technological literacy necessary for adults to make informed, everyday, technology-related decisions.

Expanding the Definition of Technology

Based on data from ITEA's two Gallup polls, the results of the committee-sponsored workshop, and informal discussions with a variety of individuals knowledgeable about technological literacy, the committee concluded that confusion about the word "technology" and the term "technological literacy" is a major challenge to improving technological literacy in the United States.

Although defining technology was not included in the statement of task for this study, the committee is aware that many people define technology as computers (and sometimes other electronic devices). A great deal of interest has been expressed in the education community and other sectors in measuring what people—adults and children—know about and can do with computer technology (e.g., NRC, 1999). Some states, testing companies (e.g., ETS), the federal government (through the No Child Left Behind Act), and others support the development of, or have

Confusion about the word "technology" and the term "technological literacy" is a major challenge to improving technological literacy in the United States.

developed assessments for, measuring computer-related literacy. The International Society for Technology in Education has developed performance standards that have been adopted or adapted by many states for the use of IT by K–12 students (ISTE, 2000)

Of course, children and adults in a modern nation like the United States benefit by being able to use computer technologies. Thus, assessments of computer or IT literacy focused on application skills will be important, particularly for students. But such assessments would be even more valuable if they also addressed other crucial aspects of technology, as discussed in *Technically Speaking* (NAE and NRC, 2002) and detailed in national educational standards for science (AAAS, 1993; NRC, 1996) and technology (ITEA, 2000). Policy makers would benefit from knowing not only how capable people are with computer technology, but also whether they can think critically and make sensible decisions about technological developments.

Recommendation 12. The U.S. Department of Education, state education departments, private educational testing companies, and education-related accreditation organizations should broaden the definition of "technological literacy" to include not only the use of educational technologies (computers) but also the study of technology, as described in the International Technology Education Association *Standards for Technological Literacy* and the National Academy of Engineering and National Research Council report *Technically Speaking*.

Conclusion

The committee's recommendations are largely interdependent. For instance, all assessments for technological literacy will benefit from the development of detailed assessment frameworks (Recommendation 11), and frameworks and assessments will improve as more becomes known about how adults and children learn technology- and engineering-related concepts (Recommendations 7, 8, and 9). This same research will also inform efforts to use new techniques, such as simulation and gaming, for assessing what people know and can do with respect to technology (Recommendation 10). And these and other novel assessment tools have the potential to improve dramatically our ability to gauge technological literacy, particularly the capabilities dimension. As educators, policy makers, and the public at large adopt a broader view of technology (Recommendation 12), assessments of technological literacy will be considered not only important, but also necessary.

Although all of the recommendations are important and should be implemented, some recommended actions will be easier and less costly to implement—and more likely to have near-term results—than others. For example, the integration of technology-related items into existing instruments (Recommendations 1, 2, 4, and 6), which would leverage already developed tests and a testing infrastructure, will be easier to accomplish than creating *de novo* assessments (Recommendations 3 and 5).

Like traditional reading literacy, science literacy, civics, and numeracy, technological literacy is considered a public good. Hence, most of the entities addressed in the recommendations are federal and state government agencies, a large number of which have an interest or role in supporting science and engineering research, developing new technologies, maintaining and protecting the nation's infrastructure, and training the technical workforce. However, many nongovernmental organizations will also benefit, directly or indirectly, from a more technologically literate public. The committee hopes that these organizations will become interested and involved in broad-based efforts to promote the assessment of technological literacy.

The Full Report

In the full report, the committee describes how the concept of technological design can be used to guide the development of assessments of technological literacy (Chapter 2). For readers not versed in the vocabulary of assessment and cognitive science, or unfamiliar with the state of research on technological learning, the report provides a primer on all three subjects (Chapter 3). Analyses of the 28 assessment instruments collected during the course of the project are also examined in detail (Chapter 4 and Appendix E).

Concrete examples of some of the general principles of assessment of technological literacy are provided in the case studies in Chapter 5. The case studies range from a nationwide sample of 7th graders to assessments of visitors to a science museum. In addition to summaries of the assessment instruments collected by the committee, the report includes excerpts of K–12 learning goals related to the study of technology from three sets of content standards (Appendix B), and an annotated bibliography of some of the research on how people learn technology-and engineering-related concepts (Appendix D).

The Executive Summary can be read online and downloaded free of charge from the website of the National Academies Press (NAP), *www.nap.edu*. The full report and individual chapters can be downloaded as PDF files for a fee, and the entire report can be ordered in hard copy, from NAP.

References

AAAS (American Association for the Advancement of Science). 1990. Science for All Americans. New York: Oxford University Press.

AAAS. 1993. Benchmarks for Science Literacy. New York: Oxford University Press.

Bloch, E. 1986. Scientific and technological literacy: the need and the challenge. Bulletin of Science, Technology and Society 6(2-3): 138–145.

ISTE (International Society for Technology in Education). 2000. National Educational Technology Standards for Students: Connecting Curriculum and Technology. Available online at: *http://cnets.iste.org/students/s_book.html* (June 29, 2005).

ITEA (International Technology Education Association). 1996. Technology for All Americans: A Rationale and Structure for the Study of Technology. Reston, Va.: ITEA.

ITEA. 2000. Standards for Technological Literacy: Content for the Study of Technology. Reston, Va.: ITEA.

ITEA. 2001. ITEA/Gallup Poll Reveals What Americans Think About Technology. A Report of the Survey Conducted by the Gallup Organization for the International Technology Education Association. Available online at: *http://www.iteaconnect.org/TAA/PDFs/Gallupreport.pdf* (October 5, 2005).

ITEA. 2004. The Second Installment of the ITEA/Gallup Poll and What It Reveals as to How Americans Think About Technology. A Report of the Second Survey Conducted by the Gallup Organization for the International Technology Education Association. Available online at: *http://www.iteaconnect.org/TAA/PDFs/GallupPoll2004.pdf* (October 5, 2005).

Lemke, M. 2004. Statement for the Assessing Technological Literacy Workshop, September 29, 2004. The National Academies, Washington, D.C. Unpublished.

Meade, S.D., and W.E. Dugger, Jr. 2004. Reporting on the status of technology education in the United States. Technology Teacher 63(October): 29–35.

NAE (National Academy of Engineering) and NRC (National Research Council). 2002. Technically Speaking: Why All Americans Need to Know More About Technology. Washington, D.C.: National Academy Press.

NAGB (National Assessment Governing Board). 2002. Mathematics Framework for the 2003 National Assessment of Educational Progress. Available online at: *http://www.nagb.org/pubs/math_framework/toc.html* (December 9, 2004).

NAGB. 2004. Science Framework for the 2005 National Assessment of Educational Progress. Available online at: *http://www.nagb.org/pubs/s_framework_05/toc.html* (October 21, 2005).

NRC (National Research Council). 1999. Being Fluent with Information Technology. Washington, D.C.: National Academy Press.

NSB (National Science Board). 2004. Science and Technology: Public Attitudes and Understanding in Science and Engineering Indicators, 2004. Available online at: *http://www.nsf.gov/sbe/srs/seind04/c7/c7h.htm* (May 25, 2005).

Petrina, S., F. Feng, and J. Kim. 2004. How We Learn (About, Through, and for Technology): A Review of Research. Paper commissioned by the National Research Council Committee on Assessing Technological Literacy. Unpublished.

Rutherford, J. 2004. Technology in the schools. Technology in Society 26(2-3): 149–160.

Waller, A. 2004. Final Report on a Literature Review of Research on How People Learn Engineering Concepts and Processes. Paper commissioned by the National Research Council Committee on Assessing Technological Literacy. Unpublished.

1
Introduction

Technology in the broadest sense is the modification of the natural world to fulfill human needs and wants. Although people often focus only on the most recent technological inventions, such as cell phones, the Internet, and MRI machines, technology also includes automobiles and airplanes, frozen food and irrigation systems, manufacturing robots and chemical processes. Virtually everyone in a modern society is profoundly influenced by technology.

At the behavioral level, Americans have traditionally been early adopters and enthusiastic users of a wide array of technologies, from automobiles and televisions to air travel and wireless telecommunications, suggesting that they not only recognize the advantages of new technologies, but also that they incorporate them into their lives and benefit from them. But, as this report shows, technological literacy is much more than simply being able and willing to use a technology.

Because technology is pervasive in our world, it is vitally important that people understand what technology is, how it works, how it is created, how it shapes society, and what factors influence technological development. The technological choices we make are important in determining our health and economic well-being, the types of jobs and recreation available to us, even our means of self-expression. How well we are prepared to make those choices depends in large part on how technologically literate we are.

Twenty years ago, Erich Bloch, the director of the National Science Foundation (NSF), noted the importance of his agency to the public awareness and understanding of technology (Bloch, 1986). More recently, other organizations concerned with the nation's science and technology enterprise, such as the American Association for the Advancement of Science and the International Technology Education Association, have called for Americans to become more technologically savvy (AAAS, 1990; ITEA, 1996). More recently, ITEA proposed standards related to technological understanding and capabilities for K–12 students (ITEA, 2000). And just a few years ago, the case for technological literacy was outlined in *Technically Speaking: Why All Americans Need to Know More About Technology*, a report from the National Academies (NAE and NRC, 2002).

How Technologically Literate Are We?

Against this background, the question naturally arises about the level of technological literacy in the American public. Most experts who have thought about the issue in depth agree that people in this country are not as technologically literate as they should be; but this is a general impression with little hard data to back it up. Unfortunately, no good measures of technological literacy are being used in the United States today. A small number of organizations and individuals—including some outside this country—have developed a variety of tests and surveys to try to get a handle on what people know or believe about technology, but most of these efforts have either been short lived or have failed to provide the kind of data necessary for drawing useful conclusions about technological literacy.

The lack of information about technological literacy contrasts sharply with the amount of information about literacy in other subject areas. For example, adults' understanding of science has been assessed for almost three decades in surveys published biennially in *Science and Engineering Indicators* (e.g., NSB, 2004). Scientific knowledge and understanding among K–12 students are evaluated in a variety of standardized tests and by the federal National Assessment of Educational Progress (NAEP). In addition, student achievement is regularly tested in other school subjects, such as mathematics, English, and history. So why not test for technology literacy?

Part of the answer is historical. Until recently, educators and policy makers did not consider technology as separate from science.

Therefore, not only has there been no testing specifically of technological literacy, there has not even been a consensus on what constitutes technological literacy. This is particularly evident in elementary and secondary schools, where technology has not been taught as a separate subject—except in limited cases, such as industrial arts classes and, more recently, computer classes. Logically then, schools have not tried to measure the technological literacy of their students. Even though science and technology—and scientific and technological literacy—are closely related, it is important that they be treated independently for the purposes of assessment.

Another part of the answer to our question is that technological literacy is difficult to assess. Technological literacy has three basic components or dimensions, each of which presents challenges for assessments. First, a technologically literate person must have a certain amount of basic knowledge about technology (e.g., an understanding of the concepts of systems, feedback, trade-offs). Second, a technologically literate person should have some basic technical capabilities, such as being able to work with a computer and to identify and fix simple problems in the technological devices used at home and in the office. More generally, he or she should able to employ an approach to solving problems that relies on aspects of a design process. This second dimension is particularly difficult to assess because it cannot be easily measured in a typical paper-and-pencil test, especially if the test is in a multiple-choice format. And third, a technologically literate person should be able to think critically about technological issues and act accordingly (e.g., should construction of a new coal-fired power plant be supported or opposed).

Many different types of assessment tools will have to be developed, depending on how the assessment data will be used and the characteristics of the population being tested. Third-grade students require a different method of assessment than eighth-grade students. An assessment developed for students will not be appropriate for assessing their teachers. And an entirely different approach will be necessary for assessing technological literacy among out-of-school adults.

In light of the importance of assessing technological literacy, several groups have called for the development of measurements of technological literacy. One of the recommendations in *Technically Speaking*, for instance, was that "NSF . . . support the development of assessment tools that can be used to monitor the state of technological literacy among

> Technological literacy has three basic components or dimensions, each of which presents challenges for assessments.

students and the public in the United States." And the *Standards for Technological Literacy* called for the development of ways to gauge learning among K–12 students, measured against the standards.

Benefits of Assessing Technological Literacy

To appreciate the benefits of assessing technological literacy, one must first appreciate the value of technological literacy itself. There are a number, and according to *Technically Speaking* some of the most important relate to improving how people—from consumers to policy makers—think and make decisions about technology; increasing citizen participation in discussion of technological developments; supporting a modern workforce, which requires workers with significant technological savvy; and ensuring equal opportunity in such areas as education and employment for people with differing social, cultural, educational, and work backgrounds. The benefits of technological literacy also address growing concerns about the state of the nation's science and engineering enterprise in the context of the global economy (NAE, 2002; NRC, 2005).

Assessments of technological literacy will have a number of benefits, too. First, they will raise the profile of technological literacy and strengthen the case for the importance of increasing the level of technological literacy. As long as technological literacy is not assessed in a rigorous or systematic way, it is unlikely to be considered a priority by policy makers or the general public. Almost by definition, making a case for boosting technological literacy will require showing that the current level of technological literacy is too low. But this cannot be done now with good quantitative measures. We live in a numbers-oriented world, and many people will only heed a call for higher technological literacy if the argument can be backed by hard data. Without numbers, the case can be dismissed altogether.

> We live in a numbers-oriented world, and many people will only heed a call for higher technological literacy if the argument can be backed by hard data.

A number of groups will benefit from good assessments of technological literacy. Perhaps the most obvious beneficiary will be the formal education community. As the K–12 system moves toward adopting the International Technology Education Association (ITEA) standards or in other ways exposes students to more technology- or engineering-based courses, schools will need to measure how well they and their students are doing. Just as schools today assess students' knowledge and understanding of science, mathematics, and English, schools tomorrow will assess students' knowledge and understanding of technology, and for the same reason—to determine the effectiveness of teaching and learning and decide where improvements should be made.

Assessments of technological literacy are also important for students training to be K–12 teachers. For schools of education to provide future teachers with the knowledge and skills to speak knowledgeably about technology, they must be able to measure the technological literacy of their graduates.

Adults who have completed their formal educations continue to learn about technology in many ways (e.g., museums and science centers; radio, television, and print media; community and social organizations). Each of these venues would benefit from knowing how much people know about technology. Museums and science centers, for instance, could use information about the technological literacy of their patrons to design exhibits that would be useful and appealing. Journalists could use assessments of technological literacy to gauge the information about technology they can expect their audience to be familiar with and to determine what they must explain in their reporting. Political scientists studying public participation in technological decision making are more likely to be interested in public attitudes and ways of thinking and acting about specific technologies, such as genetically modified foods, nuclear power, and biometrics-based security.

Many organizations, both for-profit and nonprofit, that present information to the public about technology would also benefit from assessments. For example, an agricultural business introducing a new type of genetically engineered crop or an environmental organization presenting the results of a study about air pollution in the national parks could both make more effective presentations if they had a good sense of what the public knows and believes about technology. Product developers, who must decide which features a new product will have, would benefit from knowing what sorts of technology their customers are comfortable or familiar with and which sorts they tend to dislike or avoid. For similar reasons, marketing and advertising executives in many industries would benefit from having a better sense of what the public knows and feels about different technologies.

To the extent that differences in technological literacy disadvantage a person or group, assessment can help identify these differences, thus opening the door to efforts to improve the situation. Finally, for government policy makers, assessments of technological literacy would provide a window into the hopes and fears of people regarding technology that could help guide policy decisions. Policy makers might even decide they should promote efforts to improve technological literacy in this country.

Obstacles to Assessing Technological Literacy

The developers of tools for assessing technological literacy face significant design challenges.

The developers of tools for assessing technological literacy face significant design challenges, an issue much of the rest of this report considers. With enough time and financial support, most of these difficulties can be overcome. Overcoming the obstacles to implementation of assessments, however, will require more than just time and money.

Consider, for example, assessments of the technological literacy of students in grades K–12. Children in elementary and secondary school are already subjected to a battery of standardized tests each year, and there is tremendous and understandable resistance among teachers, school administrators, and parents to giving more tests. The problem is not merely taking one more day out of the schedule to administer a technological literacy test. Once a test is added to the mix, teachers will be expected to "teach to the test" (i.e., to ensure that students have the information they need to do well on the test). Thus, teachers would have to find time in an already packed day to teach about technology.

Resistance to tests for teachers could be even greater. K–12 teachers are generally reluctant to subject themselves to any test that could be perceived as a test of professional competence, and this resistance has been supported by their professional organizations, the National Education Association and American Federation of Teachers. Some of this resistance has been overcome by provisions in the No Child Left Behind Act of 2001 (P.L. 107-110), which requires that all teachers be "highly qualified" in the subjects they teach. One way for teachers to meet this requirement is by passing a state-developed assessment (DOEd, 2005). At the post-secondary level, faculty competence is considered the purview of academic departments, which do not usually use standardized tests.

Despite these problems, testing students and teachers, who can be found in one location—their schools—and can be ordered by the school administration to take a test, would be less problematic and complicated than assessing out-of-school adults or the general public. Historically, people have been resistant to surveys of almost any kind. The response rate to surveys is so low that it is very difficult to get a good measure of the public as a whole. It would be even more difficult to convince people to submit to the kinds of performance exercises that would be necessary to assess, say, their ability to troubleshoot a technology-related problem at home, such as an appliance that stops working.

Charge to the Committee

Given the increasing importance of technology in our society, it is vital that American citizens be technologically literate. Because we do not have good ways to measure technological literacy, however, our policy makers and educators are essentially "flying blind." There are obstacles to the development and implementation of tools to measure technological literacy, but they can be overcome, and good assessments of technological literacy would have great benefits.

In response to this need, the National Academy of Engineering and National Research Council (NRC) of the National Academies, with funding from NSF, established the Committee on Assessing Technological Literacy. (Biographies of committee members appear at Appendix A.) The committee was asked to determine "the most viable approach or approaches for assessing technological literacy in three distinct populations in the United States: K–16 students, K–16 teachers, and out-of-school adults (the 'general public')."

During the course of deliberations, the committee modified one aspect of the original charge by narrowing the grade range for teacher and student populations from K–16 to K–12, or kindergarten through the end of high school. The change was made because the committee was unable to identify opportunities for assessing college students and faculty (with the exception of pre-service teachers). For K–12 students and their teachers, however, the committee found a number of opportunities for improving existing measurement tools or introducing new ones.

The charge to the committee also included the following elements:

- Assess the opportunities and obstacles to developing one or more scientifically valid and broadly useful assessment instruments for technological literacy in the three target populations.
- Recommend possible approaches to carrying out such assessments, including specification of subtest areas and actual sample test items representing a variety of formats.

The report that follows is the committee's response to that charge. In Chapter 2, the committee defines "technology" and "technological literacy" as they are used in the report. Chapter 3 describes an approach to assessments that relies heavily on the concept of technological design. In Chapter 4, the committee outlines the basics of assessment practices, relevant findings in the cognitive sciences, and research on learning in technology that are important to the design of assessments in this domain. Chapter 5 provides brief descriptions and discussions of 28 assessment instruments collected by the committee in the course of the project. Chapter 6 presents five examples illustrating how assessments of technological literacy might play out in different populations and for varying purposes. In Chapter 7, the committee discusses the potential role of computer-based assessment methods. And in Chapter 8, it presents its findings and recommendations for expanding and improving assessments of technological literacy in the United States. The appendixes include copies of K–12 learning goals related to the study of technology from three different sets of content standards, summaries of the 28 instruments discussed in Chapter 5, and bibliographies of some of the research on how people learn technology- and engineering-related concepts.

This report builds on and refers extensively to two earlier documents, *Technically Speaking* (NAE and NRC, 2002) and *Standards for Technological Literacy* (ITEA, 2000). In *Technically Speaking*, technological literacy is defined, the benefits of technological literacy are described, and the characteristics of a technologically literate person are outlined. *Standards for Technological Literacy* specifies the basic knowledge and capabilities students in grades K–12 should have to be technologically literate. The committee used these concepts and standards as guidelines in determining which assessments would be most appropriate for testing U.S. students. Both documents are discussed extensively in Chapter 2.

The committee also reviewed general information about assessments. *Knowing What Students Know: The Science and Design of Educational Assessment* (NRC, 2001) was especially helpful in this regard. For background on the science of learning, the committee relied heavily on *How People Learn: Brain, Mind, Experience, and School* (NRC, 1999). The committee also consulted many other publications and held seven face-to-face meetings, informal discussions with a number of experts in relevant fields, and a major data-gathering workshop. As noted, the committee also identified and discussed assessment instruments that measure different aspects of technological literacy.

References

AAAS (American Association for the Advancement of Science). 1990. Science for All Americans. New York: Oxford University Press.

Bloch, E. 1986. Scientific and technological literacy: the need and the challenge. Bulletin of Science, Technology and Society 138–145.

DOEd (U.S. Department of Education). 2005. New No Child Left Behind Flexibility: Highly Qualified Teachers—Fact Sheet. Available online at: *http://www.ed.gov/nclb/methods/teachers/hqtflexibility.html* (August 16, 2005).

ITEA (International Technology Education Association). 1996. Technology for All Americans: A Rationale and Structure for the Study of Technology. Reston, Va.: ITEA.

ITEA. 2000. Standards for Technological Literacy: Content for the Study of Technology. Reston, Va.: ITEA.

NAE (National Academy of Engineering). 2002. Raising Public Awareness of Engineering. Washington, D.C.: National Academy Press.

NAE and NRC (National Research Council). 2002. Technically Speaking: Why All Americans Need to Know More About Technology. Washington, D.C.: National Academy Press.

NRC (National Research Council). 1999. How People Learn: Brain, Mind, Experience, and School. Edited by J.D. Bransford, A.L. Brown, and R.R. Cocking. Washington, D.C.: National Academy Press.

NRC. 2001. Knowing What Students Know: The Science and Design of Educational Assessment. Washington, D.C.: National Academy Press.

NRC. 2005. Rising Above the Gathering Storm: Energizing and Employing America for a Brighter Economic Future. Washington, D.C.: The National Academies Press.

NSB (National Science Board). 2004. Science and Technology: Public Attitudes and Understanding. Science and Engineering Indicators, 2004. Available online at: *http://nsf.gov/statistics/seind04/* (August 16, 2005).

2
Defining Technological Literacy

To develop tools for assessing technological literacy, one must first have a clear idea of what technological literacy is. Research has shown that most people have a limited conception of "technology." In a 2004 Gallup poll, 800 adults in the United States were asked to name the first thing that came to mind when they heard the word technology. Sixty-eight percent answered computers. Only 5 percent gave the next most frequent answer, electronics (ITEA, 2004).

But technology is far more than computers and electronics. It is airplanes and automobiles, medicines and MRIs, paper and plastics. It is home building, road construction, and the manufacture of everything from turbines to toothbrushes. It is agriculture and electricity. It is books, clothing, furniture, telephones and television, fast food and home-cooked meals, kids' toys, the Space Shuttle, roller coasters, and swimming pools. In short, technology is everything that humans do or make to change the natural environment to suit their own purposes. Or, in the words of *Standards for Technological Literacy: Content for the Study of Technology*, technology is "the innovation, change, or modification of the natural environment in order to satisfy perceived human wants and needs" (ITEA, 2000, p. 242).

This broad concept of technology is widely accepted by experts who think and write about technology, science, and engineering. For example, the American Association for the Advancement of Science, in *Benchmarks for Science Literacy*, provided a sweeping definition: "In the broadest sense, technology extends our abilities to change the world: to cut, shape, or put together materials; to move things from one place to another; to reach farther with our hands, voices, and senses" (AAAS, 1993). The definition in *National Science Education Standards*, published three years later, was similar: "The goal of technology is to make modifications in the world to meet human needs" (NRC, 1996). And in 2002, in *Technically Speaking: Why All Americans Need to Know More About Technology*, technology is defined as "the process by which humans modify nature to meet their needs and wants" (NAE and NRC, 2002).

The Designed World

One way to conceptualize technology is to think of human beings as living in three interconnected worlds—the natural world, the social world, and the designed world. The natural world consists of plants and animals, rocks and minerals, rivers, streams, lakes, oceans, the soil beneath our feet, and the air we breathe—in short, everything that exists without human intervention or invention. The social world includes customs, cultures, political systems, legal systems, economies, religions, and the mores humans devise to govern their interactions and relationships. The designed world, or the world of technology, includes all of the modifications humans make to the natural world to satisfy their needs and wants.

A river is part of the natural world. The boats that travel up and down the river, the channel that has been dredged down the middle of the river, and the buoys that mark the edges of the channel are all part of the designed world. And the rules of the road that instruct a captain traveling downstream to keep the red buoys to her left and the green ones to her right are part of the social world.

The designed world, as its name implies, consists of elements that are the products of conscious design. Everything from the grocery bag to the microchip is made for a purpose, and the goal of its design is to ensure that it fulfills its purpose. As we shall see in more detail in the next chapter, design is the process by which an idea for a product is turned into a physical reality. To put it in a slightly different way, the design process turns resources—materials, tools and machines, ideas and information, energy, capital, and time—into products and systems (Box 2-1).

The most comprehensive conception of technology includes not only the designed world, but also the aspects of the social world that underlie the designed world, such as corporations that design, build, sell, operate, service, and repair technologies; government policies and regulations that apply to technologies; engineering knowledge, operating know-how, and other expertise necessary to make technologies work; and so on. Thus, technology can be thought of as a general process by which humans modify the natural world to suit their needs, and the designed world consists of the artifacts created through this process. The word technology in this report is meant to express this expansive, all-inclusive concept (except in specified cases when it is necessary to distinguish between processes and artifacts).

We sometimes fail to appreciate that humans the world over depend on technology for comfort as well as survival. In countries like the United States, technology is central to the way people go about their daily lives, to the health of the economy, and to national security. The dramatic destruction of much of New Orleans by Hurricane Katrina is an example of this dependence (Box 2-2).

Hurricane Katrina's devastating impact on New Orleans in 2005 provides dramatic evidence of our dependence on technology. Satellite and imaging technologies provided several days' warning that Katrina was headed toward the city, allowing most residents—but not some of the most vulnerable—to flee before the storm made landfall.

New Orleans as we know it could not exist without the dams and levees that held the surrounding waters at bay. And these structural barriers can work effectively only with the mechanical pumps that remove water that seeps into this below-sea-level city. The pumps are operated by electricity produced in power-generating facilities and distributed through a network of transmission lines, the "grid." When Katrina's hurricane-force winds brought down power lines all over the Gulf Coast, the pumps were no longer available to handle the inflow of water. In addition, cell phones, although they are battery operated, require cell towers to transmit messages, and these towers are also tied into the grid. Once the power was out, cell phone systems did not work, leaving authorities and citizens unable to communicate. In addition, because people could no longer call in from outside the area, individuals trapped by rising waters had little idea of the extent of the flooding or the danger they faced. Other communications technologies, television and radio, alerted the rest of the country to the developing disaster.

Without electricity to power freezers and refrigerators, home food supplies, as well as grocery store stockpiles, were soon spoiled. Katrina's storm surge disrupted the Port of New Orleans, and floodwaters blocked the main roads and rail lines into the shipyards, effectively closing one of the main export routes for American agricultural products. (Agriculture is also largely dependent on technology, from mechanized farm machinery and global positioning satellites to pesticides and chemical fertilizers.) Oil wells off the Louisiana coast were damaged, as were on-shore refineries, resulting in immediate shortages of gasoline and causing steep increases in gas prices across the entire country.

The rebuilding effort will undoubtedly be technology intensive, as major elements of the city's infrastructure will have to be redesigned to incorporate the painful lessons of Katrina.

Technological Literacy

Based on the concept of technology described above, we can now define technological literacy. In the most fundamental sense, technological literacy is a general understanding of technology. This understanding may not be comprehensive, but it must be developed enough so that a person can function effectively in a technology-dependent society where rapid technological change is the norm.

Rather than a fixed quantity, technological literacy occurs along a continuum, with types and levels of literacy varying according to the age and needs of the particular population. Consider reading literacy. If a first-grade student reads at the level of a first grader, she is considered literate. All other things being equal, a literate fifth grader is expected to have a higher level of reading capability than a first grader but a lower level than a literate high school graduate, who, in turn, will be a less skilled reader and less well-read than a literate college graduate. But all of them are considered literate.

Technological literacy is similar to the more familiar concepts of scientific literacy, mathematical literacy (sometimes called numeracy), and historical literacy, as well as the more recently described information technology "fluency" (NRC, 1999). In all of these cases, people are not expected to be experts but are expected to be comfortable enough to, say, read and understand a newspaper article that includes information about that field or to apply that knowledge in some aspect of daily life—for example, knowing that a car requires regular maintenance. Like literacy in other fields, the goal of technological literacy is to provide people with the tools they need to participate intelligently and thoughtfully in the world around them.

For the purposes of this report, we use the definition of technological literacy in *Technically Speaking: Why All Americans Need to Know More About Technology* (NAE and NRC, 2002), with one important modification. In that report, technological literacy was described as having three interrelated dimensions—knowledge, ways of thinking and acting, and capabilities. The committee renamed the ways of thinking and acting dimension as "critical thinking and decision making," which more clearly describes this important aspect of technological literacy. The change also eliminates the possible suggestion that people must have specific positions on complex or controversial issues, which was clearly not the intent of the authors of *Technically Speaking*.

The committee also made three changes in the description of the characteristics of a technologically literate person (Table 2-1). First, an element was added to the dimension of critical thinking and decision making to suggest that people must be able to systematically weigh data necessary to understanding a technological issue. Second, greater emphasis was put on design by an addition to the capability dimension that conveys the idea that people should be able to use a design-thinking[1] process to identify and solve problems important in their own lives. Finally, the characteristic related to seeking information about new technologies was moved from the critical-thinking and decision-making dimension to the capability dimension, where it fits more naturally.

---

[1]Design thinking has parallels to many other forms of critical thinking. Scientists and science educators, for example, speak of "scientific thinking" and "science inquiry." American educational philosopher John Dewey wrote at great length about the value of "systematic and logical thinking" (Dewey, 1910, 1916). Brainstorming, information gathering, making trade-offs, testing preliminary ideas, and analyzing test results are common to many methods of problem solving. Design is a very practical form of the process relevant to technological literacy.

TABLE 2-1　Characteristics of a Technologically Literate Person

Knowledge
- Recognizes the pervasiveness of technology in everyday life.
- Understands basic engineering concepts and terms, such as systems, constraints, and trade-offs.
- Is familiar with the nature and limitations of the engineering design process.
- Knows some of the ways technology has shaped human history and how people have shaped technology.
- Knows that all technologies entail risk, only some of which can be anticipated.
- Appreciates that the development and use of technology involve trade-offs and a balance of costs and benefits.
- Understands that technology reflects the values and culture of society.

Critical Thinking and Decision Making
- Asks pertinent questions, of self and others, regarding the benefits and risks of technologies.
- Weighs available information about the benefits, risks, costs, and trade-offs of technology in a systematic way.
- Participates, when appropriate, in decisions about the development and uses of technology.

Capabilities
- Has a range of hands-on skills, such as operating a variety of home and office appliances and using a computer for word processing and surfing the Internet.
- Can identify and fix simple mechanical or technological problems at home or at work.
- Can apply basic mathematical concepts related to probability, scale, and estimation to make informed judgments about technological risks and benefits.
- Can use a design-thinking process to solve a problem encountered in daily life.
- Can obtain information about technological issues of concern from a variety of sources.

Source: Adapted from NAE and NRC, 2002.

According to this description, the knowledge dimension of technological literacy includes both factual knowledge and conceptual understanding. A technologically literate person must understand the basic nature of technology, such as that technology shapes, but is also shaped by society, and should understand fundamental concepts, such as trade-offs and the balance between costs and benefits. It is also useful for people to have knowledge about specific technologies, such as medical imaging or solar power. The type and depth of knowledge varies according to the individual's circumstances.

The critical-thinking and decision-making dimension relates to the way a person approaches technological issues. A person with highly developed abilities in this area, for example, is likely to ask questions about risks and benefits when confronted with a new technology—genetically modified crops, say, or a new type of nuclear power plant. In addition, this person can participate in discussions and debates about the uses of that technology. In this sense, critical thinking and decision making is compatible with "habits of mind" described in *Science for All Americans* (AAAS, 1990).

The capabilities dimension is closely related to the use component of ITEA's definition in *Technology for All Americans* (ITEA, 1996). A technologically literate person, for example, is able to use computers and other common machines found in the home or office and to do basic troubleshooting when a machine is not working properly—determining why a computer printer will not produce a desired document, say, or checking the possible causes, such as a tripped circuit breaker, when a toaster isn't working. A key aspect of capability is being able to carry out at least a simple version of a design process to solve a problem relevant to one's life. The capabilities dimension is a determinant of how well a person can take advantage of technology in his or her personal life and of how effective that person can be in the workplace. Capabilities are related to, but distinct from, technical competence (Box 2-3).

> A key aspect of capability is being able to carry out at least a simple version of a design process.

In one area of technology—computers—an effort has been made to describe multidimensional literacy similar to technological literacy as defined in this report. In *Being Fluent with Information Technology*, three components are identified for fluency in information technology—contemporary skills, foundational concepts, and intellectual capabilities (NRC, 1999)—that correlate loosely with the three dimensions of technological literacy. Contemporary skills, comparable to technological capabilities, suggest what an individual can do with computer technology; foundational concepts, parallel to technological knowledge, suggest basic ideas about computers and their development; and intellectual capabilities, akin to critical thinking and decision making, suggest the application of information technology in complex situations and the ability to handle unintended and unexpected problems when they arise.

BOX 2-3 Distinguishing Technological Literacy from Technical Competence

Technological literacy is not the same as technical competence. Some individuals (e.g., plumbers, automobile mechanics, computer programmers, intensive care nurses, airplane pilots, CNC [computer numerically controlled] mill operators) may be very competent in the use of one or more specific technologies but may not be technologically literate in the larger sense. Most engineers, by virtue of their training and experience, also have considerable technical competence, but not necessarily technological literacy. Although technological literacy includes some hands-on ability, this may not be a high level of practical, or technical, skill.

Technical competency does not guarantee a general understanding of technology as a process that contributes to the designed world and that affects and is affected by society. Thus, technically trained individuals, even engineers, may not have the characteristics we associate with technological literacy.

The authoring committee of *Being Fluent* explains its choice of "fluency" (as opposed to "literacy") in the following way:

> Th[e] requirement of a deeper understanding than is implied by the rudimentary term "computer literacy" motivated the committee to adopt "fluency" as a term connoting a higher level of competency. People fluent with information technology . . . are able to express themselves creatively, to reformulate knowledge, and to synthesize new information. Fluency with information technology . . . entails a process of lifelong learning in which individuals continually apply what they know to adapt to change and acquire more knowledge to be more effective at applying information technology to their work and personal lives. (p. 2)

Assessment designers need a much more detailed description of technological literacy than is provided in *Technically Speaking*. The International Technology Education Association's *Standards for Technological Literacy* offers specific suggestions of what K–12 students should know and what they should be able to do with respect to technology. In addition, two sets of national science education standards (AAAS, 1993; NRC, 1996) explore the relationships among science, technology, and society. Excerpts from all three publications can be found in Appendix B.

Attitudes Toward Technology

Although the committee does not consider attitudes to be a cognitive dimension (the way knowledge, capability, and critical thinking and decision making are), attitudes toward technology can provide a context for interpreting the results of an assessment. In other words, what a person knows—or does not know—about a subject can sometimes be correlated with his or her attitude toward that subject. Individuals who do not understand the nature of technological design, for example, may not

BOX 2-4 Attitudes and the Assessment of Technological Literacy

There is no "right" or "best" attitude toward technology. An individual's attitudes are affected by many factors, including age, life experience, values, culture, education, employment, personal interests, economic status, and abilities/disabilities. An attitude can be thought of as having three components: (1) a cognitive element, or mental state involving beliefs (e.g., kids today spend too much time using cell phones); (2) an affective component, or feelings (e.g., confidence in one's ability to fix a flat tire); and (3) an action-tendency component, or a disposition to act in a certain way (e.g., the inclination to buy a hybrid car to help the environment).

"trust" technology as much as individuals who understand the design process. However, it is just as likely that individuals who are more knowledgeable may be less trustful. That is because many factors in addition to knowledge, such as personal values, culture, and religion, can affect attitudes.

Attitudes may also reveal motivations. For example, middle school girls may not believe that careers in the sciences or technology are possible, or even desirable, for them. Thus, attitudes can have cognitive, affective, and action-tendency components (Box 2-4).

Visualizing Technological Literacy

Visualizing the three dimensions of technological literacy can be very helpful to efforts to understand and discuss the concept. In a graph developed in *Technically Speaking*, each of the dimensions of technological literacy is represented as a separate axis (Figure 2-1). In addition, because the level of literacy occurs along a continuum and is different for every individual, the axes also indicate changing levels of literacy along each dimension.

In the real world, however, the three dimensions of technological literacy are interdependent and inseparable. A person cannot have technological capabilities without some knowledge, and thoughtful decision making cannot occur without an understanding of some basic features of technology. The capability dimension, too, must be informed at

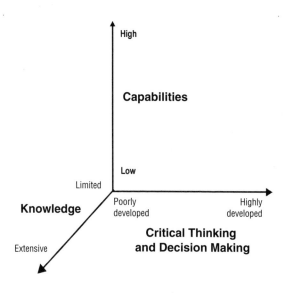

FIGURE 2-1
A graphical representation of the three dimensions of technological literacy.
Source: Adapted from NAE and NRC, 2002.

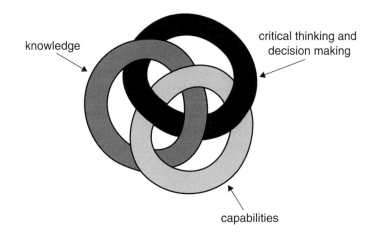

FIGURE 2-2 A visualization of the three dimensions of technological literacy as interlocking rings showing their inseparability.

knowledge

critical thinking and decision making

capabilities

some level by knowledge. Conversely, the doing component of technological literacy invariably leads to a new understanding of certain aspects of the technological world. This complex, but more accurate, idea can be represented in a number of ways. For example, the three dimensions of technological literacy can be represented as interlocking circular strands (Figure 2-2).

Assessing Technological Literacy

Once a definition of technological literacy has been developed, the next challenge, and the subject of the remainder of this report, is how to assess it. The assessment technique depends largely on the definition, and, conversely, the specifics of the definition depend on the type of assessment. An NRC report published in 2001, *Knowing What Students Know: The Science and Design of Educational Assessment*, contains a wealth of information about assessment practices generally as well as a discussion of the current status of educational assessments. The authors note, for instance, that assessments are used for three different purposes, "to assist learning, to measure individual achievement, and to evaluate programs" (NRC, 2001). The purpose of an assessment determines how the assessment is designed. As the authors point out, an assessment can be designed for more than one purpose—to measure the progress of individual students and the effectiveness of a program, for instance—but satisfying both goals inevitably requires compromises and trade-offs.

The present report is concerned with assessments of three populations: students in grades K–12, their teachers, and the general public. The committee offers different recommendations for each group. Students, for example, can be tested in schools as part of the normal assessment routine, but members of the general public must be reached in other ways—through telephone polls, perhaps, or during visits to science museums. Recommendations also vary depending on the purpose of the assessment. A museum might want to assess what the general public knows and doesn't know about technology in order to improve the design of its exhibits. A state department of education might want to assess the effectiveness of its K–12 technology program. A university school of education might want to assess whether its graduates are comfortable enough with technology to teach about it effectively.

Recommendations for approaches to assessments also take into account the three dimensions in the definition of technological literacy. Assessing technological knowledge requires different methods than assessing technological capabilities, which, in turn, is likely to require different approaches from those used to assess ways of critical thinking and decision making.

Finally, we must take into account that technological literacy does not mean the same thing to all groups. Assessments for students, for instance, who are in the process of learning about technology, must be designed to determine if they are on track to learn everything they will need to know. By contrast, assessments of out-of-school adults must measure their current level of technological literacy, which may have been acquired from life experiences, work, and other sources, and must identify strengths and weaknesses. In other words, assessments for different populations and/or purposes necessarily emphasize different aspects of technological literacy.

Assessing technological knowledge requires different methods than assessing technological capabilities.

References

AAAS (American Association for the Advancement of Science). 1990. Science for All Americans. New York: Oxford University Press.
AAAS. 1993. Benchmarks for Science Literacy. New York: Oxford University Press.
Dewey, J. 1910. How We Think. Lexington, Mass.: D.C. Heath.
Dewey, J. 1916. Essays in Experimental Logic. Chicago: University of Chicago.
ITEA (International Technology Education Association). 1996. Technology for All Americans: A Rationale and Structure for the Study of Technology. Reston, Va.: ITEA.
ITEA. 2000. Standards for Technological Literacy: Content for the Study of Technology. Reston, Va.: ITEA.

ITEA. 2004. The Second Installment of the ITEA/Gallup Poll and What It Reveals as to How Americans Think About Technology. A report of the second survey conducted by the Gallup Organization for the International Technology Education Association. Available online at: *http://www.iteaconnect.org/TAA/PDFs/ GallupPoll2004.pdf* (October 5, 2005).

NAE and NRC (National Academy of Engineering and National Research Council). 2002. Technically Speaking: Why All Americans Need to Know More About Technology. Washington, D.C.: National Academy Press.

NRC (National Research Council). 1996. National Science Education Standards. Washington, D.C.: National Academy Press.

NRC. 1999. Being Fluent with Information Technology. Washington, D.C.: National Academy Press.

NRC. 2001. Knowing What Students Know: The Science and Design of Educational Assessment. Washington, D.C.: National Academy Press.

3
Assessment as a Design Challenge

The purpose of this study, as set out in the original proposal to the National Science Foundation, was "to determine the most viable approach or approaches for assessing technological literacy in three distinct populations in the United States: K–16 students, K–16 teachers, and out-of-school adults." The committee was not asked to develop assessment tools, for which it had neither the time nor the resources, but to point the way toward that ultimate goal. To fulfill this charge, the committee decided to create a "road map" for the design of assessments of technological literacy and to provide general and specific explanations and examples of how the design process can be used to develop tools for assessing technological literacy.

The Design Process

The committee's task was similar to the tasks engineers face every day—the development of an instrument or tool to perform a particular job within given requirements and constraints. In fact, people from all walks of life face these kinds of challenges every day. Consider, for example, a restaurant manager who wants to revise her menu to reduce the fat content and maintain customer satisfaction or a group of surgeons devising a procedure to separate conjoined twins or a business executive figuring out a new corporate organizational scheme or a legislator crafting a new law. All of them are trying to solve problems by devising new entities, things that did not exist before. In short, they are engaging in design processes.

Webster's dictionary defines design as "a mental project or scheme

By its very nature, design is a messy, complex process that varies depending on what is being designed and who is designing it.

in which means to an end are laid down." The design process is a method of creating an effective design, a way of providing a structure for a creative endeavor (de Vries, 2005). By its very nature, design is a messy, complex process that varies depending on what is being designed and who is designing it. However, whether the designer is an engineer, an architect, or a professional working in the technological realm, design processes have some common elements, such as clarification of the nature of the problem, the setting of goals and limits for the project, and the delineation of the parameters of potential solutions. These elements have been formalized and are taught in engineering schools and elsewhere (Cross, 2000). In fact, the design process is a sufficiently important aspect of engineering and technology that, according to *Technically Speaking* (NAE and NRC, 2002), *Standards for Technological Literacy* (ITEA, 2002), and both sets of national science standards (AAAS, 1993; NRC, 1996), every technologically and scientifically literate person must have an understanding of it. According to ITEA, a technologically literate person must have the ability to apply the design process.

Because many members of the study committee for this report have backgrounds in engineering and technology, the committee decided to use the engineering design process to help address its charge. In fact, the engineering design process is also well suited to solving any problem that is poorly or imperfectly defined, such as the problem facing the committee.

The challenge of assessing technological literacy is difficult for several reasons. First, neither technology nor technological literacy can be easily defined. Second, although several sets of educational standards include descriptions of what a technologically literate person should know and be able to do, these standards and their associated curricula are relatively new and are largely untested. Third, the subject-matter connections among technology, mathematics, science, engineering, and history, just to name the most obvious subjects, are not well defined. Finally, assessments of technological literacy will necessarily be influenced by the large, and very complex, system of education in the United States.

The committee used a representative model of the engineering design process to organize its deliberations and, to some extent, the report as a whole. This approach had a number of benefits. First, the committee was able to approach its task in a structured, thoughtful way and to incorporate a unifying theme throughout the report. Second, the committee was able to provide a road map for others to follow in developing tools for assessing technological literacy. And third, although not part of the committee's formal task, the committee was able to promote technological literacy by demonstrating how the engineering design process can be used to address non-engineering problems.

The remainder of this chapter provides a description of how the design process was used to further the work of the committee and how it could be used to facilitate the development of assessment instruments. The chapter is organized according to the steps in a technological design process. Box 3-1 describes a simple, linear progression through a design process. Figure 3-1 provides a more realistic view of the iterative steps in a

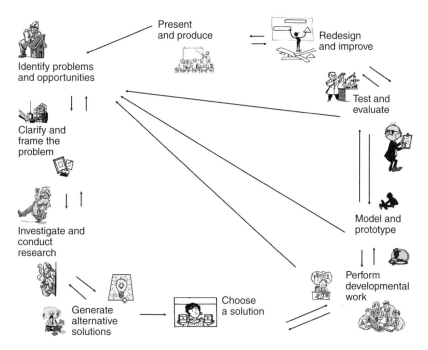

FIGURE 3-1 Design as an iterative process. Note: Typically, design begins with the identification of a problem to be solved, represented here by the detective in the upper left corner of the figure.

TABLE 3-1   Selected Design Attributes of the Committee's Study Process

Design Attribute	Committee's Study Process
Define the problem.	The problem—providing guidance on the development of assessment tools for technological literacy—which was spelled out in the committee's charge, was reviewed and refined during the first few committee meetings.
Identify constraints and criteria.	The committee planned its work to meet the constraints of time and money available for the project. During a fact-finding workshop, other constraints were identified—the report had to make a strong case for assessing technological literacy and for the feasibility of developing and implementing assessments.
Conduct relevant research.	The committee (1) collected and analyzed existing assessment instruments to provide data for brainstorming sessions; (2) commissioned reviews of the literature related to how people learn technological and engineering concepts and skills; and (3) held a workshop to gather information from stakeholders in the assessment, education, and policy communities.
Brainstorm ideas.	During seven face-to-face meetings, e-mail exchanges, and telephone conferences, the committee discussed a variety of approaches to assessment.
Identify potential solutions.	The committee developed five sample cases of assessments for different populations and different purposes, as well as a conceptual framework for organizing content for the study of technology in a way that would be useful for assessment designers.
Reiterate if necessary.	The committee revised many of its recommendations and changed other sections of the report based on input from the workshop and from external reviewers of the document.

design process. Table 3-1 illustrates how the committee's study process can be fitted to a design model.

Define the Problem

As obvious as it may seem, defining the problem, the crucial first step in the design process is often overlooked. Design problems are by nature often open-ended questions, such as "Which graphic designs will best illustrate this report?" or "What sort of emergency-response plan should the state of Louisiana put into place to deal with hurricanes more effectively?" To be certain that the design problem is thoroughly understood, the first step is to restate the problem and identify outstanding issues.

In the case of this report, the initial problem, as presented in the committee's statement of task, was "to determine the most viable approach or approaches for assessing technological literacy in three distinct populations in the United States: K–16 students, K–16 teachers, and out-of-school adults." After reflecting on the statement of task, the committee concluded that there were many reasons it would not be not feasible to treat the K–16 student and teacher populations as monolithic groups.

First, content standards have been developed for most K–12 subjects spelling out what children should know and be able to do at different grade levels, and assessments are already being used to track their achievement. By contrast, content standards and large-scale testing are not widely used in post-secondary education. Second, the high-stakes testing encouraged by the No Child Left Behind Act puts considerable pressure on K–12 teachers to follow state-developed curricula. Teachers in post-secondary institutions, although they also face many pressures, are not typically required to teach a specified curriculum. For these and other reasons, it was difficult for the committee to identify incentives for college students, college teachers, and institutions of higher education to participate in assessments of technological literacy. Thus, the committee opted to treat post-secondary students and teachers as part of the general adult population, where assessments are most likely to be done via survey methods.

Once the problem had been restated in this way, the committee attempted to clarify the context in which the problem had been posed. This process included defining technology and technological literacy (described in Chapter 2) and determining the current state of assessments of technological literacy (Chapter 5).

Finally, because the statement of a problem is always made in a particular context, it may reflect bias and even imply a particular solution. To eliminate as much bias as possible and ensure that many possible solutions were considered, the committee stressed the importance of clarifying the purpose of the design activity. The committee determined that the goal of this project was to provide a design-based road map for the development of assessments of technological literacy. Designers of specific assessment instruments can follow the road map, keeping the particular purpose or goal of that assessment in mind.

> Because the statement of a problem is always made in a particular context, it may reflect bias and even imply a particular solution.

Identify Constraints

Once a problem has been clearly defined, the next step is to identify the circumstances that limit the number of practical, or even possible, solutions. These "constraints," as engineers call them, are present in every type of design process. For example, a congressman crafting a new law is constrained by the U.S. Constitution, as well as by what is politically feasible. An architect designing a building is constrained by the budget, by local building codes, and by the materials that are available. When iron and steel beams were first developed, for example, the constraint on how tall a building could be was eliminated, and the era of skyscrapers began. Thus, constraints are not necessarily permanent or absolute. They are a function of time and place.

Constraints can be either general or specific.

Constraints can be either general or specific. General constraints, as the name implies, are issues common to many different types of problems. Specific constraints are particular to the problem at hand. Two general constraints for the development of assessments of technological literacy are time and money, limits to the amount of human and financial resources that can be devoted to the problem. For example, even though computer simulations might be an excellent way of meeting certain goals of assessment, the time and money required to develop reliable, valid simulations may be beyond the reach of many prospective users. (This constraint is discussed more fully in Chapter 7.)

There are also a variety of theoretical, practical, and policy-related constraints on the development of technological literacy assessments. First, the concept of technological literacy is not well understood or widely appreciated. The public, by and large, is not aware of or concerned about the need for a better understanding of the technological aspects of the world. Although a significant literature is available on the history, nature, and study of technology, it is not widely read outside specialized academic communities. And even though a number of federal, state, and nongovernmental groups have begun to formulate standards, curricula, instructional materials, and methods of teacher preparation, these efforts are all relatively immature. Thus, the relative newness of technological literacy in the educational landscape constrains the size and nature of the audience that might be receptive to the idea of assessment. This concern was borne out during the committee's fact-finding workshop held in September 2004 (Box 3-2).

A second constraint is the limited amount of research on, and experience with, assessments of technological literacy. The committee was able to identify only a handful of technology-related assessment instruments (see Chapter 5 for descriptions), and none of these mapped very well to the idea of technological literacy presented in *Technically Speaking*.

BOX 3-2   Input from Stakeholders

To solicit input on the idea of assessing technological literacy from the audiences the committee hoped to reach with its final report, a stakeholder workshop was convened in September 2004. About two dozen individuals representing federal and state government agencies; teachers and schools; businesses and industry; national, international, and comparative assessment programs; assessment development firms; and informal-education institutions took part.

Prior to the event, all participants were provided with copies of *Technically Speaking* and a brief summary of the project goals and objectives, and nearly all of them prepared short written statements expressing their views on the opportunities and obstacles to assessing technological literacy. An independent evaluation company, The Study Group, conducted pre- and post-workshop interviews with participants to elicit more in-depth views on the issues.

The workshop confirmed a number of the committee's assumptions about the challenges of making the case for assessment of technological literacy and yielded valuable insights that influenced the content of the report:

- The public, and at times the participants, confuse the broad concept of technology and technological literacy.
- The report must clarify the benefits of assessing technological literacy to a variety of constituencies.
- The most feasible short-term strategy is to incorporate technology-related items into existing assessments of other subjects, rather than construct assessments *de novo*.
- Businesses would be unlikely to pursue assessments of technological literacy unless it could be proved that the assessments were germane to job performance.

Thus, there is no obvious model to follow and no body of research to fall back on for assessments in this area.

This constraint is compounded because no single instrument can be effective for the many purposes for which assessments are used—to assist learning, to measure individual achievement, to evaluate programs, and so forth. Furthermore, because there are three different dimensions of technological literacy, assessment developers must decide how much of an assessment to devote to each dimension and how, or whether, to report assessment results according to performance on the three dimensions.

The most difficult dimension to assess is the capability (or doing) dimension, which includes design activities. This dimension simply cannot be fairly assessed via a paper-and-pencil test. Thus, measuring the capability dimension poses special challenges, such as the feasibility and validity of measurement methods. Measuring technological capability in out-of-school adults presents an additional challenge of engaging people who, unlike students in a classroom, are not likely to be co-located and so cannot easily participate in actual or simulated design and problem-solving tasks. Finally, the education policy environment in the United

States constrains the way the committee was able to envision assessment. With the current focus of U.S. education on high-stakes testing in mathematics, reading, and, soon, in science, few resources are available for developing assessments in other content areas, especially areas like technology that are not currently considered mainstream components of the curriculum. In addition, the amount of time in the school day that can be devoted to assessment activities is limited. Thus, the receptivity of teachers, parents, and policy makers to assessments related to technology is another serious constraint.

All of these general constraints are likely to affect the design of an assessment tool. As we will show in Chapter 6, when the design process is applied to the development of a specific type of assessment instrument, the constraints also become more specific.

Identify Design Criteria

Once the constraints have been determined, the specific criteria, or goals, for the design can be identified. The more clearly criteria are defined, the more successful the next steps in the design process will be. The criteria should be quantifiable whenever possible, but quantifiable or not, they should be stated in a way that clearly shows if they will be met by a given design. Anyone following the design process should be able to understand the reasons behind particular choices. In this project, the process of determining criteria was informed by pertinent research (described in Chapters 4 and 5), by an evaluation of the state of the art in assessments of technological literacy (Chapter 5), and by committee members' expertise.

General Criteria

Like constraints, design criteria may be general or case specific. The committee believes the following general criteria should be used to guide the development of assessments for technological literacy (specific criteria for assessments for specific purposes are spelled out in Chapter 6).

An assessment instrument must be designed to meet a specific purpose (ITEA, 2003). The purpose influences both the interpretation of the results and the design of the instrument, including the type of items included and their distribution among the dimensions of technological literacy. Some of the purposes for which an assessment might be developed are listed in Box 3-3.

Assessment data should be useful for making decisions related to the purpose of the assessment. Different assessments are necessary to address the unique characteristics of different target groups. No single assessment instrument is likely to be effective for more than one target audience.

Assessments for technological literacy should produce valid and reliable data on as many of the three dimensions of technological literacy as possible. However, it may be impractical or logistically difficult to address all three dimensions in one instrument.

Assessments of technological literacy should be informed by what has been learned from the cognitive sciences about how people learn.

Although the research base related to learning in the technological realm is relatively thin, insights into how people think about technological issues should be taken into account.

Assessments of technological literacy should reflect appropriate content standards. This criterion is especially relevant for assessments of student populations. Assessments of attitudes toward technology in out-of-school adult populations should also be designed with an eye to the important elements of knowledge and capability related to technology suggested by established standards.

Assessments for technological literacy should encourage higher order thinking (Box 3-4). An assessment provides an opportunity for students and teachers, as well as members of the general public, to demonstrate their knowledge of facts, display their conceptual understanding, and show their ability to apply that understanding to solving problems and making informed decisions.

Assessments that include items referring to specific technologies should be periodically reviewed to ensure that those references are current. Because technology is constantly changing, it is important that assessments not include out-of-date references (e.g., to long-playing records, typewriters, rotary-dial phones) that are not recognizable by the target population.

Assessments should avoid gender, race, or cultural bias, and, when appropriate, they should take into account the special needs of people with disabilities.

BOX 3-4   Characteristics of Higher-Order Thinking

Higher order thinking

- is *nonalgorithmic*, with the path of action not fully specified in advance
- tends to be *complex*, with the total path not "visible" from any single mental vantage point
- yields *multiple solutions*, each with costs and benefits, rather than a unique solution
- involves *nuanced judgment* and interpretation
- involves the application of *multiple criteria*, which sometimes conflict with one another
- often involves *uncertainty* because everything that bears on the task at hand may not be known
- involves *self-regulation* of the thinking process
- involves *imposing meaning*, or finding structure, in apparent disorder
- is *effortful*, requiring considerable mental work to make elaborations and judgments

SOURCE: Adapted from Resnick, 1987.

Conceptual Framework

Because of the broad extent of the world of technology and the numerous practical limitations on test design, boundaries around the material being assessed must be clearly delineated. One basis for setting the criteria for assessment design is to specify what the assessment will measure. Decisions must also be made about the level of detail and complexity of test items, the proportion of items devoted to particular areas of knowledge and capabilities, and the testing methods to be used.

Boundaries can be set through the development of a conceptual framework that provides a basis for test construction. Many states and the National Assessment Governing Board (NAGB), which is responsible for overseeing the development of the National Assessment of Educational Progress (NAEP), use conceptual frameworks with some common elements for developing student assessments. Most of these frameworks are closely linked to subject-specific content standards, and the most useful frameworks provide concise statements of testable material at each grade level. Frameworks for state assessments are typically based on nationally developed content standards.

NAGB has agreed to develop a framework for an assessment of technological literacy by 2008 as part of a feasibility study (Box 3-5). The committee believes that a reasonable basis for a framework for assessments of technological literacy would be the ITEA *Standards for Technological Literacy* (ITEA, 2002).

Assessment frameworks also suggest how much emphasis will be put on different areas of content, depending on the learning goals, the age of the test population, and other factors. For example, the Illinois Science Assessment Framework suggests that 20 percent of questions focus on student understanding of science inquiry and technological design; 60 percent on major scientific themes, such as living things, matter and

> NAGB has agreed to develop a framework for an assessment of technological literacy by 2008.

energy, and force and motion; and the remaining 20 percent on laboratory safety practices and connections among science, technology, and society (ISBE, 2005). Because content standards differ from state to state, the emphasis on different concepts and skills may vary. However, in all cases, there is a strong connection between the framework and relevant standards.

Assessment frameworks often provide test developers with detailed suggestions on the nitty-gritty of test construction, such as the number of test items; the number of multiple choice, short answer, and other types of questions; the relative "weight" of the parts of the assessment; the amount of time allotted for each section; and the best type of scoring (e.g., CSAP, 2004).

Finally, assessment frameworks usually suggest criteria for determining performance levels. NAEP, for instance, groups student test outcomes into three achievement levels, "basic," "proficient," and "advanced." Criteria for each level have been developed with input from subject-matter experts, parents, and others.

Frequently, the conceptual underpinnings of an assessment framework are represented as a matrix.

Frequently, the conceptual underpinnings of an assessment framework are represented as a matrix, which serves as a blueprint for the development of test specifications and, ultimately, of actual test items. Most frameworks (and matrices) are based on published documents, such as national and state content standards, that suggest desired learning outcomes. As more data become available and reveal strengths and weaknesses in the original assessment design, the framework and matrix can be revised, as needed (Wilson and Bertenthal, 2005).

Because frameworks are usually designed to fulfill the purpose of a particular assessment, the committee decided that a detailed framework might not be particularly helpful at this time. However, the committee developed a version of an assessment matrix for technological literacy that can be useful in many settings (Figure 3-2).

The committee's design of the matrix was influenced by a review of conceptual frameworks developed for subjects closely related to technological literacy. For example, in the framework for the 2005 NAEP science assessment, the content areas in the matrix are: Earth/space, physical sciences, and life sciences. The cognitive domains are three aspects of knowing and doing: conceptual understanding, scientific investigation, and practical reasoning (NAGB, 2004a).

The framework for the 2009 science assessment retains the three content categories from 2005 and creates four rather than three categories that are equivalent to the "knowing and doing" categories of the 2005

COGNITIVE DIMENSIONS

	KNOWLEDGE	CAPABILITIES	CRITICALTHINKING AND DECISION MAKING

FIGURE 3-2
Assessment matrix for technological literacy.

(Content areas listed along the left side of the matrix: TECHNOLOGY AND SOCIETY; DESIGN; PRODUCTS AND SYSTEMS; CHARACTERISTICS, CORE CONCEPTS, AND CONNECTIONS — labeled under "CONTENT AREAS")

framework. These four categories are called "science practices" and are focused on the ways scientific knowledge is used. They are: identifying scientific principles, using scientific principles, scientific inquiry, and technological design (NAGB, 2005). Underlying the science practices are four cognitive skills—"knowing that," "knowing how," "knowing why," and "knowing when and where to apply knowledge"—intended to facilitate the development of assessment items and analysis of student responses. According to the framework, technological design will be the focus of 10 percent of the 2009 NAEP items.

The 1996, 2000, and 2003 NAEP mathematics frameworks included five primary content "strands"—number sense, properties, and operations; measurement; geometry and spatial sense; data analysis, statistics, and probability; and algebra and functions—and three cognitive domains, called "math abilities"—conceptual understanding, procedural knowledge, and problem solving (NAGB, 2002). The frameworks group math abilities with "reasoning," "connections," and "communication" in a cross-cutting area of context called "mathematical power."[1]

Even from these very brief descriptions, it is apparent that the separations between the content and cognitive elements in the NAEP matrices are artificial. Indeed, many test items necessarily draw on two or more content areas and require a mix of cognitive skills. The same kind of overlap will occur in an assessment matrix for technological literacy.

---

[1]The 2005 NAEP mathematics framework retains the same five basic areas of content but eliminates the cognitive domains and adds a dimension related to the complexity of the test items themselves (NAGB, 2004b).

After looking closely at *Standards for Technological Literacy* (ITEA, 2002), *Technically Speaking: Why All Americans Need to Know More About Technology* (NAE and NRC, 2002), and the science education standards developed by AAAS (1993) and NRC (1996), both of which address the nature of technology and the relationship between technology and science, the committee adapted the three dimensions of technological literacy proposed in *Technically Speaking*—knowledge, capabilities, and critical thinking and decision making[2]—as the cognitive elements in the matrix. With the exception of the 2009 science assessment, these dimensions are conceptually consistent with the elements in NAEP's math and science frameworks (Table 3-2).

However, there are also some important differences between the committee's matrix and NAEP's matrices. First, NAEP's cognitive domains are progressive—moving from understanding to application of that understanding to what might be called critical thinking. Although the authors of *Technically Speaking* did not suggest a progression from one dimension to another, the committee believes a case can be made for an increasing cognitive complexity from knowledge to capability to critical thinking and decision making.

The committee's method of determining the content of the matrix also differs significantly from the model developed by NAEP. NAEP divides subjects into subdomains (e.g., for science, into Earth/space, physical sciences, and life sciences). By contrast, for technology, subdomains are better represented by different conceptualizations, each of which covers the whole of technology—the artifacts, or "stuff," of technology; processes (especially design) used to create technology; and the relationship between technology and society.

These conceptualizations are derived from (1) the literature on the philosophy of technology, especially *Thinking Through Technology: The Path Between Engineering and Philosophy* by Carl Mitcham (1994), where technology is described as knowledge, and (2) the ITEA standards, which are based on the same general principle. The committee defines the content in this way (rather than, for example, using categories of technologies or disciplines of engineering). The rationale for the committee's

> For technology, subdomains are better represented by different conceptualizations, each of which covers the whole of technology.

---

[2]The third dimension was called "Ways of Thinking and Acting" in *Technically Speaking*, but the committee has substituted "Critical Thinking and Decision Making," which seems a more appropriate descriptor. (See Chapter 2, pp. 33–35, for further explanation.)

TABLE 3-2 Cognitive Dimensions of the **NAEP** Science, **NAEP** Mathematics, and Committee's Technology Assessment Frameworks

	Dimension 1	Dimension 2	Dimension 3
NAEP Science Framework (for 2009 assessment)	Identifying science principles; using science principles	Scientific inquiry; technological design	See note
NAEP Science Framework (for 2005 assessment)	Conceptual understanding	Scientific investigation	Practical reasoning
NAEP Mathematics Framework	Conceptual understanding	Procedural knowledge	Problem solving
Committee on Assessing Technological Literacy	Knowledge	Capability	Critical thinking and decision making

NOTE: The 2009 NAEP science framework departs from earlier NAEP models by recasting the cognitive aspects of science knowledge and skills. These differences make it difficult to fit the new model to previous NAEP efforts and to the committee's own work. For example, there is no explicit cognitive category related to "critical thinking and decision making" or "practical reasoning." Instead, the new NAEP structure envisions critical thinking to be a cross-cutting element across all but the declarative knowledge category (i.e., "identifying scientific principles") (S. Raizen, WestEd, personal communication, April 12, 2006).

approach is that technological literacy is based on a broad understanding and conceptualization of technology, rather than on a narrow understanding of specific components of the technological world.

The committee's approach differs in three important respects from the ITEA approach. First, the ITEA standards treat the "understanding" of design and the "doing" of design separately. In the committee's matrix, one content strand encompasses both. Second, the committee uses "characteristics, core concepts, and connections" to capture the ideas ITEA lumps under "nature of technology." Third, the committee includes a content area, "products and systems," related to the "stuff" of technology. Products are the myriad individual devices and processes, from bicycles and dishwashers to automation and assembly lines, that we call technology. Systems are agglomerations of technologies that operate in complex arrangements to accomplish things that could not be accomplished by the individual components. Examples of systems include electricity generation and distribution, national and international transportation, and global communication systems. The "products and systems" category corresponds to "the designed world" in the ITEA standards, with one important difference. The committee believes this category should not be limited to the seven technologies suggested by ITEA. The groupings in the ITEA standards—medical, agricultural, and related biotechnologies; energy and power; information and communication; transportation; manufacturing; and construction—leave out some important elements (e.g., sanitation technology, nanotechnology).

Of course, no list can be complete. For one thing, new technologies are always being created while others become obsolete. But even if a comprehensive list could be compiled, it would be unmanageable. And, practically speaking, for the purposes of assessment, familiarity with some technologies will be more important than familiarity with others, depending on the purpose of the assessment and the test population. For these reasons, the committee encourages designers to be flexible in deciding which "products and systems" to include.

Table 5-2 in Chapter 5 presents a set of sample questions that illustrate how the content and cognitive elements of technological literacy might play out in each cell of the committee's matrix.

Conduct Relevant Research

Research, including reviews of the published literature and interviews with experts, can be helpful when approaching a very complex or poorly defined problem. Scientists and authorities in other fields often analyze new problems by referring to previous problems. Once they have determined the important factors in earlier cases, they may be able to apply the lessons learned to the new design problem (NRC, 1999). Following this pattern, the committee reviewed existing assessment instruments to determine the issues most important to the present task, such as identifying design criteria and constraints and possible solutions. Research was also useful for investigating whether ideas that arose during brainstorming sessions met the criteria and constraints of the problem at hand.

In fact, the committee found that research was helpful in every phase of the design process, from defining the problem to generating possible solutions. Individuals and organizations attempting to develop assessments of technological literacy based on the road map provided in this report will have to conduct even more research—pilot testing, for example—to determine how well their designs meet the criteria in real-world environments.

> The committee found that research was helpful in every phase of the design process.

Identify Potential Solutions

The heart of the design process is generating a number of possible solutions and deciding which of them is likely to be useful for solving the problem. During brainstorming sessions, the usual method of generating possible solutions, members of a design team discuss a wide range of ideas, initially with little concern for their feasibility. After listing all of the suggestions, the team begins to pare down alternatives based on constraints and to eliminate ideas that are unworkable for one reason or another.

The committee used a similar process. For example, although it was unlikely, the committee considered the possibility that one or more existing assessment instruments might adequately measure technological literacy as spelled out in *Technically Speaking*. If such an instrument had been discovered, the entire course of the project would have been different. The committee spent considerable time reading, critiquing, and discussing the collected documents, but, in the end, none was deemed adequate. Thus, this potential solution had to be abandoned. The committee was then left with the challenging task of providing guidance without the benefit of an existing model.

In most design processes, no single proposed solution meets all of the criteria, but several possible solutions fit some of the criteria. This was the case in the committee's effort to define the content and cognitive elements for assessing technological literacy, represented graphically as a two-dimensional matrix (Figure 3-2). The committee had also considered a three-dimensional alternative comprising content (materials, processes, and products of technology), context (the personal, professional, and social environment in which technology exists), and capabilities (knowledge of technology and the ability to use it). Assessment items with this alternative would be drawn from all three dimensions. Faced with these two alternatives, the committee determined which came closest to fitting all of the criteria.

This part of the design process, called "trading off" by engineers, is crucial to any design process. A so-called trade-off matrix provides a format for judging how well each potential solution satisfies each design criterion. Constructing a trade-off matrix requires gathering as much information about each alternative as possible, including the state of the art in that area, the costs and time line for implementing the alternative, and evidence demonstrating the validity and reliability of the technique.

> In most design processes, no single proposed solution meets all of the criteria.

Because there are likely to be a number of alternatives and a number of criteria, it is generally not possible within the constraints of time and money to conduct an in-depth study of each alternative and each criterion. However, once enough information has been gathered to make some qualitative comparisons, a formal trade-off analysis can be done. In the end, it is probably more important that assessment developers carefully assess how their design choices relate to the criteria and which criteria are most important for achieving the purpose of the assessment than that they use a formal matrix analysis.

The committee analyzed the two alternative conceptualizations in light of relevant content standards. The three-dimensional model had some intellectual appeal, but it differed in some dramatic ways from the organizational scheme presented in the ITEA standards. For example, ITEA considers capability to be primarily concerned with doing—using technology, problem solving, and designing, for example. Knowledge, in contrast, is mostly concerned with understanding facts and the broader concepts of technology. The two sets of science standards take a similar view of technological knowledge.

The committee's trade-off discussion focused on the question of feasibility, that is, which of the two approaches was more likely to be acceptable to educators, assessment experts, and the public at large. Even though any assessment of technological literacy is likely to face challenges, the committee decided that the three-dimensional model, despite its many interesting features, was less likely to be acceptable to key stakeholders.

Refine Possible Solutions

Although the trade-off matrix is a useful aid to decision making, it does not provide a final answer. Once the highest ranking solution or solutions have been selected, they typically require further study before the design can move to the prototype stage. Careful analysis at this stage should reveal if a particular solution holds up against the specified criteria. Because the original research is usually qualitative and is conducted rapidly, some information may be missing. At this point, all information relating to the trial solution must be entered into the analysis and a detailed design of the trial solution constructed.

This detailed design, referred to as a prototype, or pilot project, represents the first concrete step toward the creation of a real-world assessment instrument and must include at least some of the items that will be included in the final design. The prototype must be tested against specified criteria to ensure that the instrument accomplishes its purpose. If the prototype fails to meet any of the specified criteria, the design process must be repeated, after being modified to accommodate the results of the first iteration. As soon as a prototype meets the specified criteria, the design should be reconsidered with an eye toward simplifying it as much as possible.

The product of the committee's design process is this report rather than an actual assessment instrument. The principle impetus for refinements to the report was comments from the 11 outside reviewers of the document. Responses to those comments led to a host of content and organizational changes. For example, several reviewers felt that the draft report presented a potentially confusing definition of technological literacy. In response, the committee rewrote sections of the report to clarify the concept, including renaming one of the dimensions ("Ways of Thinking and Acting" was changed to "Critical Thinking and Decision Making"). Reviewers also encouraged the committee to provide a stronger connection between the recommendations in Chapter 8 and the body of the report. This, too, required significant rewriting.

Imperfect Design

Because of design constraints and the need for trade-offs among conflicting criteria, no design will be perfect. The design process is an exercise in compromise. Even if a design were theoretically perfect, the process is conducted by humans whose inherent biases and imperfections necessarily influence the process. Thus, all design products are inherently imperfect and can be improved. In the case of an assessment of technological literacy, not only is the assessment subject to refinement, but the subject being assessed is also evolving.

> The design process is an exercise in compromise.

Feedback is a crucial part of the improvement process. Engineers understand that continual improvement means feeding back the results of tests of trial solutions. In the case of assessments of technological literacy, assessment results must be tested for validity, reliability, and other stated criteria, and these results must be disseminated to test developers, researchers, and the general public. The best assessments will be designs that have been modeled, tested, evaluated, and modified over time.

Inherent Uncertainties

All technologies are human-designed products. Thus, they have both intended and unintended consequences. This is also true of assessments. For example, the recent introduction of federally mandated high-stakes testing in mathematics and reading—and science, beginning in 2007—has forced some school districts to reduce, or even cut entirely, funding for other parts of the curriculum. This result was certainly not what the drafters of the No Child Left Behind law intended.

The environment for educational assessments, or for assessments of technological literacy, or both, may change as the result of any number of factors, such as changes in leadership at the national, state, or local level. Policy makers, who must respond to political and social priorities and budget constraints, have considerable influence on the direction of educational reform.

Whether the study of technology will be a stand-alone subject or a component of science, mathematics, history, and other subjects, or both, is still an open question. Therefore, it is impossible to predict whether assessments of technological literacy will be stand-alone efforts, incorporated into assessments of other subjects, or some combination. In addition, over time research into the underlying knowledge structure of technology may lead to changes in the standards for technological literacy.

Because of these uncertainties, and because all designs are imperfect, the committee chose to provide general guidance for designing assessments of technological literacy rather than developing one or more specific assessment designs. (In Chapter 6, the committee considers how the design-based approach might play out for a variety of assessment purposes.) The road map is intended to provide a workable approach for many years, even if the environment for assessing technological literacy changes significantly.

References

AAAS (American Association for the Advancement of Science). 1993. Benchmarks for Science Literacy. Project 2061. New York: Oxford University Press.

Cross, N.G. 2000. Engineering Design Methods: Strategies for Product Design. New York: John Wiley and Sons.

CSAP (Colorado State Assessment Program). 2004. Fact Sheet for Reading. Available online at: *http://www.cde.state.co.us/cdeassess/csap/2004/Rdg_Fact_Sheet.pdf* (March 28, 2005).

de Vries, M.J. 2005. Teaching About Technology: An Introduction to the Philosophy of Technology for Non-Philosophers. Dordrecht, The Netherlands: Springer Verlag.

ISBE (Illinois State Board of Education). 2005. Illinois Science Assessment Framework. Grades 4 and 7. State Assessments Beginning Spring 2006. Available online at: *http://www.isbe.state.il.us/assessment/IAFScience.rtf* (March 28, 2005).

ITEA (International Technology Education Association). 2002. Standards for Technological Literacy: Content for the Study of Technology. Reston, Va.: ITEA.

ITEA. 2003. Advancing Excellence in Technological Literacy: Student Assessment, Professional Development, and Program Standards. Reston, Va.: ITEA.

Mitcham, C. 1994. Thinking Through Technology: The Path Between Engineering and Philosophy. Chicago: University of Chicago Press.

NAE (National Academy of Engineering) and NRC (National Research Council). 2002. Technically Speaking: Why All Americans Need to Know More About Technology. Washington, D.C.: National Academies Press.

NAGB (National Assessment Governing Board). 2002. Mathematics Framework for the 2003 National Assessment of Educational Progress. Available online at: *http://www.nagb.org/pubs/math_framework/toc.html* (December 9, 2004).

NAGB. 2004a. Science Framework for the 2005 National Assessment of Educational Progress. Available online at: *http://www.nagb.org/pubs/s_framework_05/toc.html* (October 21, 2005).

NAGB. 2004b. Mathematics Framework for the 2005 National Assessment of Educational Progress. Available online at: *http://www.nagb.org/pubs/m_framework_05/toc.html* (October 21, 2005).

NAGB. 2005. Science NAEP 2009: Science Framework for the 2009 National Assessment of Educational Progress—Prepublication Edition. Developed by WestEd and the Council of Chief State School Officers under contract to the National Assessment Governing Board (contract # ED04CO0148). Available online at: *http://www.nagb.org/pubs/naep_fw_pre_pub_edition_for_web.doc* (February 15, 2006).

NRC (National Research Council). 1996. National Science Education Standards. Washington, D.C.: National Academy Press.

NRC. 1999. How People Learn: Brain, Mind, Experience, and School. Edited by J.D. Bransford, A.L. Brown, and R.R. Cocking. Washington, D.C.: National Academy Press.

Resnick, L. 1987. Education and Learning to Think. Washington, D.C.: National Academy Press.

Wilson, M.R., and M.W. Bertenthal, eds. 2005. Systems for State Science Assessment. Washington, D.C.: The National Academies Press.

4
An Assessment Primer

Although few, if any, assessments are available in this country for technological literacy, many good assessment tools have been developed in other areas, from reading and writing to science and mathematics. Indeed, over a period of many years, a number of principles and procedures have been developed for obtaining reliable results. Although assessing technological literacy has some special requirements, the general principles developed for assessments in other areas are applicable. Thus, a logical place to begin the development of an assessment of technological literacy is with a review of what has been learned.

The overview of the field of assessments in this chapter lays the groundwork for the remainder of the report, which zeroes in on the assessment of technological literacy. The first section lays out the basics of testing and measurement—definitions, key ideas, and underlying concepts. The middle section focuses on what researchers have learned about cognition, that is, how people think and learn generally. The last section summarizes research on how people learn technological concepts and processes. Unfortunately, a great deal is still not known in this last area, a circumstance that is addressed in the committee's recommendations in Chapter 8.

Nevertheless, readers of the report, particularly those planning to design an assessment instrument for technological literacy, will want to familiarize themselves with this literature, because a clear idea of the cognitive processes involved in learning is crucial to the development of assessments and the interpretation of the results (NRC, 2001a):

[A] well-developed and empirically validated model of thinking and learning in an academic domain can be used to design and select assessment tasks that support the analysis of various kinds of student performance. Such a model can also serve as the basis for rubrics for evaluating and scoring pupils' work, with discriminating features of expertise defining the specific targets of assessment.

Testing and Measurement

Basic Vocabulary

Like any other field of knowledge, assessment has a specialized vocabulary. The terms "test" and "instrument," for instance, which are often used interchangeably, refer to a set of items, questions, or tasks presented to individuals under controlled conditions. "Testing" is the administration of a test, and "measurement" is the process of assigning numbers, attributes, or characteristics—according to established rules—to determine the test taker's level of performance on an instrument. The current emphasis on accountability in public schools, which entails accurate measurements of student performance, has renewed interest in measurement theory, which became a formal discipline in the 1930s.

"Assessment," derived from the French *assidere* (to sit beside), is defined as the process of collecting data to describe a level of functioning. Never an end in itself, an assessment provides information about what an individual knows or can do and a basis for decision making, for instance about a school curriculum. A related term, "evaluation," implies a value judgment about the level of functioning.

"Reliability" is a critical aspect of an assessment. An instrument is considered reliable if it provides consistent information over multiple administrations. For example, on a reliable test, a person's score should be the same regardless of when the assessment was completed, when the responses were scored, or who scored the responses (Moskal and Leydens, 2000). Reliability is necessary, but not sufficient, to ensure that a test serves the purpose for which it was designed. Statistically, indices of test reliability typically range from zero to one, with reliabilities of 0.85 and above signifying test scores that are likely to be consistent from one test administration to the next and thus highly reliable (Linn and Gronlund, 2000). Assuming other aspects of an assessment remain constant, reliability generally increases as the number of items or number of individuals participating increases.

"Errors of measurement" can compromise the reliability of an assessment. Even if an instrument is carefully designed and found to be highly reliable, it can never be completely free of errors of measurement (OERL, 2006). This means a test taker's true score is the sum of the observed score plus or minus measurement error. Errors can relate to the characteristics of the test taker (e.g., anxiety), the test administrator (e.g., inattention to proper test procedures), or the test environment (e.g., insufficient light or excessive noise), as well as to the accuracy of scoring.

"Validity" refers to the soundness and appropriateness of the conclusions based on test scores. Validity answers questions such as "Is the test fair?", "Does the test measure what it purports to measure?", and "Are the test results useful for the intended purpose?" (Sireci, 2005). According to current measurement theory, a test or an assessment instrument in and of itself is not considered valid or invalid. Only the inferences based on the test results are valid or invalid. Various types of evidence may be used to determine validity, and all of them must relate to the underlying concept, or construct, being measured (AERA et al., 1999; Messick, 1989).

Various types of evidence may be used to determine validity.

One of the most important types of evidence for determining validity is how well the themes, wording, and format of test items relate to a specified target-content domain, which may be based on specific learning objectives, such as those spelled out in educational standards (e.g., ITEA's *Standards for Technological Literacy*). A second type of evidence hinges on the relationship between test results and an external criterion, such as later success in college. A third type is based on a test taker's response processes. For a test of technological decision making, for example, determining the content-specific problem-solving skills used by examinees to arrive at answers could provide important evidence of validity. When test scores are used or interpreted in more than one way or in different settings, each intended use or interpretation must be validated.

In order to be valid, an assessment must be reliable, but reliability does not guarantee validity. That is, an instrument may produce highly stable results over multiple administrations but not accurately measure the desired knowledge or skill. Data from assessments should be reliable, and the inferences drawn from the data should be valid.

Central Themes

In the course of this study, the committee returned again and again to several ideas of central importance to the development of high-quality assessment instruments. Although these themes are not the only important concepts in the field of assessment, they are given special emphasis in this report, which will be read by many people outside the field. The central themes are: (1) defining purpose; (2) selecting content; (3) avoiding bias; and (4) ensuring fairness.

Defining Purpose

Any assessment instrument can only assess a small part of what a person or group of people knows, believes, or can do. Thus, before starting the design process, it is important to define the purpose of the assessment. Although an assessment may serve more than one purpose, the most effective assessments are designed to serve only one purpose; different purposes all but imply different kinds of assessments. Completely different designs would be used, for instance, to test how well museum-goers understand the lessons of a technology exhibit and to determine how well graduates of a school of education have been prepared to teach technology to elementary school students.

A designer must first establish what test takers will be expected to know about technology and what they should be able to demonstrate that they know. For students, these questions have often been answered in the form of standards. ITEA (2000) has developed content standards for K–12 students that address technological literacy. AAAS (1993) and NRC (1996) have developed national science education standards that include references to technological literacy. However, because none of these technology-related standards has been widely accepted or incorporated into education programs in the United States, the issue of assessment design can be very complicated.

In the K–12 setting, researchers have identified a number of purposes for assessments, ranging from program evaluation and instructional planning to pupil diagnosis (e.g., Brandt, 1998; McTighe and Ferrara, 1996; Stiggins, 1995). Assessments of technological literacy have two primary purposes in the K–12 setting: (1) to provide a measure of what students and teachers know about technology and how well they are

In the K–12 setting, researchers have identified a number of purposes for assessments.

able to apply it; and (2) to identify strengths and weaknesses in students' understanding, so that changes in teaching and the curriculum can be made to address those weaknesses. For an assessment of technological literacy, the designer must ask what types of information the results will provide and to whom; how the results will be interpreted; and how useful the results will be.

In contrast, the primary purpose of assessing the technological literacy of out-of-school adults should be to determine what the general populace knows and thinks about technology. At this point, little is known about the level of knowledge or practical skills of adults, and only slightly more is known about their attitudes toward technology. By contrast, a great deal is known about their political affiliations, television and movie viewing habits, health patterns, and buying trends. Assessments of technological literacy will provide information that can be used in a variety of ways, from designing museum exhibits to informing the design of new technologies.

Selecting Content

Because there are no explicit standards or expectations for what teachers and out-of-school adults should know or be able to do with respect to technology, assessment developers may wish to consider using a matrix like the one presented in Chapter 3, which is based in part on student standards, as a starting point for selecting appropriate content.

Theories of cognitive learning based on a constructivist approach to knowledge acquisition suggest that the most valuable assessment instruments for students—at both the K–12 and post-secondary levels (i.e., pre-service teachers)—are integrated with instructional outcomes and curriculum content. Developers of assessments must have an understanding of instructional goals before they can design assessments to measure whether students have indeed met those goals. However, beyond the specific outcomes of learning, assessments must also take into account learning processes, that is, how students learn; this is an important gauge of what students can do once they leave the classroom. By integrating assessments with instruction, curriculum, and standards, assessments can not only provide valuable feedback about a student's progress, but can also be used diagnostically to route students through instruction.

> Beyond the specific outcomes of learning, assessments must also take into account learning processes.

Avoiding Bias

Assessment developers must be alert to the possibility of inequities in an assessment. An item is biased if it elicits different levels of performance by individuals with the same ability but from different ethnic, sexual, cultural, or religious groups (Hambleton and Rogers, 1995). Bias can be present in various forms. If one group uses a familiar term as slang for another concept, for example, the use of that word on an assessment might cause members of that group to give the wrong answer even if they understand the concept correctly.

Pilot testing assessment items in small, sample populations is the best way to rule out bias. Suppose, for instance, that two questions seem identical, but the first has a correct response rate of 80 percent by all groups, and the second has an 80 percent correct response rate from all groups but one. Even if the bias is not apparent, the second question should not be used in the assessment.

Another kind of bias may be present for low-income students who may lack experiences that other students take for granted (e.g., family vacations, travel, visits to movie theaters and restaurants, and exposure to a variety of toys and tools). These students may present novel difficulties for developers of assessments trying to measure their knowledge, skills, and understanding.

Ensuring Fairness

The issue of fairness is closely related to bias. If no photos, illustrations, or given names of people of a student's ethnicity or race are included in a test, the student may not be motivated to do well on the test. If the only representation of a student's background has a negative connotation, the student's score may be adversely affected. Every effort should be made to avoid stereotypes and include positive examples of all groups (AERA et al., 1999; Nitko, 1996).

Assessment developers must also take into account the extent to which those being assessed have had opportunities to acquire the knowledge or practice the skills that are the subject of the test. In the classroom setting, opportunities to learn may include access to instruction and instructional materials; time to review, practice, or apply a particular concept; teacher competence; and school environment and culture (Schwartz, 1995).

Ideally, test takers, whether they are students, teachers, or out-of-school adults, should be able to participate. For test takers with special needs, the test many have to be adjusted, either through accommodations, modifications, or, in rare instances, the use of alternative items or tasks. Adjustments may vary according to the particular case. For example, individuals with visual impairments require different modifications than individuals with dyslexia, although both may have trouble reading the text of a question. When making adjustments, test developers must ensure that the modified assessment measures the same knowledge or skills as the original assessment.

Measurement Issues

Assessments can include many different types of questions and exercises, from true/false questions to the construction of a physical model that performs a certain function. Each measurement method has advantages and disadvantages, and test developers must select the ones that serve the purpose of the assessment. Additional measurement issues may arise depending on the amount of knowledge or number and types of skills an assessment attempts to capture.

> Each measurement method has advantages and disadvantages.

Selected-Response Formats

Selected-response items present test takers with a selection of responses to choose from. Formats include true/false, multiple-choice, and matching questions. One advantage of selected-response items is that they generally require less response time by test takers and are easy to score. This does not mean they are easier to develop, however. Multiple-choice items, when developed to ensure validity and reliability, can not only probe for facts, dates, names, and isolated ideas, but can also provide an effective measure of higher-order thinking skills and problem-solving abilities. Indeed, well constructed multiple-choice items can measure virtually any level of cognitive functioning.

One weakness of the selected-response format is that test takers can sometimes arrive at correct answers indirectly by eliminating incorrect choices, rather than directly by applying the knowledge intended by the test developer. In such cases, an assessment is measuring test-taking skill rather than knowledge or capability.

Constructed-Response Formats

In constructed-response questions, such as short-answer questions or essay questions, the test taker must provide a response. In general, constructed-response items provide a more in-depth assessment of a person's knowledge and ability to apply that knowledge than selected-response items. That advantage is counterbalanced, however, by the disadvantage that constructed-response questions are more difficult, time consuming, and subjective to score (Luckhel et al., 1994).

Performance-Assessment Formats

Performance assessments include exhibits, hands-on experiments, and other performance tasks, such as the construction of a device out of given materials that meets specified requirements. One advantage of performance assessments is that they can measure the capability—or "doing"—dimension of technological literacy. A disadvantage is that they are generally more time-consuming and expensive to develop and to administer than other types of assessments items. In addition, if the use of one or more performance tasks significantly reduces the total number of items in an assessment, the overall reliability of the assessment may be adversely affected (Custer et al., 2000).

Effective, Practical Formats

Many effective assessments, including some large-scale, statewide tests, combine at least two formats. In assessing technological literacy, multiple-choice and short-answer questions might be used to measure facts, knowledge, and concepts related to technological literacy, as well as the types of knowledge that can be applied in different situations. However, depending on the objective of the assessment, the latter skill might also be measured by performance tasks. Real or simulated performance tasks may be the best way for determining how well an individual can apply knowledge and concepts to solving a particular problem.

Domain of Knowledge

Often educators or researchers are interested in finding out what people know and can do related to a wide-ranging domain of knowledge.

Because the time and costs of testing would be extensive, it is usually not feasible to develop a single test to measure a very large body of knowledge. Assessment experts have devised a solution to this dilemma—giving only a fraction of the total number of items to each test subject. Dividing a large test into smaller segments and administering each segment to a portion of the population of interest is called "matrix sampling." The results are reliable at the level of the total population tested as well as for certain subgroups (e.g., by gender or age) but not at the level of the individual, and individual results are not reported. The National Assessment of Educational Progress and the Trends in International Mathematics and Science Study use matrix-sampling techniques.

So-called census testing involves giving the same test to all members of the target population. Because testing time is generally limited, an entire domain of knowledge cannot be assessed in this way. The advantage of census testing is that the results are reliable and can be reported at the level of the individual. State grade-level assessments are examples of testing by the census approach.

Reporting of Results

The way the results of an assessment are reported depends on the purpose of the assessment and the methods used in its development. The most common presentation of results is basic and descriptive—for example, the percentage of individuals who correctly respond to an item or perform a task. Other types of reporting methods include: norm-referenced interpretation; criterion-referenced interpretation; and standards-based interpretation.

Norm-Referenced Interpretations

Norm-referenced results are relative interpretations based on an individual's position with respect to a group, often called a normative sample. For example, a student might score in the 63rd percentile, which means that he or she scored better than 63 percent of the other students who took the test or, perhaps, better than 63 percent of a previous group of students who are the reference group (the norm) against which the test was standardized. Because norm-referenced results are relative, by definition some individuals score poorly, some average, and some well.

Criterion-Referenced Interpretations

Criterion-referenced interpretations are presented in absolute rather than relative terms and indicate how well individuals perform absolutely, not on how well they perform relative to others. The criterion is a desired learning outcome, often based on educational standards, and assessment items measure how well the test taker demonstrates knowledge or skill related to that goal. Criterion-referenced results may be presented as a number on a scale, a grade, or a rubric (e.g., novice, adequate, proficient). Thus, depending on the assessment and the group being assessed, few, half, or a large number of individuals (or groups) could meet the established criteria.

Standards-Based Interpretation

Standards-based interpretation is closely related to criterion-based interpretation. The No Child Left Behind Act of 2001 requires that each state develop an assessment program based on a standards-based interpretation of results, which ultimately allows for 100 percent of students, overall and disaggregated by subgroup, to be 100 percent proficient in reading, mathematics, and starting in 2007, in science.

To define proficiency, each state education agency was required to submit a workbook plan to the U.S. Department of Education for approval based on accepted standards-setting techniques, such as Bookmark or Modified Angoff (Kiplinger, 1997). Standards-based interpretation, like criterion-based interpretation, has a proficiency-defining "cut-off" score.

Cognition

In the assessment triangle described in *Knowing What Students Know* (NRC, 2001b), one corner of the triangle is cognition. In the context of the present report, cognition is a theory or set of beliefs about how people represent knowledge and develop competence in a subject domain. To test an individual's learning and knowledge, assessment designers must first understand how people learn and know things. An explicit, well conceived cognitive model of learning is the basis of any sound assessment design; the model should reflect the most scientifically credible evidence about how learners represent knowledge and develop expertise.

Most experienced teachers have an understanding of how their students learn, although that understanding may not be scientifically formulated. As researchers learn more about how people learn and understand, the new understanding should be incorporated into assessments. An assessment should not be static but should be constantly evolving to reflect the latest and best research.

Nature of Expertise

Many principles about thinking and learning are derived from studies of the nature of expertise and how it is developed. Experts have a great deal of both declarative (knowing that) and procedural (knowing how) knowledge that is highly organized and can be efficiently retrieved to solve problems. Thus, cognitive scientists have focused considerable efforts on studying expert performance in the hope of gaining insights into thinking, learning, and problem solving. These studies reveal marked differences between experts and novices (defined as individuals in the early stages of acquiring expertise).

To become an expert, a person must have many years of experience and practice in a given domain. During those years, the individual collects and stores in memory huge amounts of knowledge, facts, and information about his or her domain of expertise. For this knowledge to be useful, however, it must be organized in ways that are efficient for recall and application (Bransford et al., 1999; Chi and Glaser, 1981; Ericsson and Kintsch, 1995). Researchers have found that expert knowledge is organized hierarchically; fundamental principles and concepts are located on the higher levels of the hierarchy and are interconnected with ancillary concepts and related facts on the lower levels of the hierarchy. In addition, procedures and contexts for applying knowledge are bundled with the knowledge so that experts can retrieve knowledge in "chunks" with relatively little cognitive effort. This so-called "conditionalized knowledge" makes it possible for experts to perform high-level cognitive tasks rapidly (Anderson, 1990).

Thanks to this highly organized store of knowledge, experts can focus their short-term memory on analyzing and solving problems, rather than on searching long-term memory for relevant knowledge and procedures. In addition, experts can integrate new knowledge into their existing knowledge framework with relatively little effort. For an expert, "knowing more" means having (1) more conceptual chunks of knowledge in memory,

> Researchers have found that expert knowledge is organized hierarchically.

(2) more relations and features defining each chunk, (3) more interrelations among chunks, and (4) effective methods of retrieving and applying chunks (Chi and Glaser, 1981). In contrast, novices do not have highly organized stores of knowledge or links to related knowledge and procedures. Thus, novices must spend more cognitive effort looking for and retrieving knowledge from memory, which leaves less short-term memory for high-level tasks, such as problem solving.

> Novices must spend more cognitive effort looking for and retrieving knowledge from memory.

In a telling experiment by Egan and Schwartz (1979), expert and novice electronic technicians were shown a complex circuit diagram for just a few seconds and asked to reproduce as much of the diagram as they could from memory. The experts accurately reproduced much of the circuit diagram, whereas the novices could not. The experts were capable of such remarkable recall because they recognized the elements of the circuit as members of recognizable groups, rather than as individual elements. For example, they noticed that a particular set of resistors, capacitors, and other elements formed an amplifier of a certain typical structure and then recalled the arrangement of this amplifier chunk. When both groups were shown circuit diagrams with the elements arranged randomly, the experts had no way of identifying chunks, or functional units. In this test, experts scored no better than novices.

Experts and novices also focus on different attributes to decide on a strategy for solving a problem. In physics and mathematics, for instance, research has shown that shortly after reading a problem skilled problem solvers cue in on the underlying principles or concepts that could be applied to solve it (Chi et al., 1981; Hardiman et al., 1989; Schoenfeld and Herrmann, 1982). In contrast, unskilled problem solvers cue in on the objects and terminology, searching for a method of attack. For example, skilled problem solvers in physics decide that two problems could be solved with a similar strategy if the same principle (e.g., Newton's Second Law) applies to both problems. By contrast, unskilled problem solvers base their decisions on whether the two problems share the same surface characteristics (e.g., both contain inclined planes). Focusing on the surface characteristics is not very useful because the two problems that may look similar may require entirely different approaches.

Once an expert decides on the concepts that apply to a problem, he or she then decides on a procedure by which the concepts can be applied. Unskilled problem solvers must resort to finding and manipulating equations that contain the quantities given in the problem until they isolate the quantity or variable being asked for (Chi et al., 1981; Larkin, 1981, 1983; Mestre, 1991). Experts are also often flexible in ways novices are not. Even when experts are asked to solve a complex problem outside their immediate knowledge base, they can often use strategies (e.g., metacogition, knowledge building), or disciplinary dispositions, to come up with a solution (Wineberg, 1998).

In short, experts have a tendency to carry out qualitative analyses of problems prior to executing the quantitative solution, whereas novices tend to rely on a formulaic approach. For novices, the formulaic approach is more a necessity than a choice, because they have not yet mastered the principles and concepts of the subject and are not adept at knowing when and how to apply them. In the physical sciences, novices with reasonable skills in algebra find it easier to begin by manipulating equations, which enables them to narrow the field to the equations that might be useful by knowing which portion of the textbook the problem came from and by matching the variables in the equations to the "givens" in the problem. Only after considerable experience solving problems in this way do un-skilled problem solvers begin to realize that this approach cannot be "generalized." At that point, they may begin to shift to concept-based problem-solving strategies.

Cognitive research related to expertise raises a number of questions relevant to assessments of technological literacy:

- What assumptions can be made about the conditions and time necessary to acquire technological literacy?
- How can technological literacy be assessed in ways that do not encourage short-term exam coaching?
- What defines the key principles/concepts and procedural knowledge in different areas of technology, and what types of assessments can test for these high-level constructs?
- How should naïve and skilled problem solving in technology be characterized, and what types of assessments can distinguish between them?
- What constitutes cuing on surface characteristics and cuing on deep structures in technological problem solving, and how does one assess an individual's place along this spectrum?

Knowledge Transfer

One dimension of technological literacy is the ability to reason about technology coherently and abstractly from a broad perspective as a basis for making informed decisions about environmental, health, economic, political, scientific, and other issues that affect society. Thus, assessing technological literacy is largely about measuring the ability to transfer and apply knowledge in different contexts. In fact, knowledge transfer is a major goal in all education. Teaching in school and university classrooms and lecture halls is based on the premise that what a student learns in school will be useful in other settings both in and out of school (e.g., other courses, other disciplines, the workplace).

Knowledge transfer is difficult to achieve.

All of the research indicates that knowledge transfer is difficult to achieve. For example, classic studies of analogical transfer illustrate that transferring relevant knowledge from one situation to another in a different context, even if the tasks are isomorphic (i.e., they share the same structure), is not routine (Gick and Holyoak, 1980; Hayes and Simon, 1977; Reed et al., 1974, 1985). Most students can transfer knowledge only after being given hints pointing out that the two situations are isomorphic. Recently, Blanchette and Dunbar (2002) found that even students who spontaneously draw analogical inferences from one domain to another do not infer enough similarities to support a full-fledged transfer of knowledge. These studies suggest that the ability to transfer knowledge is context-bound, which presents educators with the challenge of structuring lessons to encourage transfer.

Research shows that several factors affect transfer. First, although it seems obvious, there must be an initial acquisition of knowledge (Brown et al., 1983; Carey and Smith, 1993; Chi, 2000). In many studies, a failure to transfer knowledge was attributable to insufficient initial learning (e.g., Brown, 1990; Klahr and Carver, 1988; Littlefield et al., 1988). The quality of initial learning is also important for transfer. Rote learning does not facilitate transfer; learning with understanding does (Bransford et al., 1983; Mandler and Orlich, 1993; see also the review of the literature in Barnett and Ceci, 2002). If students try to learn too many topics quickly, they may simply memorize isolated facts and have little opportunity to organize the material in a meaningful way or to link new knowledge to related knowledge.

The context of learning also affects transfer. If students perceive that knowledge is tightly bound to the context in which it is learned, transfer to contexts with even superficial differences becomes significantly more difficult (Bjork and Richardson-Klavhen, 1989; Carraher, 1986; Eich, 1985; Lave, 1988; Mestre, 2005; Saxe, 1989). For example, students who learn to solve arithmetic-progression problems can transfer the method to similar physics problems involving velocity and distance, but students who learn to solve the physics problems first have difficulty transferring the method to arithmetic-progression problems involving the same basic principles (Bassok and Holyoak, 1989). Apparently, after learning physics equations in a specific context, students are unable to recognize that they are applicable in a different context.

Prior knowledge can affect transfer and can lead to the application of inappropriate knowledge to a situation (referred to as negative transfer). There is a great deal in the literature on misconceptions in the sciences indicating that students come to science classes with fragmented knowledge and many misconceptions about how the physical and biological world works (diSessa and Sherin, 1998; Etkina et al., 2005; McDermott, 1984). For example, when children who believe Earth is flat are told that it is round, they may understand this to mean that Earth is round like a pancake, with people standing on top of the pancake (Vosniadou and Brewer, 1992). When told that Earth is round like a ball, children may envision a ball with a pancake on top, upon which people could stand. Thus, misconceptions can adversely affect learning (because students may misconstrue new knowledge that conflicts with prior knowledge) and problem solving (because inappropriate knowledge may be applied).

Cognitive research related to knowledge transfer has raised several questions relevant to the assessment of technological literacy:

- What test items would assess the transfer of key technological principles from one context to another?
- Are teaching practices and curricula in technology education guided by our best understanding of how to promote knowledge transfer?

Metacognition

Cognitive scientists use the term "metacognition" to refer to the process of consciously keeping track of thinking processes and adjusting understanding while learning to solve problems. Learners develop metacognitive strategies, such as monitoring understanding through self-regulation, planning, monitoring success, and correcting errors, to assess their readiness for high-level performance and to become more aware of themselves as learners (Bransford et al., 1999). Reflecting on one's learning, a major component of metacognition, does not typically occur in the classroom, possibly because of the lack of opportunity, because instructors do not emphasize its importance, or because metacognition develops slowly. In the physical sciences, for example, if students are unable to make any progress in solving a problem and are asked to identify the difficulty, they tend to say only that they are "stuck" and not to analyze what they need to make progress. In short, they have a metacognitive awareness of their level of understanding but are unable to bring conditional knowledge of learning strategies to bear on the task.

There are some notable examples of metacognitive strategies being used to improve learning in various domains. In mathematics, for example, teachers have had success with techniques that combine problem-solving instruction with control strategies for generating alternative problem-solving approaches, evaluating among several courses of action, and assessing progress (Schoenfeld, 1985). And in science, a middle-school curriculum that incorporates metacognitive strategies, such as scaffolded inquiry, reflection, and generalization, has met with considerable success in teaching force and motion (White and Frederiksen, 1998).

Metacognition can be important in the development of technological literacy.

Metacognition can be important in the development of technological literacy. Students whose instruction and curricula in technology education include metacognitive components, should show observable improvement in technological literacy over time. The development of metacognitive strategies for technology education thus has indirect implications for the assessment of technological literacy.

Cognitive research related to metacognition has raised a number of questions relevant to the assessment of technological literacy:

- How does metacognition develop in specific technology content areas?
- How is self-monitoring accomplished for technology, and does it differ from self-monitoring in other domains?
- What modes of instruction encourage self-monitoring?

Conceptual Change

Cognitive scientists have also examined how people form concepts and how they give up one concept in favor of another. In science learning, for example, although no consensus has been reached on the ontological status of students' emerging conceptual knowledge, some theories are emerging. One theory posits that portions of students' knowledge have the qualities of "naïve theories," which have an impact on students' scientific explanations and judgments (Carey, 1999; Chi et al., 1994; Hatano and Inagaki, 1996; Ioannides and Vosniadou, 2002; McCloskey, 1983a,b; Smith et al., 1997; Vosniadou and Brewer, 1992; Vosniadou and Ioannides, 1998). Although proponents of this theory do not argue that students' naïve theories have the robustness and consistency of scientists' theories, they do argue that some of children's knowledge is organized into cognitive entities that are activated as bundled units and applied remarkably consistently in similar contexts. According to this theory, encouraging conceptual change requires eliciting and exposing counterproductive knowledge, confronting and refuting that knowledge, and finally offering new ideas to replace the erroneous information (Strike and Posner, 1985).

Others argue that students' knowledge of science is sensitive to context and unstructured to the point that it cannot be described as a "theory." According to this view, students' knowledge is composed of diverse, fine-grained elements that lack the coherence and integration necessary for theories. This granular knowledge is variously described as "resources" (Hammer and Elby, 2003; Hammer et al., 2005) and "knowledge in pieces" (diSessa, 1988, 1993; diSessa and Sherin, 1998; diSessa and Wagner, 2005; diSessa et al., in press). In the knowledge-in-pieces view, instead of activating and applying precompiled knowledge bundles (as suggested in the naïve-theories view), students activate and combine knowledge pieces to reason about scientific situations; however, the knowledge pieces are highly sensitive to contextual variations, and if a context is changed slightly, a new, or modified set of knowledge pieces is activated (Mestre et al., 2004). Thus, conceptual change is more correctly described as conceptual development or refinement because concepts are fluid rather than well formed. To encourage conceptual change, then, instructors must help students both develop knowledge pieces or resources relevant to the situation and then activate students' existing productive resources they may not have considered relevant (Smith et al., 1994).

Cognitive research related to conceptual change has raised several questions relevant to the assessment of technological literacy:

- What is the "conceptual ecology" (diSessa, 2002; Smith et al., 1994) of technological knowledge among different age groups, and how does that knowledge affect technological problem solving and knowledge transfer?

- What counterproductive knowledge about technology do students and adults possess, and how difficult is it to restructure this knowledge in ways that support effective reasoning?
- How well do current theories of conceptual change in science map to what occurs in technological learning?

Research on Technological Learning

Technological literacy is a dynamic characteristic developed over a lifetime. To understand how individuals learn to design, solve technological problems, and make decisions and judgments about technological issues, in other words how they become technologically literate, we must attend to the research into how children and adults learn technological concepts and processes.

To inform the committee's deliberations, two reviews of the literature related to how people learn technology-related concepts were commissioned. One review focused on work in the field of technology education (Petrina et al., 2004); the other examined research in the field of engineering (Waller, 2004). (For selected bibliographies from these reviews, see Appendix D.) As noted in the preceding section, there are a number of unanswered questions about key aspects of how people think and learn in the realm of technology. But some useful work has been done, and those interested in designing assessments for technological literacy will benefit by taking it into account.

Learning Related to Technology[1]

Very few empirical studies have been done on learning related to technology using a conceptual framework of forms, levels, and the development of competence and expertise. This can be attributed to two factors: (1) the field of technology education is young compared with the field of cognitive psychology; and (2) cognitive scientists, psychologists, and science-education researchers have conducted few studies of any kind on learning related to technology.

One of the few studies that refers explicitly to the insights of

---

[1]This section includes material adapted from Petrina et al., 2004.

cognitive science was published in 1997 by Thomson, who used concept mapping to investigate how students conceptualize technology. Concept mapping is a method of organizing knowledge hierarchically, showing cause-effect relationships among different knowledge components. Concept maps by experts reflect the organization and structure of their knowledge, whereas concept maps by novices tend to reflect their less integrated, less structured knowledge. Thomson concluded that, although concept mapping might be useful for assessing student knowledge structures, a great deal of work remains to be done to validate the use of concept mapping in technology-education research.

Other studies indicate that young students readily identify tangible objects as technology. They not only commonly associate technology with computers, but they also recognize buildings, machines, and vehicles as technology (Hill and Anning, 2001a,b; Rennie and Jarvis, 1995). Based on the number of examples of technology children identified in images, texts, and words, Jarvis and Rennie (1996, 1998) concluded that conceptions of technology became more sophisticated with increasing age.

Davis, Ginns, and McRobbie (2002) investigated the conceptual understanding of particular aspects of technology, such as material properties. In one study, seven- and eight-year-olds described features of materials they used in a bridge-building lesson. Although they had difficulty expressing the features of composition, such as strength, they understood that by increasing the volume of materials they could basically increase the strength of the structure.

Children understand the *concept* of technology to be primarily objects, but they understand design to be a *process*. Children learn the processes of technology by participating in design activities (e.g., Foster and Wright, 2001; Hmelo et al., 2000; Roth, 1998). Using a classic "apprenticeship" model of situated cognition, Druin (1999, 2002) and other researchers have been investigating how students apply their expertise to the design of common children's artifacts—animation, fantasy spaces, games, storybooks, and toys. These studies have shown that children are capable of playing different roles on design teams (e.g., user, tester of technology, design inventor, and critic). Other studies have shown that children prefer participatory models to independent-inventor models and that they feel most creative when they embed their design work in narratives or stories (Bers, 2001; Druin, 2002; Druin and Fast, 2002; Druin and Hendler, 2001; Kafai et al., 1997; Orr, 1996; Taxen et al., 2001).

Children understand the *concept* of technology to be primarily objects, but they understand design to be a *process*.

Researchers have also studied the development of visualization and spatial skills in adolescents and younger teens, who are capable of working with simple symbolic, mathematical models, but who respond most readily to computer and concrete, three-dimensional (3-D) models. Although these children tend to have complex imaginations, unless they have sketching and drawing skills, they have difficulty representing the designs in their mind's eye in two-dimensional space. For example, Welch et al. (2000) found that 12- to-13-year-old novice designers approach sketching differently than professional designers, who use sketching to explore ideas and solutions. Although adolescents and teens may not be adept at sketching and drawing, they tend to develop design ideas by working with 3-D models. These and other observations by researchers raise questions about the differences between school-based design and professional design (Hill and Anning, 2001a,b).

Novices and experts approach technological design tasks differently, just as they do in other domains of learning. Both novice and expert designers manage a range of concurrent cognitive actions, but novices lack metacognitive strategies for organizing their activities (Kavakli and Gero, 2002). In a study of how expert, novice, and naïve designers approach the redesign of simple mechanical devices, Crismond (2001) found that all three groups relied more heavily on analytic strategies than on evaluation or synthesis. Not surprisingly, expert designers were able to generate more redesign ideas than designers with less experience.

Research on the development of expertise has also focused on the relationship of procedural to conceptual knowledge, both of which appear to be necessary for successful design, for novices as well as experts. In addition, the content of the procedural knowledge is determined by the design problem to be solved. In other words, different design problems require different approaches. The connection between procedural and conceptual knowledge in educational settings was investigated by Pomares-Brandt (2003) in a study of students' skills in retrieving information from the Internet. In this study, a lack of conceptual knowledge of what the Internet is and how it functions had a negative impact on information-retrieval skills.

Critical thinking and decision making in children, as in adults, suggest the level of reasoning necessary to making sensible choices regarding technological issues. Taking advantage of the relative comfort in distance afforded by virtual reality, researchers have used digital simulations to prompt students to reason through a variety of moral dilemmas

---

Novices and experts approach technological design tasks differently.

(e.g., Bers, 2001; Wegerif, 2004). Researchers in Germany found that when ethics was taught in school it was often perceived to be "just another school subject" or misunderstood to be religious instruction (Schallies et al., 2002). About 60 percent of the more than 3,000 high school students surveyed in this study did not think they had been prepared in school to deal with the types of ethical decisions that commonly face practitioners in science and technology.

Researchers are also beginning to explore the roles students negotiate in relation to technology (Jenson et al., 2003; Selwyn, 2001, 2003; Upitis, 1998; Zeidler, 2003). Students' identities are increasingly defined through these roles in terms of competence, interests, and status. Ownership of cell phones or MP3 players, for example, confers status in a culture in which students are heavily influenced by media pressure from one direction and peer pressure from another.

Ethical decision making by adults may be commonplace, but research suggests it is difficult to specify how ethical decisions are made (Petrina, 2003). Research on software piracy reveals that moral reasoning on technological issues has contingencies. For instance, university students typically recognize unethical behavior, but make decisions relative to their desires. Nearly three-quarters of 433 students in one study acknowledged participating in software piracy, and half of these said they did not feel guilty about doing so (Hinduja, 2003).

Learning Related to Engineering[2]

Historically, research on engineering education has mostly been done by engineering faculty and has focused on changing curricula, classrooms, and content rather than on measuring the impact of these changes on what students know and can do. Recently, however, as academic engineering faculty increasingly collaborate with faculty in other disciplines, such as education, psychology, and sociology, the types of research questions being asked and the assumptions being made are beginning to change. Because of the shift toward investigating how people learn engineering, most of the available research is based on qualitative methodologies, such as verbal protocol analysis and open-ended questionnaires.

Research on how individuals learn the engineering design process

---

[2]This section includes material adapted from Waller, 2004.

is focused mostly on comparing novice and experienced designers. These studies indicate that novices use a trial-and-error approach, consider fewer issues when describing a problem, ask for fewer kinds of information, use fewer types of design activities, make fewer transitions between design activities, and produce designs of lower quality than experienced designers (e.g., Adams et al., 2003; Ahmed et al., 2003; Atman et al., 1999; Mullins et al., 1999).

Other findings are also relevant to assessing design activity: (1) the choice of task affects problem-solving behavior; (2) more evaluation occurs in the solving of complex problems than simple problems; (3) students draw on personal experiences with the problem situation to generate solutions; and (4) sketching not only allows the problem solver to store information externally, but also allows him or her to experiment with reality, iterate the solution space, and reason at the conceptual and systems level.

Assessing mental models can be very tricky.

Assessing mental models can be very tricky because questions about different, but parallel, situations evoke different explanations. In addition, people who have more than one model for a concept (e.g., electricity as flow and electricity as a field phenomenon) may use the simpler model to explain a situation unless they are asked specifically for the most technically precise explanation. Since the early 1980s, researchers have been trying to capture the mental models children, students, and adults use to understand concepts and processes, such as combustion, electricity, and evaporation (e.g., Borges and Gilbert, 1999; Tytler, 2000; Watson et al., 1997). However, because the vast majority of studies on conceptual change involve single or comparative designs, rather than longitudinal designs, the conclusions require assumptions of equivalence of samples and populations.

Taken together, these studies indicate several features of mental models: (1) they are developed initially through everyday experiences; (2) they are generally simple, causal models of observable phenomena; and (3) they are applied consistently according to the individual's rules of logic (which may not match those accepted in the scientific community). In addition, individuals can hold alternative conceptions simultaneously without apparent conflict. Thus, different questions may elicit different models from the same individual.

One way of measuring students' conceptual understanding, rather than their ability to apply formulae, is through a concept inventory. First developed in physics education in the Force Concept Inventory (Hestenes et al., 1992), concept inventories consist of multiple-choice questions that require a substantial understanding of concepts rather than simple calculation skills or commonsense understanding. By including a variety of distractors, such assessments reveal the extent and nature of student misconceptions about a topic. In engineering education, 15 concept inventories are in various stages of development (Box 4-1).

Thus far, no studies have addressed general engineering concepts, such as systems, boundaries, constraints, trade-offs, goal setting, estimation, and safety. Some of these are obliquely included in analyses of design behavior, but no study addresses how participants specifically include these concepts. In addition, not a single study investigates what the general public understands about these concepts, much less how they come to understand them.

When applying the findings of studies of how people learn engineering design and content, several caveats must be observed. First, engineering students and practitioners are not a random sample of the general population; therefore findings based on this specialized population may not apply to other populations. Second, learning preferences not only affect the way people learn, but also how they interact with assessment instruments, and engineering concepts can be expressed in many different ways (e.g., mathematics, diagrams, analogies, and verbal descriptions). Thus, a robust assessment instrument should accept several different expressions of concepts as "correct." Third, engineering design is ultimately a collaborative process, with goals, boundaries, constraints, and criteria negotiated by a wide variety of stakeholders. Therefore, an authentic assessment of design skills should include a component that reflects the

---

BOX 4-1   Concept Inventories Under Development, by Topic

Electronics	Electromagnetics	Dynamics
Waves	Circuits	Thermal and transport processes
Thermodynamics	Fluid mechanics	Computer engineering
Strength of materials	Materials	Statistics
Signals and systems	Chemistry	Heat transfer

Source: Waller, 2004.

---

negotiation, teamwork, and communication skills necessary for successful design processes.

Fourth, because design is context sensitive, researchers must be cautious in comparing results across cultures (including cultures within the United States) (Herbeaux and Bannerot, 2003). The values underlying choices and trade-offs between groups may be very different, as may the communication and negotiation processes. And, because understanding depends in part on everyday experiences, assessors must be careful to select examples and situations that do not reflect socioeconomic or cultural differences. For example, some children may not have experience with clothes drying on a line, while others may never have seen a light wired to a dimmer switch. If these items are used, an assessment instrument may indicate differences in conceptual understanding that actually reflect socioeconomic and/or cultural differences among study participants.

References

AAAS (American Association for the Advancement of Science). 1993. Benchmarks for Science Literacy. Project 2061. New York: Oxford University Press.

Adams, R.S., J. Turns, and C.J. Atman. 2003. Educating effective engineering designers: the role of reflective practice. Design Studies 24(2003): 275–294.

AERA (American Educational Research Association), APA (American Psychological Association), and NCME (National Council on Measurement in Education). 1999. Fairness in Testing and Test Use: Standards 7.3 and 7.4. Pp. 79–82 in Standards for Educational and Psychological Testing. Washington, D.C.: AERA.

Ahmed, S., K.M. Wallace, and L.T.M. Blessing. 2003. Understanding the differences between how novice and experienced designers approach design tasks. Research in Engineering Design 14(2003): 1–11.

Anderson, J.R. 1990. Cognitive Psychology and Its Implications. San Francisco: Freeman.

Atman, C.J., J.R. Chimka, K.M. Bursic, and H. Nachtmann. 1999. A comparison of freshman and senior engineering design processes. Design Studies 20(2): 131–152.

Barnett, S.M., and S.J. Ceci. 2002. When and where do we apply what we learn?: a taxonomy for far transfer. Psychological Bulletin 128(4): 612–637.

Bassok, M., and K.J. Holyoak. 1989. Interdomain transfer between isomorphic topics in algebra and physics. Journal of Experimental Psychology: Learning, Memory, and Cognition 15(1): 153–166.

Bers, M.U. 2001. Identity construction environments: developing personal and moral values through design of a virtual city. Journal of the Learning Sciences 10(4): 365–415.

Bjork, R.A., and A. Richardson-Klavhen. 1989. On the Puzzling Relationship Between Environment Context and Human Memory. Pp. 313–344 in Current Issues in Cognitive Processes: The Tulane Flowerree Symposium on Cognition, edited by C. Izawa. Hillsdale, N.J.: Lawrence Erlbaum Associates.

Blanchette, I., and K. Dunbar. 2002. Representational change and analogy: how analogical inferences alter target representations. Journal of Experimental Psychology: Learning, Memory, and Cognition 28(4): 672–685.

Borges, A.T., and J.K. Gilbert. 1999. Mental models of electricity. International Journal of Science Education 21(1): 95–117.

Brandt, R. 1998. Assessing Student Learning: New Rules, New Realities. Washington, D.C.: Educational Research Services.

Bransford, J.D., B.S. Stein, N.J. Vye, J.J. Franks, P.M. Auble, K.J. Mezynski, and G.A. Perfetto. 1983. Differences in approaches to learning: an overview. Journal of Experimental Psychology: General 3: 390–398.

Bransford, J.D., A.L. Brown, and R.R. Cocking. 1999. How People Learn: Brain, Mind, Experience, and School. Washington, D.C.: National Academy Press.

Brown, A.L. 1990. Domain-specific principles affect learning and transfer in children. Cognitive Science 14(1): 107–133.

Brown, A.L., J.D. Bransford, R.A. Ferrara, and J. Campione. 1983. Learning, Remembering, and Understanding. Pp. 78–166 in Cognitive Development, vol. 3, edited by J. Flavell and E.M. Markman. New York: John Wiley and Sons.

Carey, S. 1999. Sources of Conceptual Change. Pp. 293–326 in Conceptual Development: Piaget's Legacy, edited by E.K. Scholnick, K. Nelson, S. Gelman, and P. Miller. Mahwah, N.J.: Lawrence Erlbaum Associates.

Carey, S., and C. Smith. 1993. On understanding the nature of scientific knowledge. Educational Psychologist 28(3): 235–251.

Carraher, T.N. 1986. From drawings to buildings: mathematical scales at work. International Journal of Behavioral Development 9(4): 527–544.

Chi, M.T.H. 2000. Self-explaining: The Dual Processes of Generating Inference and Repairing Mental Models. Pp. 161–238 in Advances in Instructional Psychology: Educational Design and Cognitive Science, vol. 5, edited by R. Glaser. Mahwah, N.J.: Lawrence Erlbaum Associates.

Chi, M.T.H, and R. Glaser. 1981. The Measurement of Expertise: Analysis of the Development of Knowledge and Skills as a Basis for Assessing Achievement. Pp. 37–47 in Design, Analysis and Policy in Testing, edited by E.L. Baker and E.S. Quellmalz. Beverly Hills, Calif.: Sage Publications.

Chi, M.T.H., P.J. Feltovich, and R. Glaser. 1981. Categorization and representation of physics problems by experts and novices. Cognitive Science 5(2): 121–152.

Chi, M.T.H., J.D. Slotta, and N. De Leeuw. 1994. From things to processes: a theory of conceptual change for learning science concepts. Learning and Instruction 4(1): 27–43.

Crismond, D. 2001. Learning and using science ideas when doing investigate-and-redesign tasks: a study of naïve, novice, and expert designers doing constrained and scaffolded design work. Journal of Research in Science Teaching 38(7): 791–820.

Custer, R.L., M. Hoepfl, B. McAlister, J. Schell, and J. Scott. 2000. Using Alternative Assessment in Vocational Education. Information Series No. 381. ERIC Clearinghouse on Adult, Career, and Vocational Education.

Davis, R.S., I.S. Ginns, and C.J. McRobbie. 2002. Elementary school students' understandings of technology concepts. Journal of Technology Education 14(1): 35–50.

diSessa, A.A. 1988. Knowledge in Pieces. Pp. 49–70 in Constructivism in the Computer Age, edited by G. Forman and P. Pufall. Hillsdale, N.J.: Lawrence Erlbaum Associates.

diSessa, A.A. 1993. Toward an epistemology of physics. Cognition and Instruction 10(2-3): 105–225.

diSessa, A.A. 2002. Why "conceptual ecology" is a good idea. Pp. 29–60 in Reconsidering Conceptual Change: Issues in Theory and Practice, edited by M. Limón and L. Mason. Dordrecht, The Netherlands: Kluwer Academic Pulishers.

diSessa, A.A., and B.L. Sherin. 1998. What changes in conceptual change? International Journal of Science Education 20(10): 1155–1191.

diSessa, A.A., and J.F. Wagner. 2005. What Coordination Has to Say About Transfer. Pp. 121–154 in Transfer of Learning from a Modern Multidisciplinary Perspective, edited by J.P. Mestre. Greenwich, Conn.: Information Age Publishing.

diSessa, A A., N. Gillespie, and J. Esterly. In press. Coherence vs. fragmentation in the development of the concept of force. Cognitive Science.

Druin, A., ed. 1999. The Design of Children's Technology. San Francisco: Morgan Kaufman.

Druin, A. 2002. The role of children in the design of new technology. Behaviour and Information Technology 21(1): 1–25.

Druin, A., and C. Fast. 2002. The child as learner, critic, inventor, and technology design partner: an analysis of three years of Swedish student journals. International Journal of Technology and Design Education 12(3): 189–213.

Druin, A., and J. Hendler, eds. 2001. Robots for Kids: Exploring New Technologies for Learning Experiences. San Francisco: Morgan Kaufman.

Egan, D.E., and B.J. Schwartz. 1979. Chunking in recall of symbolic drawings. Memory and Cognition 7: 149–158.

Eich, E. 1985. Context, memory, and integrated item/context imagery. Journal of Experimental Psychology: Learning, Memory, and Cognition 11(4): 764–770.

Ericsson, K.A., and W. Kintsch. 1995. Long-term working memory. Psychological Review 102(2): 211–245.

Etkina, E., J. Mestre, and A. O'Donnell. 2005. The Impact of the Cognitive Revolution on Science Learning and Teaching. Pp. 119–164 in The Cognitive Revolution in Educational Psychology, edited by J.M. Royer. Greenwich, Conn.: Information Age Publishing.

Foster, P., and M. Wright. 2001. How children think and feel about design and technology: two case studies. Journal of Industrial Teacher Education 38(2): 40–64.

Gick, M.L., and K.J. Holyoak. 1980. Analogical problem solving. Cognitive Psychology 12(3): 306–355.

Hambleton, R., and J. Rogers. 1995. Item bias review. Practical Assessment, Research and Evaluation 4(6). Available online at: *http://pareonline.net/getvn.asp?v=4&n=6.*

Hammer, D., and A. Elby. 2003. Tapping epistemological resources for learning physics. Journal of the Learning Sciences 12(1): 53–91.

Hammer, D., A. Elby, R. Scherr, and E. Redish. 2005. Resources, Framing, and Transfer. Pp. 89–119 in Transfer of Learning from a Modern Multidisciplinary Perspective, edited by J.P. Mestre. Greenwich, Conn.: Information Age Publishing.

Hardiman, P.T., R. Dufresne, and J.P. Mestre. 1989. The relation between problem categorization and problem solving among experts and novices. Memory and Cognition 17(5): 627–638.

Hatano, G., and K. Inagaki. 1996. Cognitive and Cultural Factors in the Acquisition of Intuitive Biology. Pp. 683–708 in Handbook of Education and Human Development: New Models of Learning, Teaching and Schooling, edited by D.R. Olson and N. Torrance. Malden, Mass.: Blackwell Publishers Inc.

Hayes, J.R., and H.A. Simon. 1977. Psychological Differences Among Problem Isomorphs. Pp. 21–41 in Cognitive Theory, vol. 2, edited by N.J. Castellan Jr., D.B. Pisoni, and G.R. Potts. Hillsdale, N.J.: Lawrence Erlbaum Associates.

Herbeaux, J.-L., and R. Bannerot. 2003. Cultural Influences in Design. Paper presented at the American Society for Engineering Education Annual Conference and Exposition, June 22–25, 2003, Nashville, Tenn. Available online at: *http://asee.org/acPapers/2003-549_Final.pdf* (April 5, 2006).

Hestenes, D., M. Wells, and G. Swackhammer. 1992. Force concept inventory. The Physics Teacher 30(3): 141–158.

Hill, A.M., and A. Anning. 2001a. Comparisons and contrasts between elementary/primary "school situated design" and "workplace design" in Canada and England. International Journal of Technology and Design Education 11(2): 111–136.

Hill, A.M., and A. Anning. 2001b. Primary teachers' and students' understanding of school situated design in Canada and England. Research in Science Education 31(1): 117–135.

Hinduja, S. 2003. Trends and patterns among online software pirates. Ethics and Information Technology 5(1): 49–61.

Hmelo, C., D. Holton, and J. Kolodner. 2000. Designing to learn about complex systems. Journal of the Learning Sciences 9(3): 247–298.

Ioannides, C., and S. Vosniadou. 2002. The changing meanings of force. Cognitive Science Quarterly 2(1): 5–62.

ITEA (International Technology Education Association). 2000. Standards for Technological Literacy: Content for the Study of Technology. Reston, Va.: ITEA.

Jarvis, T., and L. Rennie. 1996. Understanding technology: the development of a concept. International Journal of Science Education 18(8): 979–992.

Jarvis, T., and L. Rennie. 1998. Factors that influence children's developing perceptions of technology. International Journal of Technology and Design Education 8(3): 261–279.

Jenson, J., S. de Castell, and M. Bryson. 2003. "Girl talk": gender equity and identity discourses in a school-based computer culture. Women's Studies International Forum 26(6): 561–573.

Kafai, Y., C.C. Ching, and S. Marshall. 1997. Children as designers of educational multimedia software. Computers in Education 29(2-3): 117–126.

Kavakli, M., and J. Gero. 2002. The structure of concurrent actions: a case study on novice and expert designers. Design Studies 23(1): 25–40.

Kiplinger, V.L. 1997. Standard-setting procedures for the specification of performance levels on a standards-based assessment. Available online at: *http://www.cde.state.co.us/cdeassess/csap/asperf.htm* (October 14, 2005).

Klahr, D., and S.M. Carver. 1988. Cognitive objectives in a LOGO debugging curriculum: instruction, learning, and transfer. Cognitive Psychology 20: 362–404.

Larkin, J.H. 1981. Enriching Formal Knowledge: A Model for Learning to Solve Problems in Physics. Pp. 311–334 in Cognitive Skills and Their Acquisition, edited by J.R. Anderson. Hillsdale, N.J.: Lawrence Erlbaum Associates.

Larkin, J.H. 1983. The Role of Problem Representation in Physics. Pp. 75–98 in Mental Models, edited by D. Gentner and A.L. Stevens. Hillsdale, N.J.: Lawrence Erlbaum Associates.

Lave, J. 1988. Cognition in Practice: Mind, Mathematics and Culture in Everyday Life. Cambridge, U.K.: Cambridge University Press.

Linn, R.L., and N.E. Gronlund. 2000. Measurement and Assessment in Teaching, 8th ed. Upper Saddle River, N.J.: Prentice-Hall.

Littlefield, J., V. Delclos, S. Lever, K. Clayton, J. Bransford, and J. Franks. 1988. Learning LOGO: Method of Teaching, Transfer of General Skills, and Attitudes Toward School and Computers. Pp. 111–136 in Teaching and Learning Computer Programming, edited by R.E. Mayer. Hillsdale, N.J.: Lawrence Erlbaum Associates.

Luckhel, R., D. Thissen, and H. Wainer. 1994. On the relative value of multiple-choice, constructed-response, and examinee-selected items on two achievement tests. Journal of Educational Measurement 31(3): 234–250.

Mandler, J.M., and F. Orlich. 1993. Analogical transfer: the roles of schema abstraction and awareness. Bulletin of the Psychonomic Society 31(5): 485–487.

McCloskey, M. 1983a. Intuitive physics. Scientific American 248(4): 122–130.

McCloskey, M. 1983b. Naive Theories of Motion. Pp. 299–313 in Mental Models, edited by D. Gentner and A. Stevens. Hillsdale, N.J.: Lawrence Erlbaum Associates.

McDermott, L.C. 1984. Research on conceptual understanding in mechanics. Physics Today 37(7): 24–32.

McTighe, J., and S. Ferrara. 1996. Assessing Learning in the Classroom. Washington, D.C.: National Education Association.

Messick, S. 1989. Validity. Pp. 13–103 in Educational Measurement, 3rd ed., edited by R.L. Linn. New York: Macmillan.

Mestre, J.P. 1991. Learning and instruction in pre-college physical science. Physics Today 44(9): 56–62.

Mestre, J.P., ed. 2005. Transfer of Learning from a Modern Multidisciplinary Perspective. Greenwich, Conn.: Information Age Publishing.

Mestre, J., T. Thaden-Koch, R. Dufresne, and W. Gerace. 2004. The Dependence of Knowledge Deployment on Context among Physics Novices. Pp. 367–408 in Proceedings of the International School of Physics, "Enrico Fermi" Course CLVI, edited by E.F. Redish and M. Vicentini. Amsterdam: ISO Press.

Moskal, B.M., and J.A. Leydens. 2000. Scoring rubric development: validity and reliability. Available online at: *http://pareonline.net/getvn.asp?v=7&n=10* (January 26, 2006).

Mullins, C.A., C.J. Atman, and L.J. Shuman. 1999. Freshman engineers' performance when solving design problems. IEEE Transactions on Education 42(4): 281–287.

Nitko, A. J. 1996. Bias in Educational Assessment. Pp. 91–93 in Educational Assessment of Students, 2nd ed. Englewood Cliffs, N.J.: Merrill.

NRC (National Research Council). 1996. National Science Education Standards. Washington, D.C.: National Academy Press.

NRC. 2001a. The Science and Design of Educational Assessment. Pp. 44–51 in Knowing What Students Know: The Science and Design of Educational Assessment.. Washington, D.C.: National Academy Press.

NRC. 2001b. Knowing What Students Know: The Science and Design of Educational Assessment. Washington, D.C.: National Academy Press.

OERL (Online Evaluation Resource Library). 2006, Alignment Table for Instrument Characteristics—Technical Quality. Available online at: *http://oerl.sri.com/instruments/alignment/instralign_tq.html* (January 26, 2006).

Orr, J.E. 1996. Talking About Machines: An Ethnography of a Modern Job. Ithaca, N.Y.: ILR Press.

Petrina, S. 2003. "Two cultures" of technical courses and discourses: the case of computer-aided design. International Journal of Technology and Design Education 13(1): 47–73.

Petrina, S., F. Feng, and J. Kim. 2004. How We Learn (About, Through, and for Technology): A Review Of Research. Paper commissioned by the Committee on Assessing Technological Literacy. Unpublished.

Pomares-Brandt, P. 2003. Les nouvelles technologies de l'information et de la communication dans les enseignements technologiques. Unpublished Ph.D. dissertation. Université de Provence, Aix-Marseille.

Reed, S.K., G.W. Ernst, and R. Banerji. 1974. The role of analogy in transfer between similar problem states. Cognitive Psychology 6(3): 436–450.

Reed, S.K., A. Dempster, and M. Ettinger. 1985. Usefulness of analogous solutions for solving algebra word problems. Journal of Experimental Psychology: Learning, Memory, and Cognition 11(1): 106–125.

Rennie, L., and T. Jarvis. 1995. Three approaches to measuring children's perceptions about technology. International Journal of Science Education 17(6): 755–774.

Roth, W.-M. 1998. Designing Communities. Dordrecht, The Netherlands: Kluwer Academic Publishers.

Saxe, G. B. 1989. Transfer of learning across cultural practices. Cognition and Instruction 6(4): 325–330.

Schallies, M., A. Wellensiek, and A. Lembens. 2002. The development of mature capabilities for understanding and valuing in technology through school project work: individual and structural preconditions. International Journal of Technology and Design Education 12(1): 41–58.

Schoenfeld, A.H. 1985. Mathematical Problem Solving. New York: Academic Press.

Schoenfeld, A.H., and D.J. Herrmann. 1982. Problem perception and knowledge structure in expert and novice mathematical problem solvers. Journal of Experimental Psychology: Learning, Memory, and Cognition 8(4): 484–494.

Schwartz, W. 1995. Opportunity to Learn Standards: Their Impact on Urban Students. ERIC/CUE Digest no. 110. Available online at: *http://www.eric.ed.gov/ ERICDocs/data/ericdocs2/content_storage_01/0000000b/80/2a/24/a0.pdf* (January 26, 2006).

Selwyn, N. 2001. Turned on/switched off: exploring children's engagement with computers in primary school. Journal of Educational Computing Research 25(3): 245–266.

Selwyn, N. 2003. Doing IT for the kids: re-examining children, computers and the "information society." Media, Culture and Society 25(4): 351–378.

Sireci, S.G. 2005. The Most Frequently Unasked Questions About Testing. Pp. 111–121 in Defending Standardized Testing, edited by R.P. Phelp. Mahwah, N.J.: Lawrence Erlbaum Associates.

Smith, C., D. Maclin, L. Grosslight, and H. Davis. 1997. Teaching for understanding: a study of students' preinstruction theories of matter and a comparison of the effectiveness of two approaches to teaching about matter and density. Cognition and Instruction 15(3): 317–393.

Smith, J.P., A.A. diSessa, and J. Roschelle. 1994. Misconceptions reconceived: a constructivist analysis of knowledge in transition. Journal of the Learning Sciences 3(2): 115–163.

Stiggins, R. 1995. Assessment literacy for the 21st century. Phi Delta Kappan 77(3): 238–245.

Strike, K.A., and G.J. Posner. 1985. A Conceptual Change View of Learning and Understanding. Pp. 211–231 in Cognitive Structure and Conceptual Change, edited by L.H.T. West and A.L. Pines. New York: Academic Press.

Taxen, G., A. Druin, C. Fast, and M. Kjellin. 2001. KidStory: a technology design partnership with children. Behaviour and Information Technology 20(2): 119–125.

Thomson, C. 1997. Concept Mapping as an Aid to Learning and Teaching. Pp. 97–110 in Shaping Concepts of Technology: from Philosophical Perspectives to Mental Images, edited by M.J. de Vries and A. Tamir. Dordrecht, The Netherlands: Kluwer Academic Publishers. Reprinted from International Journal of Technology and Design Education 7(1-2).

Tytler, R. 2000. A comparison of year 1 and year 6 students' conceptions of evaporation and condensation: dimensions of conceptual progression. International Journal of Science Education 22(5): 447–467.

Upitis, R. 1998. From hackers to Luddites, game players to game creators: profiles of adolescent students using technology. Journal of Curriculum Studies 30(3): 293–318.

Vosniadou, S., and W.F. Brewer. 1992. Mental models of the Earth: a study of conceptual change in childhood. Cognitive Psychology 24(4): 535–585.

Vosniadou, S., and C. Ioannides. 1998. From conceptual development to science education: a psychological point of view. International Journal of Science Education 20(10): 1213–1230.

Waller, A. 2004. Final Report on a Literature Review of Research on How People Learn Engineering Concepts and Processes. Paper commissionied by the Committee on Assessing Technological Literacy. Unpublished.

Watson, J.R., T. Prieto, and J.S. Dillon. 1997. Consistency of students' explanations about combustion. Science Education 81(4): 425–443.

Wegerif, R. 2004. The role of educational software as a support for teaching and learning conversations. Computers and Education 43: 179–191.

Welch, M., D. Barlex, and H.S. Lim. 2000. The strategic thinking of novice designers: discontinuity between theory and practice. Journal of Technology Studies 25(2): 34–44.

White, B.Y., and J.R. Frederiksen. 1998. Inquiry, modeling, and metacognition: making science accessible to all students. Cognition and Instruction 16(1): 3–118.

Wineburg, S. 1998. Reading Abraham Lincoln: an expert/expert study in historical cognition. Cognitive Science 22(3): 319–346.

Zeidler, D., ed. 2003. The Role of Moral Reasoning on Socioscientific Issues and Discourse in Science Education. Dordrecht, The Netherlands: Kluwer Academic Publishers.

5
Review of Instruments

To provide a basis for deliberations, the committee collected and analyzed assessments that have been used or might be used to measure an aspect of technological literacy, even if they were not designed explicitly for that purpose. In fact, only about one-third of the assessment "instruments" collected by the committee were explicitly designed to measure technological literacy. Of these, only a handful was based on a conceptual model of technological literacy like the one presented in *Technically Speaking* or *Standards for Technological Literacy*. Indeed, the universe of assessments of technological literacy is very small.

A combination of formal methods (e.g., database searches) and informal methods (e.g., inquiries to knowledgeable individuals and organizations) were used to collect assessment instruments. The committee believes most of the relevant assessment instruments were evaluated, but, because the identification process was imperfect, the portfolio of instruments should not be considered comprehensive.

Altogether, the committee identified 28 assessment instruments of several types, including formal criterion- or norm-referenced tests, performance-based activities intended to measure an aspect of design or problem-solving ability, attitude or opinion surveys, and informal quizzes. Item formats ran the gamut from multiple-choice and short-answer questions to essays and performance tasks. About half the instruments had been used more than once; a very few had been administered many times over the course of a decade or more. The others, such as assessments developed as research for Ph.D. dissertations, had been used once, if at all.

The population of interest for most of the instruments was K–12 students. Teachers were the target population for two, the Praxis Technology Education Test (ETS, 2005) and the Engineering K–12 Center Teacher Survey (ASEE, 2005). The rest were designed to test out-of-school adults. Although the focus of this project is on assessment in the United States, the committee also studied instruments developed in Canada, England, and Taiwan. The approaches to assessment in non-U.S. settings provided useful data for the committee's analysis.

The purposes of the assessment tools varied as much as the instruments themselves. They included diagnosis and certification of students, input for curriculum development, certification of teachers, resource allocation, program evaluation, guidance for public policy, suitability for employment, and research. The developers of these assessments could be divided into four categories: state or federal agencies, private educational organizations, academic researchers, and test-development or survey companies.

Table 5-1 provides basic information about the instruments, according to target population. More detailed information on each instrument, including sample items and committee observations, is provided in Appendix E.

The committee reviewed each instrument through critiques written by committee members, telephone conferences, and face-to-face discussions. In general, the reviews focused on two aspects of the assessments: (1) the type and quality of individual test items; and (2) the format or design of the assessment. The reviews provided an overview of current approaches to assessing technological understanding and capability and stimulated a discussion about the best way to conduct assessments in this area.

Although a number of the instruments reviewed were thoughtfully designed, no single instrument struck the committee as completely adequate to the task of assessing technological literacy. This is not surprising, considering the general challenge of developing high-quality assessments; the multifaceted nature of technological literacy; the characteristics of the three target populations; the relatively small number of individuals and organizations involved in designing assessments for technological literacy; and the absence of research literature in this area. And as noted, only a few of the instruments under review were designed explicitly to assess technological literacy in the first place.

> No single instrument struck the committee as completely adequate to the task of assessing technological literacy.

TABLE 5-1 Technological-Literacy-Related Assessment Instruments

Name	Developer	Primary Purpose	Frequency of Administration
K–12 Students			
Assessment of Performance in Design and Technology	Schools Examinations and Assessment Council, London	Curriculum development and research.	Once in 1989.
Design Technology	International Baccalaureate Organization	Student achievement (part of qualification for diploma).	Regularly since 2003.
Design-Based Science	David Fortus, University of Michigan	Curriculum development and research.	Once in 2001–2002.
Design Team Assessments for Engineering Students	Washington State University	Assess students' knowledge, performance, and evaluation of the design process; evaluate student teamwork and communication skills.	Unknown.
Future City Competition —Judges Manual	National Engineers Week	To help rate and rank design projects and essays submitted to the Future City Competition.	Annually since 1992.
ICT Literacy Assessment[a]	Educational Testing Service	Proficiency testing.	Launched in early 2005.
Illinois Standards Achievements Test— Science	Illinois State Board of Education	Measure student achievement in five areas and monitor school performance.	Annually since 2000.
Industrial Technology Literacy Test[b]	Michael Allen Hayden, Iowa State University	Assess the level of industrial-technology literacy among high school students.	Once in 1989 or 1990.
Infinity Project Pretest and Final Test	Geoffrey Orsak, Southern Methodist University	Basic aptitude (pretest) and student performance.	Ongoing since 1999.
Information Technology in a Global Society	International Baccalaureate Organization	Student evaluation.	Semiannually at the standard level since 2002; higher-level exams will be available in 2006.
Massachusetts Comprehensive Assessment Systems— Science and Technology/	Massachusetts Department of Education	Monitor individual student achievement, gauge school and district performance, satisfy	Annually since 1998.

continued

TABLE 5-1   Continued

Name	Developer	Primary Purpose	Frequency of Administration
Engineering		requirements of No Child Left Behind Act.	
Multiple Choice Instrument for Monitoring Views on Science-Technology-Society Topics	G.S. Aikenhead and A.G. Ryan, University of Saskatchewan	Curriculum evaluation and research.	Once in September 1987–August 1989.
New York State Intermediate Assessment in Technology[b]	State Education Department/State University of New York	Curriculum improvement and student evaluation.	Unknown.
Provincial Learning Assessment in Technological Literacy[b]	Saskatchewan Education	Analyze students' technological literacy to improve their understanding of the relationship between technology and society.	Once in 1999.
Pupils' Attitudes Toward Technology (PATT-USA)[b]	E. Allen Bame and William E. Dugger, Jr., Virginia Polytechnic Institute and State University; Marc J. de Vries, Eindhoven University	Assess student attitudes toward and knowledge of technology.	Dozens of times in many countries since 1988.
Student Individualized Performance Inventory	Rodney L. Custer, Brigitte G. Valesey, and Barry N. Burke, with funding from the Council on Technology Teacher Education, International Technology Education Association, and the Technical Foundation of America	Develop a model to assess the problem-solving capabilities of students engaged in design activities.	Unknown.
Survey of Technological Literacy of Elementary and Junior High School Students[b]	Ta Wei Le, et al., National Taiwan Normal University	Curriculum development and planning.	Once in March 1995.
Test of Technological Literacy[b]	Abdul Hameed, Ohio State University	Research.	Once in April 1988.
TL50: Technological Literacy Instrument[b]	Michael J. Dyrenfurth, Purdue University	Gauge technological literacy.	Unknown.
WorkKeys—Applied Technology[c]	American College Testing Program	Measure job skills and workplace readiness.	Multiple times since 1992.

TABLE 5-1   Continued

Name	Developer	Primary Purpose	Frequency of Administration
K–12 Teachers			
Engineering K–12 Center Teacher Survey	American Society for Engineering Education	Inform outreach efforts to K–12 teachers.	Continuously available.
Praxis Specialty Area Test: Technology Education[a]	Educational Testing Service	Teacher licensing.	Regularly.
Out-of-School Adults			
Armed Services Vocational Aptitude Battery	U.S. Department of Defense	Assess potential of military recruits for job specialties in the armed forces and provide a standard for enlistment.	Ongoing in its present form since 1968.
Awareness Survey on Genetically Modified Foods	North Carolina Citizens' Technology Forum Project Team	Research on public involvement in decision making on science and technology issues.	Once in 2001.
Eurobarometer: Europeans, Science and Technology	European Union Directorate General for Press and Communication	Monitor changes in public views of science and technology to assist decision making by policy makers.	Surveys on various topics conducted regularly since 1973; this poll was conducted in May/June 2001.
European Commission Candidate Countries Eurobarometer: Science and Technology	Gallup Organization of Hungary	Monitor public opinion on science and technology issues of concern to policy makers.	Periodically since 1973; this survey was administered in 2002.
Gallup Poll on What Americans Think About Technology[b]	International Technology Education Association	Determine public knowledge and perceptions of technology to inform efforts to change and shape public views.	Twice, in 2001 and 2004.
Science and Technology: Public Attitudes and Public Understanding	National Science Board	Monitor public attitudes, knowledge, and interest in science and technology issues.	Biennially from 1979 to 2001.

[a]Also administered to community and four-year college students.
[b]Designed explicitly to measure some aspects of technological literacy.
[c]Also used in community college and workplace settings.

Mapping Existing Instruments to the Dimensions of Technological Literacy

Only about one-third of the instruments collected were developed with the explicit goal of measuring technological literacy. Only two or three of these were designed with the three dimensions of technological literacy spelled out in *Technically Speaking* in mind. Nevertheless, the committee found the three dimensions to be a useful lens through which to analyze all of the instruments. When viewed this way, some instruments and test items appeared to be more focused on teasing out the knowledge component than testing capability. Others were more focused on capability or critical thinking and decision making. In some cases, the instruments and items addressed aspects of two or even all three dimensions of technological literacy.

Knowledge Dimension

Every assessment instrument examined by the committee assumed some level of technological knowledge on the part of the person taking the test or participating in the poll or survey. Because the three dimensions are interwoven and overlapping (see Chapter 2), even assessments focused on capability or ways of thinking and acting tap into technological knowledge. The committee did not undertake a precise count but estimated that one-half to three-quarters of the assessment instruments were mostly or entirely designed to measure knowledge.

The knowledge dimension is evident in the handful of state-developed assessments, which are designed to measure content standards or curriculum frameworks that spell out what students should know and be able to do at various points in their school careers. Massachusetts and Illinois, for example, have developed assessments that measure technological understanding as part of testing for science achievement. The Massachusetts Comprehensive Assessment System (MCAS) science assessment instrument (MDE, 2005a,b) reflects the addition in 2001 of "engineering" to the curriculum framework for science and technology (MDE, 2001). In the 2005 science assessment, 9 of the 39 5th-grade items and 10 of the 39 8th-grade items targeted the technology/engineering strand of the curriculum. In the 5th-grade test, 6 of the 9 questions were aligned with state standards for engineering design; the others were aligned with standards for tools and materials. Questions in the 8th-grade exam were related to standards for transportation, construction, bioengineering, and manufacturing technologies; engineering design; and materials, tools, and machines.

Multiple-choice items that are well crafted can elicit higher order thinking. The 2002 8th-grade MCAS, for example, included the following item:

An engineer designing a suspension bridge discovers it will need to carry twice the load that was initially estimated. One change the engineer must make to her original design to maintain safety is to increase the

A. length of wires in tension
B. diameter of wires in tension
C. height of support towers
D. length of the bridge

To arrive at the suggested correct answer (B), students must be able to define "load" and "tension" in an engineering context. But they must also make the connection between the diameter and strength of the load-bearing structure (the wire in this case). A student would be more likely to be able to answer this question if he or she had participated in design activities in the classroom, such as building a bridge and testing it for load strength.

Open-ended questions can also probe higher-order thinking skills. Although these kinds of questions are more time consuming to respond to and more challenging to score, they can provide opportunities for test takers to demonstrate deeper conceptual understanding. To assess students' understanding of systems, for instance, a question on the New York State Intermediate Assessment in Technology requires that students fill in a systems-model flow chart for one of four systems (a home heating system, an automotive cooling system, a residential electrical system, or a hydroponic growing system).

Recent versions of the Illinois science assessment (ISBE, 2003) were developed with the Illinois Learning Standards in mind (ISBE, 2001a,b). The standards spell out learning goals related to technological design and relationships among science, technology, and society (STS). Of the 70 multiple-choice items on the 2003 assessment, 14 were devoted to STS topics, and 14 were devoted to "science inquiry," which includes technological design. As in the Massachusetts assessment, design-related items required that students demonstrate an understanding of the design process, although they were not asked to take part in an actual design task as part of the test.

Even when learning standards are the basis for the assessment design, the connection between the standards and individual test items is not always clear. A sample question for the 4th-grade Illinois assessment, for instance, asks students to compare the relative energy consumption of four electrical appliances. The exercise is intended to test a standard that suggests students should be able to "apply the concepts, principles, and processes of technological design." However, the question can be answered without knowing the principles of technological design.

The Illinois State Board of Education has devised a Productive Thinking Scale (PTS) by which test developers can rate prospective test items according to the degree of conceptual skill required to answer them (Box 5-1). Similar in some ways to Bloom's taxonomy (Bloom et al., 1964), PTS is specifically intended to be used for developing multiple-choice items. The state tries to construct assessments with most questions at level 3 or level 4; level 1 items are omitted completely; level 2 questions are used only if they address central concepts; level 5 items are used sparingly; and level 6 items are not used because the answers are indeterminate. Level 4, 5, and 6 items seem likely to encourage higher order thinking. Although PTS is used for the development of science assessments, the same approach could be adapted to other subject areas, including technology.

BOX 5-1   Productive Thinking Scale

Content Knowledge	**Process Knowledge**
Level 1: Recall of conventional uses, such as names or vocabulary	Level 1: Recall of conventional uses, such as norms or units
Level 2: Reproduction of empirical facts or effects	Level 2: Reproduction of research sequences or instruments
Level 3: Reproduction of empirical theories or causes	Level 3: Reproduction of methodological reasons
Level 4: Production of one-step problem solving	Level 4: Production of research designs for single-variable control
Level 5: Production of multistep problem solving	Level 5: Production of research designs for multivariable control
Level 6: Creation of new theory	Level 6: Creation of new methods

Source: ISBE, 2003.

From 1977 through 1999, the federal National Assessment of Educational Progress (NAEP) periodically asked 13- and 17-year-olds the same set of science questions as part of an effort to gather long-term data on achievement. The committee commissioned an analysis of responses to the few questions from this instrument that measure technological understanding (Box 5-2).

The Canadian Provincial Learning Assessment in Technological Literacy, an instrument administered in 1999 in Saskatchewan, includes a number of items intended to test 5th-, 8th-, and 11th-graders' conceptions of technology and the effect of that understanding on responsible citizenship, among other issues (Saskatchewan Education, 2001). Student achievement was measured in five increasingly sophisticated

---

BOX 5-2 Selected Data from the NAEP Long-Term Science Assessment, 1977–1999

In 1985, responses to technology-related questions in the 1976–1977 and 1981–1982 NAEP long-term science assessment were analyzed as part of a dissertation study (Hatch, 1985). The analysis included more than 50 questions common to assessments of 13- and 17-year-olds that met the author's definition of technological literacy. In later editions of the test, which involved about 16,000 students, many of these questions were dropped. As part of its exploration of this "indirect" assessment of technological literacy, the committee asked Dr. Hatch to analyze data from all five times the test was administered, the most recent in 1999. Among the 12 questions common to both age groups, two were of particular interest to the committee:

- Would installing storm windows and insulation in your home help to save resources?
  In 1977, 94 percent of 17-year-olds and 92 percent of 13-year-olds answered "yes."
  In 1999, only 65 and 53 percent, respectively, answered "yes."
- What happens to the sulfur dioxide released by a factory's smoke stack?
  In 1977, only 31 percent of 17-year-olds and 20 percent of 13-year-olds chose the correct answer, "The sulfur dioxide eventually falls back to Earth as acid rain."
  By 1999, the percentage of correct answers had jumped to 68 percent for 17-year-olds and 54 percent for 13-year-olds.

It is impossible to state with confidence the reasons for the dramatic changes in students' apparent understanding of the benefits and negative consequences of technology use. The differences undoubtedly have something to do with changes in government and private-sector concerns about energy use and air pollution over this span of time.

This example illustrates why items that mention specific technologies must be periodically reviewed for currency. Because storm windows have largely been replaced by double- or triple-glazed windows, a student faced with this same question today might not be able to answer it, simply because she did not understand what was being asked.

More important, from the committee's perspective, this example illustrates the potential value of time-series data for tracking changes in technological literacy.

SOURCE: Hatch, 2004.

FIGURE 5-1 Level 5 exemplar of eighth-grade student responses to a question about technology, Saskatchewan 1999 Provincial Learning Assessment in Technological Literacy. Source: Saskatchewan Education, 2001.

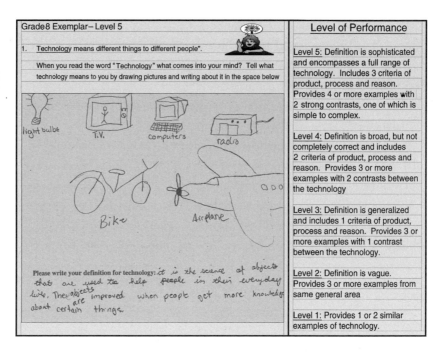

levels according to a rubric developed by a panel of teachers, business leaders, parents, students, and others. Students who cited computers as the only example of technology, for instance, were classified at the lowest level. Students who had a more comprehensive understanding of technology as artifacts made by people to extend human capabilities scored significantly higher (Figure 5-1).

A great many of the knowledge-focused assessments reviewed by the committee relied heavily on items that required test takers to recall facts or define terms. Although knowledge of certain facts and terminology is essential to the mastery of any subject, this type of item has a major drawback because it does not tap into deeper, conceptual understanding. The following question from an assessment intended for high school students is illustrative (Hayden, 1989).

A compact disk can be used to store:

A. numbers
B. music
C. pictures
D. language
E. all of the above

In this question, the suggested correct answer is E, all of the above. One might disagree with the wording of the answers (e.g., is "language" or the printed word stored on a CD?). But the significant issue is that the question focuses on the superficial aspects of CD technology rather than the underlying concepts, such as that information can take multiple forms and that digitization facilitates the storage, retrieval, and manipulation of data. A correct answer does little more than demonstrate a familiarity with some of the capabilities of one type of data-storage device. Although there is a place in assessments for testing factual knowledge, questions of this type could easily dominate an assessment given the number of technologies about which one might reasonably ask questions. In addition, because of the pace of technological development, narrowly targeted items may quickly become obsolete as one technology replaces another.

Nearly one-third of the 100 items in the Pupils' Attitude Toward Technology instrument address the knowledge dimension of technological literacy. The assessment, developed in the 1980s by a Dutch group headed by Marc de Vries, has been used in many countries, including the United States (Bame et al., 1993). The test includes statements with which students are asked to indicate agreement or disagreement. The statements deal with basic and important ideas about the nature of technology, such as the relationship between technology and science, the influence of technology on daily life, and the role of hands-on work in technological development.

High school students and out-of-school adults considering entering the military can choose to take the Armed Services Vocational Aptitude Battery (ASVAB). The ASVAB has eight sections, including items on auto and shop knowledge, mechanics, and knowledge of electronics. Sample items in ASVAB test-preparation books require mostly technical rather than conceptual understanding (e.g., Kaplan, 2003). This reflects the major purpose of the test, which is to identify individuals suited for specialty jobs in the armed forces. ASVAB is notable because it is an online, "adaptive" testing option for adult test takers. In adaptive testing, a right or wrong answer to a question determines the difficulty of the next question.

A group of engineering schools, the Transferable Integrated Design Engineering Education Consortium, has developed an instrument for testing knowledge of the design process (TIDEE, 2002). This is the only assessment in the committee's analysis explicitly intended for college

> Narrowly targeted items may quickly become obsolete as one technology replaces another.

students. The Design Team Knowledge Assessment, parts of which are completed by individuals and parts of which are completed by teams, consists of extended-response and essay questions.

The Praxis Specialty Area Test for Technology Education was designed to assess teachers' knowledge (ETS, 2005). Seventy percent of the 120 multiple-choice questions on the exam address knowledge of specific categories of technology (e.g., information and communication, construction); the remaining items test familiarity with pedagogical concepts. The focus on specific technologies reflects the historical roots of technology education in industrial arts. According to Educational Testing Service, the Praxis test is being "aligned" more closely with the ITEA *Standards for Technological Literacy* to reflect a less vocational, more academic and engineering-oriented view of technology studies.

The following sample item from the Praxis test highlights another potential shortcoming of items that assess only factual knowledge.

The National Standards for Technology Education published in 2000 by the International Technology Education Association are titled:

A. A Conceptual Framework for Technology
B. Standards for Technological Literacy
C. Technology Education: The New Basic
D. Technology for All Americans
E. The Technology Teacher

In this example, the suggested correct answer is B, Standards for Technological Literacy. A stickler might point out that the full title of the ITEA document is *Standards for Technological Literacy: Content for the Study of Technology*, which means that none of the answers is correct. More important, however, the value of demonstrating knowledge of the title of this document is not evident. An item that tests a prospective teacher's knowledge of the contents of the standards would have greater value.

In adult populations, assessment instruments tend to take the form of surveys or polls, and the test population is typically a small, randomly selected sample of a larger target population. Two attempts to gather information about what American adults know and think about technology in 2001 and 2004 were public opinion polls conducted for

ITEA by the Gallup organization (ITEA, 2001, 2004). Six questions from the 2001 survey were repeated in the 2004 poll, including two in the knowledge dimension. One was an open-ended question intended to elicit people's conceptions of technology, the vast majority of which were narrowly focused on computers. The second, a multiple-choice question, was intended to assess people's knowledge of how everyday technologies, such as portable phones, cars, and microwave ovens, function. Nearly half of the respondents thought, incorrectly, that there was a danger of electrocution if a portable phone were used in the bathtub. One knowledge-related question that appeared only in the 2001 poll was intended to assess people's conceptions of design, but the bulk of the questions (17 in 2001 and 16 in 2004) were focused on attitudes and opinions about technology and technological literacy.

For more than 20 years, the National Science Board (NSB) sponsored the work of Jon Miller in the development of a time series of national surveys to measure the public understanding of and attitudes toward science and technology. The summary results of these surveys were published in a series of reports called *Science and Engineering Indicators* (NSB, 1981, 1983, 1986, 1988, 1990, 1992, 1994, 1996, 1998, 2000), and more detailed analyses were published in journals and books (Miller, 1983a,b, 1986, 1987, 1992, 1995, 1998, 2000, 2001, 2004; Miller and Kimmel, 2001; Miller and Pardo, 2000; Miller et al., 1997). Questions about the operating principle of lasers and the role of antibiotics in fighting disease illustrate the kinds of technology-oriented items included in this series.

Adults have also been surveyed about their technology savvy for more specific purposes. In 2001, for example, researchers at North Carolina State University administered a 20-question, multiple-choice test to 45 people taking part in an experimental "citizens' consensus conference" on genetically modified foods. Questions focused on participants' understanding of the purposes, limits, and risks of genetic engineering. Although this test was not reviewed by the committee, some of the same researchers were involved more recently in the development of a test to assess adult knowledge of and attitudes toward nanotechnology (Cobb and Macoubrie, 2004).

Capability Dimension

One of the distinguishing characteristics of technological literacy is the importance of "doing." Described in *Technically Speaking* as the "capability" dimension, doing includes a range of activities and abilities, including hands-on tool skills and, most significantly, design skills. The ITEA *Standards for Technological Literacy* suggests that K–12 students should understand the attributes of design and be able to demonstrate design skills. Using an iterative design process (see Figure 3-1) to identify and solve problems provides insights into how technology is created that cannot be gained any other way.[1] The problem-solving nature of design, with its cognitive processes of analysis, comparison, interpretation, evaluation, and synthesis, also encourages higher order thinking.

Assessing technology-related capability is difficult, however. For one thing, little is known about the psychomotor processes involved. In addition, the cost of developing and administering assessments that involve students in design activities tends to be prohibitive, at least for large-scale assessments, because of the time and personnel required. However, the committee believes there are some promising approaches to measuring design and problem-solving skills that avoid some of these time and resource constraints. (These approaches are discussed in detail in Chapter 7.)

Many attempts have been made to develop standardized instruments for capturing design behavior in educational settings. Custer, Valesey, and Burke (2001) created the Student Individualized Performance Inventory (SIPI), which tests four dimensions: clarification of the problem and design; development of a plan; creation of a model/prototype; and evaluation of the design solution. A student's performance in each dimension is rated as expert, proficient, competent, beginner, or novice. SIPI has been used several times for research purposes (Rodney Custer, Illinois State University, personal communication, May 5, 2005).

Problem solving in a technological context is the focus of the American College Testing (ACT) WorkKeys applied technology assessment, which is intended to help employers compare an individual's workplace skills with the skills required for certain technology-intensive jobs. The 32 multiple-choice test items present real-world problems ranging in difficulty from simple to highly complex. Sample items on the ACT website (*http://www.act.org/workkeys/assess/tech/*) require test takers to

---

[1]A similar argument has been made about the role of inquiry in science. Content standards for K–12 science education (AAAS, 1993; NRC, 1999), for example, stress the importance of students doing "inquiry-based" science projects, in large part because such activities are thought to convey the techniques and thinking processes of real scientists.

decide on the placement of a thermostat in a greenhouse; safely place a load on a trailer pulled by a pickup truck; troubleshoot a bandsaw that will not turn on; and diagnose a hydraulic car lift that is malfunctioning. Multiple-choice tests of capability must be interpreted cautiously, however. A test taker who picks the correct "solution" to a problem-solving task in the constrained environment of multiple choice may not fare nearly as well in an open-ended assessment, where potential solutions may not be spelled out, or in the real world, where the ability to work with tools and materials may come into play. Assessment of capability is one area where computer-based simulation may play a useful role (see Chapter 7).

In the United Kingdom, design and technology have been a mandatory part of the pre-college curriculum since 1990. To test students' design skills, the Assessment of Performance in Design and Technology project developed a 90-minute paper-and-pencil assessment based on carefully tested design tasks intended to measure design capabilities, communication skills, and conceptual understanding of materials, energy, and aesthetics. The assessment was administered to a sample of 10,000 15-year-olds in the United Kingdom in the late 1980s (Kimbell et al., 1991). A small subset of the 10,000 also completed a half-day collaborative modeling exercise, and a subset of these students took part in a design activity that lasted for several months. The research team also developed a rubric for calculating an overall (holistic) score and subtest scores for each student. Figure 5-2 shows an example of a highly rated design effort (holistic score of 5 on a scale of 0 to 5). The rubric has since been adapted for use in assessments of student-selected design and technology projects throughout the United Kingdom.

The British design and technology curriculum centers on doing "authentic" design tasks, activities that represent a believable and—for the student—meaningful challenge. Children in the early grades might be asked to devise a bed for a favorite stuffed animal; children in the middle grades might design a temperature-controlled hutch in which to keep the class rabbit; older students might develop an all-terrain skateboard or an automatic fish feeder for an aquarium.

From an assessment standpoint, performance on the designing and making activity—from the articulation of a design brief to the review of a working prototype—is of primary interest in the United Kingdom. This means that specific knowledge, specific capabilities, and specific ways of critical thinking and decision making are relevant only insofar as they advance a student's design work. In the British model for assessing

> Assessment of capability is one area where computer-based simulation may play a useful role.

FIGURE 5-2 Drawings, models, and final product from a design project for an all-terrain skateboard developed by a 17-year-old student at Saltash Community School in Cornwall, England. The student lived on a farm with no hard surfaces suitable for a traditional skateboard. (a) early-stage concept sketch, (b) Lego model, (c) detail sketch, component of final steering mechanism, (d) completed skateboard, and (e and f, facing page) late-stage concept sketches, steering mechanism.

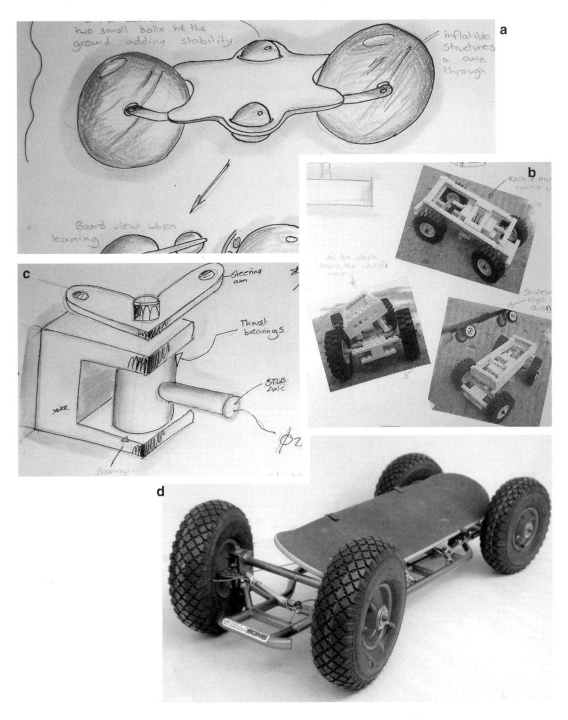

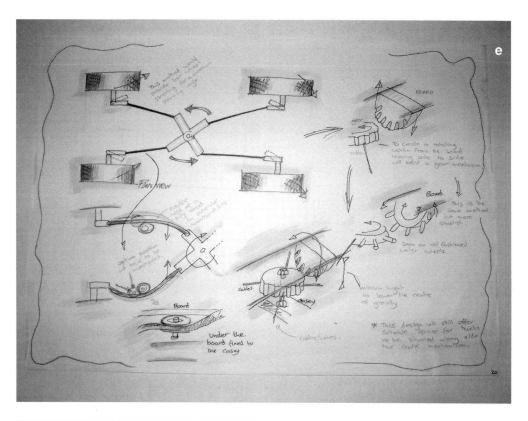

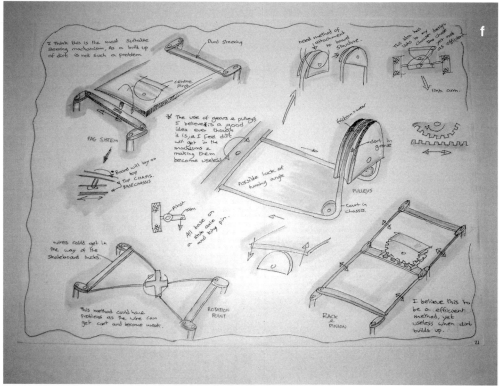

technological literacy, there is almost no interest in determining what students know, independent of specific design challenges. However, there is considerable interest in how students *use* their knowledge, whether they recognize when they are missing key information, and how skillfully they gather new data. In the end, how well or poorly a student scores in the assessment process is a function of how well his or her performance aligns with the elements of good design practice.

In contrast, in the United States, curriculum in technology, as in most subjects, is centered on the acquisition of specific knowledge and skills. Although design activities may be used to reinforce or aid students in the acquisition of certain concepts and capabilities, performance on a design task is not usually the primary basis for assessment. Instead, assessments are based mostly on content standards, which represent expert judgments about the most important knowledge and skills for students to master.

The committee found a great deal to commend the British approach to assessing design-related thinking. For one thing, the design-centered method much more closely mimics the process of technology development in the real world and seems likely to promote higher order thinking. Engineers and scientists in industry or in academic or government laboratories identify and then attempt to solve practical problems using some version of an iterative design methodology. This is a fairly open-ended process, at least at the beginning. For another thing, the design-centered method of assessment reinforces many key notions in technology that cannot easily be taught any other way. The ideas that design always involves some degree of uncertainty and that no human-designed product is without shortcomings are more likely to be understood at a deeper level by someone who has engaged in an authentic design challenge than by someone who has not.

The Saskatchewan Education 1999 Provincial Learning Assessment in Technological Literacy required that students demonstrate capability in two areas: (1) the use of information technology; and (2) performance on design-related tasks. Over a period of two to three hours, students used word-processing software and an Internet Web browser, adjusted controls on a clock radio to specified settings, conducted a paper-and-pencil design task (a plan for a playground [grades 5 and 8] and a plan for a small town [grade 8]), and built and tested multipart devices (levers and balances [grade 5] and Lego model cars [grades 8 and 11]). Student performance was rated according to five performance levels

> The committee found a great deal to commend the British approach to assessing design-related thinking.

that focused almost exclusively on the quality of the product rather than the design process.

In 2001, the International Baccalaureate Organization (IBO) began offering a Design Technology curriculum that emphasizes the use of scientific information and "production techniques" to solve problems (IBO, 2001). End-of-course assessments include three paper-and-pencil exams that include a mixture of multiple-choice, short-answer, and extended-response items. As part of their coursework, IB students also take part in individual and group design projects. Teachers use a detailed rubric to assess how well students meet expectations related to project planning; data collection, processing and presentation; conclusions and evaluation; manipulative skills; and personal skills.

The committee also reviewed the assessment component of the Future City Competition, an annual extracurricular, design-related challenge available to K–12 students as part of National Engineers Week (*http://www.new.org*). The Future City Competition encourages teams of middle-school students to design a city using Sim City™ software and, separately, to build a small, model city that satisfies the theme of the contest for that year. The computer-design entries are judged by volunteers with varied backgrounds, including engineering. The score sheet for the computer-designed city includes whether the city design incorporates certain features, such as transportation and recreation. The score sheet for the built model assigns points for creativity, accuracy and scale, transportation, a moving-part component, and attractiveness.

The committee found no instruments that required teachers to demonstrate the kind of technological capability envisioned in *Technically Speaking* and broadened by the committee to include design-related skills. The ACT WorkKeys assessment was the only instrument that targeted technological capability in out-of-school adults, although it is also used in K–12 schools and community colleges. Undoubtedly, there are other assessments that test technical proficiency or skill in job-specific areas, such as computer-network administration or computer numerically controlled milling. But these assessments are beyond the scope of this project.

Critical-Thinking and Decision-Making Dimension

The critical thinking and decision-making dimension of technological literacy suggests a process that includes asking questions, seeking and weighing information, and making decisions based on that information. Critical thinking is a form of higher order thinking that has historical roots dating back to the Greek philosophers. The National Council for Excellence in Critical Thinking Instruction defines critical thinking this way (Paul and Nosich, 2004):

> Critical thinking is the intellectually disciplined process of actively and skillfully conceptualizing, applying, analyzing, synthesizing, or evaluating information gathered from, or generated by, observation, experience, reflection, reasoning, or communication, as a guide to belief and action.

Critical thinking and decision making may be the most cognitively complex dimension of technological literacy. Not only does it require knowledge related to the nature and history of technology and the role of engineers and others in its development, it also requires that individuals be aware of what they do not know so they can ask meaningful questions and educate themselves in an appropriate manner.

The committee found very few assessments that addressed this aspect of technological literacy. One of them was the assessment for Information in a Global Society, a program of study developed by IBO, which includes a two-hour-long paper-and-pencil exam with several open-ended questions. The 2002 assessment included questions related to the use of school identification cards, the development of an online business, Web publishing, Web-based advertising, and video camera surveillance in public spaces. As part of each question, students were asked to discuss and weigh the importance of the social and/or ethical concerns raised by the use of that technology. Examiners used a rubric-like marking scheme to score this part of the assessment.

The Saskatchewan Education 1999 Provincial Learning Assessment in Technological Literacy also addressed critical thinking by requiring that students make and defend decisions concerning the uses and management of technology. Eighth- and 11th-grade students, for instance, watched a videotaped drama involving a union leader, Ed, who was forced to decide between retaining jobs for his fellow employees and supporting an expensive solution to his company's waste-disposal problem. The open-ended assessment asked students to decide which option Ed should select and to discuss how difficult societal issues like this might be solved.

Attitudes Toward Technology

As noted in Chapter 2, a person's attitudes toward technology can provide a context for interpreting the results of an assessment. The committee found that assessments of general, or public, literacy related to technology tend to focus on people's awareness, attitudes, beliefs, and opinions rather than on their knowledge, capabilities, or critical thinking skills.

Assessments conducted periodically over an extended period of time can track changes in public views on specific issues, such as the use of nuclear power or the development of genetically modified foods. This is one purpose of the data available in *Science and Engineering Indicators* published by NSB, which address attitudes toward federal funding of scientific research, as well as specific topics, such as biotechnology and genetic engineering, space exploration, and global warming. They also reveal a good deal about people's beliefs, as distinct from their attitudes. For instance, in 2004, the *Indicators* focused on the belief in various pseudosciences, such as astrology (NSB, 2004). Recent versions of the NSB reports have compared the attitudes or beliefs of Americans with those of citizens of other countries.

Assessment of attitudes, beliefs, and opinions are often used by government decision makers and others to gauge the effectiveness of public communication efforts or the need for new policies. In the case of technology, measuring attitudes can provide insights into the level of comfort with technology; the role of the public in the development of a technology; and whether public concerns about technology are being heard by those in positions of power. In order to communicate risk effectively, it is necessary to understand the attitudes of those who are being warned (Morgan et al., 2002). The Eurobarometer surveys, for example, which are conducted periodically in the European Union, attempt to measure public confidence in certain technologies, such as the Internet, genetically modified foods, fuel-cell engines, and nanotechnology. Eurobarometer surveys typically involve about 1,000 people (15 and older) in each member country (currently 25 countries).

The American Association for Engineering Education (ASEE, 2005) developed the Survey of Teachers' Attitudes About Engineering, an online assessment instrument for gauging the views of K–12 teachers about engineering, engineers, and engineering education (Box 5-3). ASEE plans to use the results of this survey, which includes 44-multiple-choice

> Measuring attitudes can provide insights into the level of comfort with technology.

questions, to improve its outreach efforts to the K–12 education community. As of spring 2005, about 400 teachers had taken the survey. Responses are scored on a five-part Likert scale (strongly agree, agree, neutral, disagree, strongly disagree).

The Boston Museum of Science, home to the National Center for Technological Literacy (*http://www.mos.org/doc/1505/*), has developed several instruments intended to elicit student and teacher conceptions (and misconceptions) of engineering and technology (Christine Cunningham, Boston Museum of Science, personal communication, May 10, 2005). Based on the Draw a Scientist Test (Finson, 2002), the museum's "What Is Technology?" test and the "What Is Engineering?" test ask students to look at 16 pictures accompanied by short descriptions and select the ones that express their ideas about technology or engineering. The museum uses similar tests with teachers who take part in its Engineering Is Elementary Program.

Not all attitudinal assessments or surveys target adults. Views on Science, Technology, and Society (VOSTS), for example, was developed by researchers at the University of Saskatchewan and administered to some 700 Canadian high school students in the early 1990s. The purpose of the assessment was to eliminate ambiguities in student interpretations of multiple-choice questions (Aikenhead and Ryan, 1992). The developers of the 114 VOSTS items relied heavily on student essays and interview responses in developing position statements about science and technology; scientists; and the nature and development of scientific and technological knowledge. The questionnaire reflects the entire range of students' views. Because there are no obviously wrong answers, students chose the answer that most closely reflected their views (Box 5-4).

Sample Question

When a new technology is developed (for example, a better type of fertilizer), it may or may not be put into practice. The decision to use a new technology depends on whether the advantages to society outweigh the disadvantages to society.

Your position, basically: (Please read from A to G, and then choose one.)

A. The decision to use a new technology depends mainly on the benefits to society, because if there are too many disadvantages, society won't accept it and may discourage its further development.
B. The decision depends on more than just the technology's advantages and disadvantages. It depends on how well it works, its cost, and its efficiency.
C. It depends on your point of view. What is an advantage to some people may be a disadvantage to others.
D. Many new technologies have been put into practice to make money or gain power, even though their disadvantages were greater than their advantages.
E. I don't understand.
F. I don't know enough about this subject to make a choice.
G. None of these choices fits my basic viewpoint.

The attitudes portion of the Pupils' Attitudes Toward Technology instrument consists of 58 statements and a five-part Likert scale for responses. Each item is related to a student's interest in technology, perception of technology and gender, perception of the difficulty of technology as a school subject, perception of the place of technology in the school curriculum, and ideas about technological professions (Box 5-5).

Filling the Assessment Matrix

The conceptual matrix proposed in Chapter 2 is intended as guidance for assessment developers. The matrix can be made less theoretical

BOX 5-5   Pupils' Attitudes Toward Technology (PATT)

Sample Attitudinal Statements[a]

Technology is as difficult for boys as it is for girls.
I would rather not have technology lessons at school.
I would enjoy a job in technology.
Because technology causes pollution, we should use less of it.

  [a]Responses given on a five-part Likert scale: agree, tend to agree, neutral, tend to disagree, disagree.

by filling the 12 cells with examples of assessment items that address the content and cognitive specifications of each cell. To this end, the committee reviewed the items in the portfolio of collected assessment instruments to identify those that might fit into the matrix (Table 5-2). For instance, the committee found questions that might be placed in the cell in the upper left-hand corner of the matrix representing the cognitive dimension of knowledge and the content domain related to technology and society.

Some of the items fit the cells better than others, and, because they come from different sources, the style of question and target populations vary. Of course, one would not use this piecemeal approach to design an actual assessment, and the quality of most of the selected items is not nearly as high as for the items one would devise from scratch. Nevertheless, this exercise demonstrates the potential usefulness of a matrix and gives the reader a sense of the scope of the cognitive and content dimensions of an assessment of technological literacy.

Table 5-2 begins on next page.

TABLE 5-2 Assessment Matrix for Technological Literacy with Items from Selected Assessment Instruments

	Technology and Society	Design
Knowledge	In the late 1800s the railroad was built across Canada. What effects did this have on life in Saskatchewan? A. More people settled in Saskatchewan. B. The natural landscape of Saskatchewan changed significantly. C. The weather of Saskatchewan changed. D. A and B E. All of the above[a] What impact (or effects) do people living longer have? A. The development of new business enterprises to look after the wants and needs of the elderly. B. People are happier and there is no real impact on society. C. More taxes are collected to provide care for the elderly. D. A and C. E. All of the above[b] Someone concerned about the environment would prefer to buy A. Drinks in glass bottles B. Eggs in a plastic carton C. Boxes covered with wax paper D. Books made of nonrecycled paper[c]	Marcus designed a television stand like the one shown below for his family. 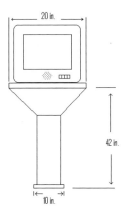 His father is worried that the stand could tip over. Look at the measurements in the drawing. How can Marcus improve the design so the stand would be less likely to tip over? A. Make the base wider. B. Make the stand taller. C. Make the top narrower. D. Use a different material.[d] If you were designing a product that has to be easily serviced, you would assemble it with A. welded joints B. epoxy resin C. rivets D. threaded screws[e]
Capabilities	Business and industry use technology in a variety of ways. Sometimes the technology that is used has negative results. The automobile industry makes	A group of young people have investigated the needs of people with small gardens and decided to make a floor and wall plant holder. They have

Products and Systems	Characteristics, Core Concepts, and Connections

Products and Systems

Which of the following is a key factor that enables an airplane to lift?
A. Air pressure beneath the wing is greater than that above the wing.
B. Pressure within the airplane is greater than that of the outside.
C. Engine power is greater than that of friction.
D. The plane's wing is lighter than air.[f]

Using a portable phone while in the bathtub creates the possibility of being electrocuted. (True or False)[g]

To find the depth of the ocean, some ships send a sound wave to the ocean floor and record the time it takes to return to the detector. The kind of wave used by this detector is the same as that used by
A. bats to detect objects in the dark.
B. snakes to detect warm-blooded prey, such as mice.
C. police cars to detect the speed of motorists.
D. airports to detect the location of airplanes in the sky.[h]

Which system would locate a lost person with the appropriate signal sending devices?
A. Geographical information system (GIS)
B. Global positioning system (GPS)
C. Computer simulation system
D. Robotics system[i]

(This assessment item requires a clock radio)
1) Set the time on the clock for 9:00 AM
2) If you hold the FWD down and count for 20 seconds, what is the new reading of the clock?

Characteristics, Core Concepts, and Connections

Indicate whether you believe each item to be "definitely technology," "might be technology," "not technology," or "don't know"
1. cup
2. telephone
3. airplane
4. book
5. bridge
6. computer
7. gun
8. jeans
9. TV commercial
10. clock
11. trombone
12. old stone axe
13. cheese
14. deer
15. cough medicine
16. microwave
17. flower
18. restaurant
19. river
20. house plan[j]

A bicycle is considered a complex machine because it is
A. used to perform a task.
B. made from natural materials.
C. made up of more than one simple machine.
D. complicated to build and repair.[k]

Technical developments and scientific principles are related because:
A. Science and technology have identical characteristics.
B. Technological innovations always precede a scientific explanation.
C. Scientific discoveries always precede a scientific explanation
D. Sometimes technical developments give scientists something to explain and sometimes scientific discoveries lead to technical development.
E. They are not related.[l]

continued

TABLE 5-2 Continued

	Technology and Society	Design
Capabilities (contd.)	use of robotics for many reasons: to create products that are uniform, to ensure accuracy, to save time, and to perform dangerous tasks. —Identify and describe one positive effect of robotics on manufacturing and one negative effect of robotics on the employees in the automobile industry. —Why would a company use a technology even though it will have negative effects?[m]	decided that the plant holder must be able to do the four things shown here. Your task today is to take this idea and develop it as far as you can in the time available. Design a floor and wall plant holder that: a) stands on the floor or can be fixed to a wall b) stacks or links together so that they can be arranged in a variety of ways c) has a rainwater drainage and storage system d) has a self-watering system[n] An igloo is a structure that is used for survival in extremely cold environments with snowstorms. The structure is typically made of blocks of ice laid one on another in order to form the shape of a dome. Describe how you would test this structure to evaluate its ability to withstand static and dynamic forces: Describe how you would test this structure to evaluate its thermal insulation:[o]
Critical Thinking and Decision Making	"Technology makes the world a better place to live in!" Do you totally agree with the above statement? Discuss in full detail, using specific examples, your viewpoint on the impact and responsibilities involving technology and technological developments.[q] When a new technology is developed (for example, a better type of fertilizer), it may or may not be put into practice. The decision to use a new technology depends on whether the advantages to society outweigh the disadvantages to society. Your position basically: A. The decision to use a new technology depends mainly on the benefits to society, because if there are too many disadvantages, society won't accept it and may discourage its further development. B. The decision depends on more than just the technology's advantages and disadvantages. It	A new prototype for a refrigerator that contains a computer and has a computer display screen mounted in its door has been developed. The display screen uses touch-screen technology. As well as standard computer programs, the computer runs a database on which the user can maintain a record of the refrigerator contents including sell-by. Explain three reasons for conducting market research before starting the design of the new refrigerator-computer for sale in the global marketplace.[t] Why would tightly closed windows be a good design choice in cold climates but not a good design choice in hot climates?[u]

3) How many minutes did the clock reading advance?
4) Set the time of the clock for 9:00 AM
5) If you hold the FFWD down and count for
   10 seconds what is the reading of the clock?
6) How many minutes did the clock reading advance?
7) Approximately how many times faster is the FFWD
   than the FWD?
8) You are preparing to go to bed and have decided
   you want to wake up at 6:30 AM and listen to the
   radio for 2 hours straight while lying in bed.
   Unfortunately the clock radio is located across the
   room from your bed and you don't want to get up
   to adjust it in the morning. How can you preset the
   clock radio the night before to meet your needs
   for the next morning?[p]

Explain the benefits of using standards for mobile
phones.[v]

On the internet, people and organizations have no
rules to follow and can say just about anything they
want. Do you think this is good or bad? Explain.[w]

When you put food in a microwave oven, it heats up
rapidly. On the other hand, when you hold an
barely warms at all. Give two reasons for this.[x]

People have frequently noted that scientific research
has created both beneficial and harmful consequences.
Would you say that, on balance, the benefits of
scientific research have outweighed the harmful
results, or have the harmful results of scientific
research been greater than its benefits?[y]

We always have to make trade-offs (compromises)
between the positive and negative effects of science.
Your position basically:

There are always trade-offs between benefits and
negative effects:
A. because every new development has at least one
   negative result. If we didn't put up with the negative
   results, we would not progress to enjoy the
   benefits.
B. because scientists cannot predict the long-term
   effects of new developments, in spite of careful
   planning and testing. We have to take the chance.
C. because things that benefit some people will be
   negative for someone else. This depends on a

continued

TABLE 5-2 Continued

	Technology and Society	Design
Critical Thinking and Decision Making (contd.)	depends on how well it works, its cost, and its efficiency. C. It depends on your point of view. What is an advantage to some people may be a disadvantage to others. D. Many new technologies have been put into practice to make money or gain power, even though their disadvantages were greater than their advantages. E. I don't understand. F. I don't know enough about this subject to make a choice. G. None of these choices fits my basic viewpoint.[r] What do you think are the 3 most important pieces of technology ever made? —Why do you think the 3 items you listed above are the most important? —Explain how the first item you picked has affected society. —How did society influence the development of the first item you picked?[s]	

[a]1999 Provincial Learning Assessment in Technological Literacy, Saskatchewan Education. Student Test Booklet Day 1, Sample A, page 8, question 24, Intended level: 8th grade.

[b]1999 Provincial Learning Assessment in Technological Literacy, Saskatchewan Education. Student Test Booklet Day 1, Sample A, page 4, question 8. Intended level: 8th grade.

[c]Illinois Standards of Achievement Test–Science. Intended level: 4th grade students (page 37, question 59).

[d]MCAS Spring 2003 Science and Technology/Engineering. Intended level: grade 5, page 235, question 30.

[e]Test of Technological Literacy, Dissertation by Abdul Hameed, Ohio State University, 1988. page 173, question 9. Intended level: 7th and 8th grade.

[f]Technological Literacy of Elementary and Junior High School Students (Taiwan), question 55.

[g]ITEA/Gallup Poll on Americans' Level of Literacy Related to Technology. Table 11, page 5, March 2002. Intended level: adults.

[h]Illinois Standards of Achievement Test–Science (page 19, question 4). Intended level: 4th grade students.

[i]International Baccalaurate: Information Technology in a Global Society. Standard Level, Paper 1, N02/390/S(1), page 3, question 4. Intended level: high school.

[j]1999 Provincial Learning Assessment in Technological Literacy, Saskatchewan Education. Student test booklet day 1, Sample A, Part A, question 1. Intended level: 5th, 8th and 11th grade.

[k]MCAS Spring 2003 Science and technology/Engineering (page 233, question 26). Intended level: grade 5.

[l]The Development and Validation of a Test of Industrial Technological Literacy (Hayden Dissertation), page 178, question 33. Intended level: high school.

[m]New York State Intermediate Assessment in Technology. Question 18. Intended level: 7th and 8th grade.

[n]Assessment of Performance in Design and Technology, The Final Report of the APU Design and Technology Project, 1985–1991, figure 7.5, page 104. Intended Level: students aged 15 years.

[o]Design-Based Science (Fortus Dissertation), Structures for extreme environments content test, question 19. Intended level: 9th and 10th grade.

person's viewpoint.

D. because you can't get positive results without first trying a new idea and then working out its negative effects.

E. but the trade-offs make no sense. (For example: Why invent labour saving devices which cause more unemployment? or Why defend a country with nuclear weapons which threaten life on Earth?)

There are NOT always trade-offs between benefits and negative effects:

F. because some new developments benefit us without producing negative effects.

G. because negative effects can be *minimized* through careful planning and testing.

H. because negative effects can be *eliminated* through careful planning and testing. Otherwise a new development is not used.

I. I don't understand.

J. I don't know enough about this subject to make a choice.

K. None of these choices fits my basic viewpoint.[z]

---

[p]1999 Provincial Learning Assessment in Technological Literacy, Saskatchewan Education. Performance station test, sample B, performance station 3 clock radio, stage 4, page 9 (questions 1–8). Intended level: 8th grade.

[q]1999 Provincial Learning Assessment in Technological Literacy, Saskatchewan Education. Thread 2, page 33. Intended level: 11th grade.

[r]The Development of a Multiple Choice Instrument for Monitoring Views on Science-Technology-Society Topics. Intended Level: 12th grade.(80133).

[s]1999 Provincial Learning Assessment in Technological Literacy, Saskatchewan Education. Student Test Booklet Day 2, Sample A, page 7, question 4a, b, c, d. Intended level: 8th grade.

[t]International Baccalaureate: Design Technology. Fall 2004 exam N04/DESTE/HP3/ENG/TZ0/XX, Higher Level, Paper 3, page 12, question F4.

[u]Design-Based Science (Fortus Dissertation). Structure for extreme environments content test, question 17. Intended level: 9th and 10th grade.

[v]International Baccalaureate: Design Technology. Fall 2004 exam N04/4/DESTE/HP3/ENG/TZ0/XX, page 20, question H4, Higher Level, Paper 3.

[w]1999 Provincial Learning Assessment in Technological Literacy, Saskatchewan Education. Student Test Booklet Day 2, Sample A, page 4, question 3e. Intended level: 8th grade.

[x]Design-Based Science (Fortus Dissertation). Safer cell phones content assessment, page 6, question 16. Intended level: 9th and 10th grade.

[y]NSF Indicators, Public Understanding of Science and Technology—2002, page 7–14, Appendix Table 7-18. Intended level: adults.

[z]The Development of a Multiple Choice Instrument for Monitoring Views on Science-Technology-Society Topics, question 40311. Intended level: 12th grade.

References

AAAS (American Association for the Advancement of Science). 1993. Benchmarks for Science Literacy. Project 2061. New York: Oxford University Press.

Aikenhead, G.S., and A.G. Ryan. 1992. The Development of a New Instrument: Monitoring Views on Science-Technology-Society (VOSTS). Available online at: *http://www.usask.ca/education/people/aikenhead/vosts_2.pdf* (May 20, 2005).

ASEE (American Society for Engineering Education). 2005. Teachers' Survey Results. ASEE Engineering K–12 Center. Available online at: *http://www.engineeringk12.org/educators/taking_a_closer_look/survey_results.htm* (October 5, 2005).

Bame, E.A., M.J. de Vries, and W.E. Dugger, Jr. 1993. Pupils' attitudes towards technology: PATT-USA. Journal of Technology Studies 19(1): 40–48.

Bloom, B.S., B.B. Mesia, and D.R. Krathwohl. 1964. Taxonomy of Educational Objectives. New York: David McKay.

Cobb, M.D., and J. Macoubrie. 2004. Public perceptions about nanotechnology: risks, benefits and trust. Journal of Nanoparticle Research 6(4): 395–405.

Custer, R.L., G. Valesey, and B.N. Burke. 2001. An assessment model for a design approach to technological problem solving. Journal of Technology Education 12(2): 5–20.

ETS (Educational Testing Service). 2005. Sample Test Questions. The Praxis Series, Specialty Area Tests, Technology Education (0050). Available online at: *http://ftp.ets.org/pub/tandl/0050.pdf* (May 27, 2005).

Finson, K.D. 2002. Drawing a scientist: what do we know and not know after 50 years of drawing. School Science and Mathematics 102(7): 335–345.

Hatch, L.O. 1985. Technological Literacy: A Secondary Analysis of the NAEP Science Data. Unpublished dissertation, University of Maryland.

Hatch, L.O. 2004. Technological Literacy: Trends in Academic Progress—A Secondary Analysis of the NAEP Long-term Science Data. Draft 6/16/04. Paper commissioned by the National Research Council Committee on Assessing Technological Literacy. Unpublished.

Hayden, M.A. 1989. The Development and Validation of a Test of Industrial Technological Literacy. Unpublished dissertation, Iowa State University.

Hill, R.B. 1997. The design of an instrument to assess problem solving activities in technology education. Journal of Technology Education 9(1): 31–46.

IBO (International Baccalaureate Organization). 2001. Design Technology. February 2001. Geneva, Switzerland: IBO.

ISBE (Illinois State Board of Education). 2001a. Science Performance Descriptors—Grades 1–5. Available online at: *http://www.isbe.net/ils/science/word/descriptor_1-5.rtf* (April 11, 2005).

ISBE. 2001b. Science Performance Descriptors—Grades 6–12. Available online at: *http://www.isbe.net/ils/science/word/descriptor_6-12.rtf* (April 11, 2005).

ISBE. 2003. Illinois Standards Achievement Test—Sample Test Items: Illinois Learning Standards for Science. Available online at: *http://www.isbe.net/assessment/PDF/2003ScienceSample.pdf* (August 31, 2005).

ITEA (International Technology Education Association). 2001. ITEA/Gallup Poll Reveals What Americans Think About Technology. A Report of the Survey Conducted by the Gallup Organization for the International Technology Education Association. Available online at: *http://www.iteaconnect.org/TAA/PDFs/Gallupreport.pdf* (October 5, 2005).

ITEA. 2004. The Second Installment of the ITEA/Gallup Poll and What It Reveals as to How Americans Think about Technology. A Report of the Second Survey Conducted by the Gallup Organization for the International Technology Education Association. Available online at: *http://www.iteaconnect.org/TAA/PDFs/GallupPoll2004.pdf* (October 5, 2005).

Kaplan. 2003. ASVAB—The Armed Services Vocational Aptitude Battery. 2004 Edition. New York: Simon and Schuster.

Kimbell, R., K. Stables, T. Wheeler, A. Wosniak, and V. Kelly. 1991. The Assessment of Performance in Design and Technology. The Final Report of the APU Design and Technology Project 1985–1991. London: School Examinations and Assessment Council.

MDE (Massachusetts Department of Education). 2001. Science and Technology/Engineering Curriculum Framework. Available online at: *http://www.doe.mass.edu/frameworks/scitech/2001/0501.doc* (April 11, 2005).

MDE. 2005a. Science and Technology/Engineering, Grade 5. Released test items. Available online at: *http://www.doe.mass.edu/mcas/2005/release/g5sci.pdf* (August 31, 2005).

MDE. 2005b. Science and Technology/Engineering, Grade 8. Released test items. Available online at: *http://www.doe.mass.edu/mcas/2005/release/g8sci.pdf* (August 31, 2005).

Miller, J.D. 1983a. The American People and Science Policy: The Role of Public Attitudes in the Policy Process. New York: Pergamon Press.

Miller, J.D. 1983b. Scientific literacy: a conceptual and empirical review. Daedalus 112(2): 29–48.

Miller, J.D. 1986. Reaching the Attentive and Interested Publics for Science. Pp. 55–69 in Scientists and Journalists: Reporting Science as News, edited by S. Friedman, S. Dunwoody, and C. Rogers. New York: Free Press.

Miller, J.D. 1987. Scientific Literacy in the United States. Pp. 19–40 in Communicating Science to the Public, edited by D. Evered and M. O'Connor. London: John Wiley and Sons.

Miller, J.D. 1992. From Town Meeting to Nuclear Power: The Changing Nature of Citizenship and Democracy in the United States. Pp. 327–328 in The United States Constitution: Roots, Rights, and Responsibilities, edited by A.E.D. Howard. Washington, D.C.: Smithsonian Institution Press.

Miller, J.D. 1995. Scientific Literacy for Effective Citizenship. Pp. 185–204 in Science/Technology/Society as Reform in Science Education, edited by R.E. Yager. New York: State University of New York Press.

Miller, J.D. 1998. The measurement of civic scientific literacy. Public Understanding of Science 7: 1–21.

Miller, J.D. 2000. The Development of Civic Scientific Literacy in the United States. Pp. 21–47 in Science, Technology, and Society: A Sourcebook on Research and Practice, edited by D.D. Kumar and D. Chubin. New York: Plenum Press.

Miller, J.D. 2001. The Acquisition and Retention of Scientific Information by American Adults. Pp. 93–114 in Free-Choice Science Education, edited by J.H. Falk. New York: Teachers College Press.

Miller, J.D. 2004. Public understanding of, and attitudes toward scientific research: what we know and what we need to know. Public Understanding of Science 13: 273–294.

Miller, J.D., and L. Kimmel. 2001. Biomedical Communications: Purposes, Audiences, and Strategies. New York: Academic Press.

Miller, J.D., and R. Pardo. 2000. Civic Scientific Literacy and Attitude to Science and Technology: A Comparative Analysis of the European Union, the United States, Japan, and Canada. Pp. 81–129 in Between Understanding and Trust: The

Public, Science, and Technology, edited by M. Dierkes and C. von Grote. Amsterdam: Harwood Academic Publishers.

Miller, J.D., R. Pardo, and F. Niwa. 1997. Public Perceptions of Science and Technology: A Comparative Study of the European Union, the United States, Japan, and Canada. Madrid: BBV Foundation.

Morgan, G., B. Fischhoff, A. Bostrom, and C.J. Atman. 2002. Risk Communication: A Mental Models Approach. New York: Cambridge University Press.

NRC (National Research Council). 1999. How People Learn: Brain, Mind, Experience, and School. Edited by J.D. Bransford, A.L. Brown, and R.R. Cocking. Washington, D.C.: National Academy Press.

NSB (National Science Board). 1981. Science Indicators, 1980. Washington, D.C.: Government Printing Office.

NSB. 1983. Science Indicators, 1982. Washington, D.C.: Government Printing Office.

NSB. 1986. Science Indicators, 1985. Washington, D.C.: Government Printing Office.

NSB. 1988. Science and Engineering Indicators, 1987. Washington, D.C.: Government Printing Office.

NSB. 1990. Science and Engineering Indicators, 1989. Washington, D.C.: Government Printing Office.

NSB. 1992. Science and Engineering Indicators, 1991. Washington, D.C.: Government Printing Office.

NSB. 1994. Science and Engineering Indicators, 1993. Washington, D.C.: Government Printing Office.

NSB. 1996. Science and Engineering Indicators, 1996. Washington, D.C.: Government Printing Office.

NSB. 1998. Science and Engineering Indicators, 1998. Washington, D.C.: Government Printing Office.

NSB. 2000. Science and Engineering Indicators, 2000. Washington, D.C.: Government Printing Office.

NSB. 2004. Science and Engineering Indicators, 2004. Washington, D.C.: Government Printing Office.

Paul, R., and G.M. Nosich. 2004. A Model for the National Assessment of Higher-Order Thinking. Available online at: *http://www.criticalthinking.org/resources/articles/a-model-nal-assessment-hot.shtml* (January 19, 2006).

Saskatchewan Education. 2001. 1999 Provincial Learning Assessment in Technological Literacy. May 2001. Available online at: *http://www.learning.gov.sk.ca/branches/cap_building_acct/afl/docs/plap/techlit/1999techlit.pdf.*

TIDEE (Transferable Integrated Design Engineering Education). 2002. Assessments. Available online at: *http://www.tidee.cea.wsu.edu/resources/assessments.html* (August 31, 2005).

6
From Theory
to Practice:
Five Sample Cases

M uch of the discussion about assessing technological literacy in this report is by necessity general and applicable to many different settings. But in the real world, assessments must be done on a case-by-case basis, and each assessment will be tailored to fulfill a specific purpose. Thus, it is useful to see how the general principles might apply in particular situations. In this chapter, examples are given for five different settings, ranging from classrooms throughout a state to a museum or other informal-learning institution. Two of the examples deal with assessing students, one with assessing teachers, and two with assessing segments of the general population. The choice of cases was influenced considerably by the committee's charge, which was focused on these same three populations.

Many of the sample cases inform one or more of the recommendations in Chapter 8. For example, Case 2, a national sample-based assessment, addresses some of the same issues designers of the National Assessment of Educational Progress, Trends in Mathematics and Science Study, and Programme for International Student Assessment may face in adapting those instruments to measuring technological literacy (Recommendations 1 and 2). Case 3, an assessment of teachers, addresses concerns that will undoubtedly arise as researchers develop and pilot test instruments for assessing pre-service and in-service teachers (Recommendation 5). Cases 4 and 5, assessments of broad populations and informal-learning institutions, address the committee's suggestion that efforts to assess the technological literacy of out-of-school adults be expanded (Recommendation 6). Although none of the recommendations specifically addresses Case 1, a statewide census assessment of students, the committee believes state leaders in education and other readers will benefit from seeing how this type of testing might play out.

Beyond the call for modified or new assessments, the discussion of determining content for an assessment of teachers (Case 3) illustrates the need for careful development of assessment frameworks (Recommendation 11). And the cases related to broad populations (Case 4) and visitors to a museum or other informal-education institution (Case 5) suggest the importance of new measurement methods (Recommendation 10).

Even though the sample cases touch on many of the issues facing designers of assessments, they are meant to be descriptive rather than prescriptive. Each case includes a rationale and purpose for the assessment, suggests a source for deriving the assessment content, proposes a way of thinking about performance levels, and addresses some administrative, logistical, and implementation issues. The committee intends this chapter to be a springboard for discussion about designing and carrying out assessments of particular groups and for particular purposes.

When reviewing the examples in this chapter, readers should keep in mind the discussion of the design process in Chapter 3. Design is a process in which experience helps. When experienced designers are faced with a problem, they immediately ask themselves if they have encountered similar problems before and, if so, what the important factors were in those cases. The committee adopted the same approach, beginning with a review and analysis of existing studies and instruments, the identification and incorporation of useful aspects of those designs into the sample design, the identification of needs that had not been met by existing designs, and attempts to devise original ways to meet those needs. Anyone who intends to design an assessment of technological literacy will have to go through a similar process.

During the committee's deliberations, considerable time was spent discussing the value of including a sample assessment for an occupational setting. Ultimately, the committee decided not to include an occupational assessment for two reasons. First, the goal of most technical training and education for specific occupations is to provide a high level of skill in a limited set of technologies (see Box 2-2), rather than to encourage proficiency in the three dimensions of technological literacy spelled out in *Technically Speaking*. Second, two industry participants in a data-gathering workshop (one from the food industry and one from the automotive industry) expressed the view that a measure of overall

> The committee intends this chapter to be a springboard for discussion.

technological literacy would be of little value to employers, who are more concerned with workers' job-related skills.[1]

Case 1: Statewide Grade-Level Assessment

Description and Rationale

In Case 1, the target population is students in a particular state and in particular grades. The exact grades are not important, but for the sake of illustration we assume that they include one elementary grade (3rd, 4th, or 5th grade), one middle school grade (6th, 7th, or 8th grade), and one high school grade (9th, 10th, 11th, or 12th). So, for example, the test population might consist of all 4th-, 8th-, and 11th-graders in Kentucky public schools.

A statewide assessment has many similarities to large-scale national assessments and small, school-based assessments. But there are also important differences. For instance, a statewide assessment generally falls somewhere between a national assessment and a school-based assessment in terms of the timeliness of results and the breadth and depth of knowledge covered. But the most important difference is that a statewide assessment provides an opportunity for assessors to calculate individual, subgroup, and group-level scores. In addition, aggregate scores can be determined at the state, district, school, and classroom levels. Disaggregated scores can be determined for student subgroups, according to variables such as gender, race/ethnicity, and socioeconomic status.

The assessment in this sample case is in some ways—such as the targeted test group and how the data are analyzed—similar to assessments currently used by states to meet the requirements of the No Child Left Behind Act of 2001 (NCLB). To comply with this legislation, states are required to test students' proficiency in reading/language arts and mathematics annually in grades 3 through 8 and at least once in grades 10 through 12. States must also include assessments of science proficiency in three designated grade spans by 2007. Results are generally reported within about four months of administration of the assessment.

---

[1]Some proponents of technological literacy, including the authoring committee of *Technically Speaking*, have suggested that there may be at least an indirect link between general technological literacy and performance in the workplace (NAE and NRC, 2002, pp. 40–42).

The rationale for a statewide assessment of technological literacy is to encourage changes in standards, curriculum, and teacher education to support the goal of increasing technological literacy for all students. With the possible exception of Massachusetts, states do not currently have the curricular building blocks in place to justify a statewide assessment of technological literacy. However, an assessment on such a large scale conducted in even a single state could demonstrate the feasibility and value of determining what students know and can do with respect to technology and could provide momentum for changes in standards, curriculum, and teacher education across the country.

Purpose

In this example, the primary purpose of the statewide assessment of technological literacy is to improve teaching and learning related to technology. Typically, statewide assessments serve a powerful accountability function, providing data that can be used to track student achievement trends by school, school district, and the state as a whole. In an area of content as new as technological literacy, however, the goal of improving teaching and learning looms large. As technological literacy becomes more established as a school subject, however, assessment data may increasingly be used for accountability purposes.

In this sample case, assessment results can be used to inform policy makers at the state and district levels and provide data for instructional leaders at the district, school, and classroom levels. This assessment could either be designed to provide a snapshot of technological literacy in the target populations or to provide data on specific content standards for technological literacy, which in turn may be aligned with national standards, such as those developed by ITEA (2000).

A statewide assessment of technological literacy could not only tell educators what students at these age levels know and what they can do with respect to technology, but could also provide information related to specific standards. For example, they could determine if there was a difference in performance between boys and girls on ITEA Standard 19, which relates to understanding and being able to select and use manufacturing technologies. In short, data from such an assessment would enable educators to answer a large variety of questions useful for improving teaching and learning.

Content

The ITEA *Standards for Technological Literacy* (ITEA, 2000) the
AAAS *Benchmarks for Science Literacy* (AAAS, 1993), the NRC *National
Science Education Standards* (NRC, 1996), and especially state-specific
content standards, would be logical starting points for determining the
content of the assessment. All of these documents suggest "benchmark"
knowledge and skills that a technologically literate individual should have.
To be useful for an assessment, however, the benchmarks must be
"operationalized, " that is, the most important technology concepts and
capabilities must first be identified and then made specific enough to
clarify the range of material to be covered in the assessment. This is a step
in the process of developing an assessment framework for technological
literacy, as discussed in Chapter 3.

To be useful for
an assessment,
benchmarks
must be
"operationalized."

In addition, existing assessments may be reviewed to determine if
any items are aligned with, and measure, the operationalized benchmarks.
If not, technology-related content may have to be added. A review of the
general guidelines for student assessments developed by ITEA may also
be helpful (ITEA, 2004a).

The assessment framework must specify the emphasis, or weight,
given to items in each dimension of technological literacy. The weighting
process must be based on many factors, including the purpose of the
assessment, the time allotted for testing, the developers' views of
the importance of each dimension of technological literacy, and expert
judgments about reasonable expectations for students in these grades.
Table 6-1 shows how the weighting process might work.

Performance Levels

In this sample case, the state would derive a scale score for each
student. If similar technology-related concepts were tested for more than
one grade level (e.g., manufacturing processes for grades 3–5 and 6–8), the
state might use cross-grade vertical scaling, which would enable scorers to
compare the mastery of material by students at different grade levels.
Using within-grade scaling, which is more common, the performance
levels in each grade would be examined independently.

To provide scores in a useful form for policy makers and instructional leaders, the state board of education might establish performance

TABLE 6-1 Sample Weighting for Grades 6–8 Items Assessing Knowledge, Capability, and Critical Thinking and Decision Making Related to Manufacturing Technologies, by Percentage of Items Devoted to Topic

	Benchmark Topics			
	Manufacturing Systems	Manufacturing Goods	Chemical Technologies	Materials Use
Knowledge	20 percent	10 percent	10 percent	10 percent
Capability	10 percent	10 percent		
Critical Thinking and Decision Making		10 percent	10 percent	10 percent

SOURCE: Adapted from ITEA, 2000.

levels to group students according to subjective achievement standards for increasingly sophisticated levels of performance (e.g., novice, competent, proficient, and expert). Performance-level descriptors must realistically capture what a child of a given age might know and be able to do.

Reporting could be done either on the overall assessment or on separate subscales or dimensions of the assessment. If separate subscales or dimensions were used, separate performance levels could be defined for each. If the idea is to report subscale- or dimension-specific scores, the assessment must be designed so that the items in each subscale or dimension support reliable scoring.

Once state and local educators received descriptive and diagnostic data, they could interpret the results in context and identify achievement gaps. Based on diagnostic information, educators could determine which standards had been mastered by most students and which subjects required more or better instruction. Based on assessment results, educators could then focus their instruction and professional development practices to improve student learning.

If the assessment were given regularly, perhaps biennially, the resulting data would provide a measure of whether the level of technological literacy had increased, stayed the same, or declined. Results over time could reveal trends among subgroups of students. If the assessment includes items that measure student attitudes and opinions about technology or technology careers, that information could be correlated with performance data. In this way, the data could be used by K–12 educators to assist with course planning and career counseling.

Administration and Logistics

A statewide assessment would be administered to all students in three grade levels, one elementary (grades 3–5), one middle school (grades 6–8), and one high school (grades 9–12), in every school in the state. The assessment should take no more than two sessions, lasting no more than 90 minutes each, and should use both census and matrix-sampling techniques.[2] Combining census and matrix-sampling approaches would have several advantages. It would reduce the time required to administer the assessment, because not every student would see every question. By making sure all students were presented with a core set of items (the census portion of the instrument), a general measure of technological literacy could be obtained.

> Combining census and matrix-sampling approaches would have several advantages.

The matrix portion of the assessment would enable the collection of additional diagnostic measures of performance related to specific areas of content, such as student knowledge of the influence of technology on history. The assessment should include a mix of multiple-choice, constructed-response, and design-based performance items, possibly including simulations.

Teachers would require rudimentary training to administer the test, particularly the hands-on design or online computer-based components. Administrators and policy makers would also have to be educated about the dimensions of technological literacy, the purpose of the assessment, and potential uses of the data obtained from the assessment.

Obstacles to Implementation

With the notable exception of state testing conducted to fulfill the requirements of NCLB, assessments like the one described here usually have no direct consequences for students, teachers, or schools if student scores are low. Without the threat of punitive consequences for poor outcomes, teachers may be less inclined to spend time preparing students for the assessment, and students may be less inclined to take the test seriously.

A statewide assessment of technological literacy would also have resource constraints, especially today, when states are already spending considerable sums to meet the assessment and reporting requirements of

---

[2]Matrix sampling and census testing are explained in Chapter 4 in the section on Measurement Issues.

NCLB. For example, the Maryland State Department of Education recently spent more than $5 million to develop and implement, within two years, new reading/language arts and mathematics assessments for 9th graders (M. Yakimowski-Srebnick, director of assessments, Council of Chief State School Officers, personal communication, June 16, 2005). Although some of the costs of an assessment, particularly related to test administration, might be reduced by using computer-based testing methods (see Chapter 7), it would still be difficult to convince states that are already "feeling the pinch" of NCLB to add a statewide assessment of technological literacy.

Furthermore, traditional paper-and-pencil tests alone generally do not provide an adequate measure of capabilities related to technological design. Thus, some states are beginning to explore nontraditional testing methodologies, such as computer simulations, to assess hands-on tasks and higher order thinking. Developing and testing these methods, however, requires considerable resources and time.

Turf issues within the academic community might introduce additional challenges for a statewide assessment. For instance, the mathematics and science-education communities might argue that an assessment of technological literacy would divert attention and resources from their efforts to improve student learning in their content areas. Many educators might be concerned about the amount of time taken away from instruction, above and beyond the time required to prepare for mandated assessments.

Another potential challenge for states might be providing opportunities for students with special needs to participate in the assessment. Adjustments would have to be made for students with physical or cognitive disabilities, limited proficiency in English, or a combination of these to ensure full and fair access to the test. Adjustments must be made on a case-by-case basis. For instance, a student with a visual impairment would not require the same test accommodation as someone with dyslexia, even though both have trouble reading small, crowded text. Common accommodations include extending time, having test items read aloud, and allowing a student to dictate rather than write answers. It is also important that accommodations be used only to offset the impact of disabilities unrelated to the knowledge and skills being measured (NRC, 1997).

Some students with special needs might require alternative assessment approaches, such as evaluation of a collection of work (portfolio), a one-on-one measure of skills and knowledge, or checklists filled out

> Turf issues within the academic community might introduce additional challenges.

by persons familiar with a student's ability to demonstrate specific knowledge or skills (Lehr and Thurlow, 2003); typically, a very small percentage of students, on the order of 1 percent, require alternative assessments. Because a test score may not be a valid representation of the skills and achievement of students with disabilities, high-stakes decisions about these students should take into account other sources of evidence, such as grades, teacher recommendations, and other examples of a student's work (NRC, 1999a).

Finally, because it is often difficult or impractical for states to collect meaningful data related to socioeconomic status, assessment results might inadvertently be reported in ways that reinforce negative racial, ethnic, or class stereotypes. Concerns about stereotyping might even arouse resistance to the implementation of a new assessment.

Sample Assessment Items[3]

---

1. Manufacturing changes the form of materials through a variety of processes, including separation (S), forming (F), and combining (C). Please indicate which process is associated most closely with each of the following:

a. bending
b. sawing
c. gluing
d. cutting

2. One common way of distinguishing types of manufactured goods is whether they are "durable" or "nondurable." In your own words, explain *two* ways durable goods differ from nondurable goods. Then sort the following products into two groups, according to whether they are durable or nondurable: toothbrush, clothes dryer, automobile tire, candy bar, bicycle, pencil.

---

[3]For a statewide assessment, items would be based on a framework derived from rigorously developed content standards. In this example, items were derived from content specified for grades 6 through 8 in the *ITEA Standards for Technological Literacy.*

3. Manufacturing, like all aspects of technology, has had significant impacts on society, and not all of these have been anticipated or welcome. Innovations in manufacturing in the past quarter-century have included the use of robotics, automation, and computers. Using examples from only one manufacturing sector, describe some of the positive and negative impacts these manufacturing innovations have had on life in the United States.

Case 2: Matrix-Sample Assessment of 7th Graders

Description and Rationale

Case 2 involves a matrix-sample-based assessment of the technological literacy of 7th graders throughout the United States. Sample-based assessments differ from other types of assessments in that individual scores are rarely, if ever, reported. Instead, the focus is on discovering and tracking trends. In this case, one might want to follow the changes over time in the average level of technological literacy of 7th graders. Sampling can also reveal geographic variations, such as state-by-state differences in scores and variations among subgroups, such as gender, race/ethnicity, type of school, population density, poverty level, and other demographic variables, depending on the design of the sample.

In matrix sampling,[4] individual students are not tested on all test items. This is done mainly to accommodate the time constraints of test administration. Even though no single student sees every item, every question is administered to a large enough subset of the sample to ensure that the results are statistically valid. Another important feature of a matrix sample is that the large number of questions ensures that all three dimensions of technological literacy are assessed. The assessment described here is similar in structure to assessments conducted through the National Assessment of Education Progress (NAEP).

The rationale for conducting a national, sample-based assessment of students would be to draw public attention to the state of

---

[4]Matrix sampling is described in more detail in Chapter 4 in the section on Measurement Issues.

technological literacy in the country's middle-school population. In the same way the release of NAEP results in science and mathematics encourages examination of how learning and teaching occur in these subjects, data on technological literacy would provide an impetus for a similar analysis related to the learning and teaching of technology. If the results indicated significant areas of weakness, they might provide an impetus for education reform. Periodic administration of the assessment would provide valuable time-series data that could be used to monitor trends.

Purpose

A national sample assessment of technological literacy among U.S. 7th graders could provide a "snapshot" of technological literacy in this population that would be useful for policy makers. Like the statewide assessment described in Case 1, educators could use these data to get a sense of what students at this age know and what can they do with respect to technology. With a national assessment, however, administrators at the school, district, and state levels could determine how their students' scores compared with student scores in other areas of the country, and national education officials could get a sense of the overall technological literacy of 7th graders. Unlike the assessment in Case 1, of course, the sample assessment would not provide information about individual students. This assessment would be a policy tool, rather than a classroom tool.

If a national sample assessment were repeated periodically, it would show whether technological literacy was increasing, staying the same, or declining around the country. If similar assessments were conducted in other countries, it would be possible to make some cautionary comparisons across national boundaries. If the assessment revealed student attitudes about technology or technology careers, that information could be correlated with performance data to determine how attitudes influence the level of technological literacy.

> This assessment would be a policy tool, rather than a classroom tool.

Content Specifications

The ITEA *Standards for Technological Literacy*, AAAS *Benchmarks for Science Literacy*, and the NRC *National Science Education Standards* would be useful starting points for determining the content of a national sample assessment, just as they would be for the statewide assessment described in Case 1. Each of these documents suggests "benchmarks" of knowledge and skills a technologically literate individual should have. An assessment framework for a national sample assessment should specify the most important technology concepts and capabilities for 7th-grade students, and the specifications should be detailed enough to clarify the range of material to be covered. Test developers would also have to create a detailed test- and item-specifications document.

Performance Levels

The development of performance levels would be as important for a national sample-based assessment as it would be for the statewide assessment described in Case 1. The processes for developing performance standards, for disaggregating scores according to subscales or dimensions of technological literacy, and for reporting results would be the same for both.

Administration and Logistics

A national sample-based assessment should be administered to a representative sample of 7th graders attending public and nonpublic schools in the United States. (The 2000 NAEP science assessment national sample included about 47,000 children in grades 4, 8, and 12 [DoEd, 2003].) The assessment should take about 50 minutes and should include a mix of multiple-choice, constructed-response, and design-based performance items. An additional 10 minutes could be allocated for completion of accompanying surveys to gauge attitudes and collect demographic information. Teachers would require some training in administering the test, particularly the hands-on design component.

Obstacles to Implementation

Resources and time for designing, administering, and reporting results would be the most significant constraints on a national sample assessment of technological literacy. For example, it costs the federal government about $1.2 million to develop the content framework and item and test specifications for the science portion of the NAEP, which is administered every four years (S. Shakrani, deputy executive director, National Assessment Governing Board, personal communication, August 23, 2004). The development and validation of test items, data collection, analysis, and reporting consume another $2.8 million every test year. For an assessment of technological literacy, in addition to the usual expenses involved in creating and administering a large-scale assessment, additional resources might be necessary to develop specialized assessment tools—such as computer simulations—for measuring the capability dimension. (Cost issues related to simulation are discussed in detail in Chapter 7.)

There may also be other obstacles to overcome. Many decision makers, whose support would be necessary for the development of a national sample-based assessment, might have a limited understanding of technological literacy themselves. In addition, as might be true for a statewide assessment, the mathematics and science education communities might object to a separate assessment of technological literacy on the grounds that it would divert attention and resources from their efforts to improve student learning in their content areas. Finally, because the matrix-sampling approach does not allow for the reporting of individual scores, students and their teachers might not take the test as seriously as other assessments.

Sample Assessment Item

The objective of this sample item, which would constitute most, perhaps all, of the assessment for measuring the capability dimension of technological literacy, would be to gauge a student's knowledge of the design process and his or her ability to carry out a design task. Other items, in multiple-choice, extended-response, and open-response formats, would address the other dimensions of technological literacy. See Table 6-2 for the performance rubric.

Explanation of the Problem

Design and Test a Straw Bridge.

An outdoor jogging and biking path is being built for people to use for exercise. The best site for the path requires that at one location it cross a stream 6 meters wide. The bridge for this crossing must be strong enough to hold several people at once and must prevent them from falling off the edge.

Directions

Select a bridge design that meets the problem constraints, and build a model of it with plastic straws and tape.

Constraints

The model bridge should span a 25-cm space, hold the weight of at least five spice containers, and prevent them from falling off. Only the materials provided can be used to build the model.

Documentation

Use your log sheets to show the drawings you make of potential bridge designs, to describe the process you use to design and select your bridge, and to record your test results.

Materials Provided

15 plastic drinking straws, each one 10 inches long
10 inches of masking tape
  5 spice containers (~4 cm in diameter, 10 cm tall) filled with sand
    or water
  2 large cardboard bricks
    log sheets

Time Limit

25 minutes

Case 3: National-Sample Assessment of Teachers

Description and Rationale

Case 3 involves an assessment of technological literacy for a national sample of pre-service and in-service K–12 teachers. The sample would be designed to include generalists (e.g., elementary school teachers) as well as teachers in specific academic disciplines—science, mathematics, social studies/history, fine arts, and language arts. The sample would also

TABLE 6-2   Performance Rubric for Sample Task

Performance Standard	Performance Level Basic	Proficient	Advanced
Generates and visualizes possible solutions.	Student identifies a single solution that meets some of the constraints and would adequately solve the problem. However, the solution may or may not be feasible.	Student generates solutions that are feasible, meet the constraints, and make efficient use of resources. The design expresses an element of creativity. More than one solution may be presented, but many of them are similar. Student tends to think "inside the box."	Student generates creative and efficient solutions. All solutions meet the constraints and address the original problem. A number of the solutions are feasible. Student is innovative and thinks "outside the box."
Selects a design solution.	Student selects a solution based on limited attention to criteria. The solution may or may not be feasible. The selection process tends to be tentative and uncertain.	Student selects solutions on the basis of efficiency and effectiveness. The solutions are checked against the constraints. Student provides a basic rationale for the design but tends not to have an alternative solution in case the initial choice does not work.	Student provides detailed reasons for selecting a particular solution. Student may provide a backup or alternate solution in case the first solution fails. Student tries to be innovative and to find the best possible solution.

Source: Adapted from Custer et al., 2001.

include teachers of technology, who are routinely assessed during their pre-service education, to provide a basis for comparison.

The rationale for developing an assessment of this sort would be to make efforts to improve technological literacy in the United States more effective. Contemporary models of education reform emphasize that multiple elements of the educational system must be addressed to achieve meaningful, lasting change (e.g., AAAS, 1998; Bybee, 1997). In this view, simply developing content standards is not sufficient. Curricula and instructional materials must also be reworked to align with the standards, goals and methods of teacher education must be reassessed, and assessments must be created that link to what is being taught in the classroom. Knowing what a representative sample of U.S. teachers know and can do with respect to technology would be essential to reforms intended to improve the technological literacy of both teachers and their students.

Purpose

A sample-based assessment of teachers could have several purposes. Education researchers could use the data, along with information from other sources, to build a model of adult learning related to technology. Anyone involved in in-service teacher education could draw on the assessment results to enrich existing activities with technology content (e.g., through summer workshops); results could also be used to design new materials and programs. For schools of education, the assessment could provide a rough indication of how well new teachers are being prepared to think technologically (beyond using computers).

Content

The ITEA *Standards for Technological Literacy*, the AAAS *Benchmarks for Science Literacy*, and the NRC *National Science Education Standards* would be useful starting points for determining the content of a teacher assessment. However, these documents suggest the knowledge and skills for technologically literate students; because of differences in age, maturity, and expectations for content knowledge of teachers, the standards would not be directly transferable.

Thus, a careful framework-development process would be necessary to support assessment in this population. Assessment designers might consider creating a set of items to measure "general" technological literacy to be administered to all teachers in the sample; items targeting more discrete knowledge and skills would be given to a subset of subject-matter specialists. The balance between general and subject-specific items would vary, depending on the purpose of the assessment.

Content specialists in technology as well as in the subjects taught by the teachers in the sample population should be involved in the framework-development process. Standards and benchmarks in non-technology subjects that state or imply a requirement for technological knowledge, capabilities, or critical thinking should be examined. One helpful resource in this regard is the compendium of K–12 education standards created by Mid-Continent Research for Education and Learning (MCREL, 2004). The framework-development process should be informed by the realities of current teacher education. For this reason, those involved in developing and administering teacher pre- and in-service education programs should also be involved.

To the extent that computers and other educational technologies are used to support the development of technological literacy in students, assessments for teachers should include items measuring their knowledge and capability in this domain. The skills, foundational concepts, and intellectual capabilities considered essential to information-technology fluency (NRC, 1999b) would be a reasonable basis upon which to develop such items.

Performance Levels

Establishing performance levels for an assessment of teachers would be challenging. First, the only current basis for deriving descriptions of what might constitute sub-par, adequate, or exemplary teacher technological literacy would be the Praxis test, which is given to a limited target population (technology teachers) for the purpose of licensure. Thus, assessment designers would be charting new territory in many ways. Second, sensitivities to the provisions for highly qualified teachers in NCLB might increase the concerns of potential test takers. If assessment results suggest that teachers are not knowledgeable or capable "enough" in technology, the very individuals and institutions (i.e., schools of education) the assessments are designed to help might resist participating. Third, setting discipline-specific benchmarks would require the involvement of experts in various dimensions of technological literacy and experts familiar with K–12 curricula in the subjects of interest. For all of these reasons, setting performance levels and reporting results for this assessment must be approached with considerable care and sensitivity.

Administration and Logistics

The assessment should last no more than two hours and should include at least one performance task. If possible, testing should be done in a way that encourages teacher participation and reassures them that the results will not be seen by school system administrators involved in personnel oversight and evaluation. One possibility would be to have the assessment administered online by a third-party testing firm. Virtually all teachers have access to computers and the Internet, or can easily obtain access, and there are numerous examples of successful online surveys and tests of professionals, ranging from physicians to journalists and policy makers.

> The assessment should include at least one performance task.

Obstacles to Implementation

A large-scale assessment of teachers' technological literacy would be a major undertaking with significant resource constraints. Because this would be a sample-based assessment, the most significant constraint would be the time and expertise required to design and carry out appropriate sampling procedures. Like assessments for students and out-of-school adults, the other two target populations, designing this assessment would pose technical, logistical, and financial challenges associated with measuring the capability dimension. As a rule, performance assessments, including assessments of technological capability, are time consuming and expensive to design, administer, and score.

Another constraint might be the difficulty of persuading teachers and facility administrators that an assessment would be worthwhile. Teachers have limited time for activities not directly related to their classroom duties, and many teachers and their unions might be wary of an assessment process that could have uncertain outcomes and consequences. This resistance might be overcome by a combination of compensation for participation and assurances that individual scores would not be provided to school administrators. However, if scores were completely disconnected from accountability measures, this would become a low-stakes assessment, thus making it less likely that teachers would take the test seriously.

Sample Assessment Items

Test Items for Generalists

1. An electric generator is used to convert what into what? (knowledge dimension)

a. Solar energy into electric energy
b. Electric energy into solar energy
c. Mechanical energy into electric energy
d. Electric energy into mechanical energy

2. Which device receives, analyzes, and processes incoming information like motion, heat, and light? (knowledge dimension)

a. A sensor
b. A monitor
c. A radio
d. An air coil

3. Develop a basic sketch of the heating system in a typical home. The sketch should include the major components as well as a feedback system that enables the system to function automatically. Describe in words how the system works to deliver heat throughout the home. (knowledge and capabilities dimensions)

4. Hydrogen-powered engines for cars may provide some advantages over existing fuel sources. Focus on either the ethical, social, political, or environmental impact of this significant technological change, and identify the negative and positive consequences. (critical thinking and decision making dimension)

5. Identify a key selling feature (e.g., high gas mileage) of hybrid vehicles and describe two of the associated trade-offs (e.g., less engine power) involved in optimizing that feature. (knowledge and critical thinking and decision making dimensions)

Subtest Item for Social Studies Teachers

How have technological inventions changed the nature of conflict between nations?

a. Describe the changes in technology used in wars of the 18th century and wars of the 20th century? (knowledge dimension)
b. How have these changes impacted the decision to go to war? (critical thinking and decision making dimension)

Case 4: Assessments for Broad Populations

Description and Rationale

In addition to information about the technological literacy of students and teachers, information about the technological literacy of segments of the general population in the United States—people who are affected by, or likely to join in a debate about, a particular new technology—can be extremely helpful. Public opinion researchers call this assessing a "broad population," by which they mean any group sufficiently numerous and widely distributed so that a measurement involves sampling rather than surveying every member of the group. Segments of any of the three population groups—students, teachers, and out-of-school adults—could be part of a broad population. For example, a family of one parent and two young children attending a baseball game could be part of the broad population of "family visitors to sporting events."

The rationale for assessing broad populations is simple. If broad populations are not assessed, a large segment of the general population for which we might want data about technological literacy might be missed. K–12 students and teachers together comprise only about 19 percent of the U.S. population.[5] In addition, assessment in these groups is almost always linked to a structured curriculum. In contrast, assessments of broad populations reveal the understanding, skills, and attitudes acquired by people through life experiences.

Broad population assessments might also provide opportunities to gauge how the dimensions of technological literacy play out in the situations and environments of everyday life, rather than in the somewhat artificial environment of the classroom. Researchers, policy makers, and the education and business communities might all benefit from information about the nature of technological literacy outside the formal education environment.

> K–12 students and teachers together comprise only about 19 percent of the U.S. population.

---

[5]This estimate is based on data from the 2001–2002 school year, the most recent period for which accurate data on teachers are available. There were approximately 2.7 million public school K–12 teachers, according to the National Center for Education Statistics (Young, 2003a). There were approximately 425,000 private elementary and secondary school teachers (Broughman and Pugh, 2004). The K–12 public school student population was approximately 47 million in the 2001–2002 school year (Young, 2003b), and there were about 5.3 million private school students that year (Broughman and Pugh, 2004). According to the Population Division of the U.S. Census Bureau (2005) the U.S. population in 2001 was about 285 million.

Purpose

Assessments of broad populations might be conducted for many different purposes. One way of thinking about a broad population assessment was introduced in 1975 by Benjamin Shen in a discussion of scientific literacy (rather than technological literacy). Shen distinguished three types of literacy: (1) consumer scientific literacy; (2) civic scientific literacy; and (3) cultural scientific literacy. If this framework is applied to technology, three broad populations can be identified: (1) technology consumers, (2) policy-attentive citizens, and (3) the general public.

Technology Consumers

Technology consumers include most adolescents and adults in the United States. The people in this group tend to seek out information about specific technologies—for example, technologies related to health and medical issues—but they are generally more interested in the value and risks of specific technologies than in general issues of public policy. As a group, technology consumers have been studied intensely by technology developers and manufacturers, who routinely conduct studies of users—or potential users—of specific technologies. But much of this information is proprietary and not available for analysis by outsiders. Additional studies of this group would be enlightening, especially assessments comparing attitudes toward, and knowledge of, different technologies.

> Assessments of broad populations might be conducted for many different purposes.

Policy-Attentive Citizens

Policy-attentive citizens, mostly adults but also some well informed teenagers, have a high level of interest in public policy as it relates to one or more specific technologies. Researchers have identified "attentive publics" for science and technology policy, energy policy, space policy, and biomedical policy (Miller, 1983a, 1986, 1992, 1995, 2004a; Miller and Kimmel, 2001; Miller and Pardo, 2000; Miller et al., 1997). In addition, some people are interested in the widespread effects of technology in general on economic and social life.

Policy-oriented audiences tend to want more sophisticated information about technology and tend to have a deeper understanding of technology than technology consumers. Assessments of this population would be particularly useful for characterizing the role of the public in the making of technology-related policies.

The General Public

Everyone in a society is affected by and, in turn, helps shape technology. Thus, the level of "cultural" technological literacy—roughly speaking, the awareness and attitudes of the members of a society toward technology in general and toward specific technologies in particular—can be an important factor in the health of a society. An assessment of cultural technological literacy would provide information about the acceptance of technology by society and about people's awareness of how technology shapes their lives.

An assessment of cultural technological literacy would necessarily be less structured than assessments of technology consumers or policy-attentive citizens. Assessments of knowledge of and attitudes toward technology could provide useful information for educators and media that produce informal science educational products intended for the general adult population; social scientists hoping to improve their understanding of public attitudes; and policy makers attempting to get a perspective on the workforce in relation to national competitiveness in technology-related areas. Assessment data might also be valuable to people who communicate information about technological issues to the general public, such as journalists, designers of museum exhibits, and designers of public-health campaigns (Friedman et al., 1986, 1999).

Content

Some questions for surveys and assessments of broad populations might be derived from the National Science Board (NSB) longstanding survey series on scientific literacy (Miller, 1983b, 1987, 1995, 1998, 2000, 2004a). In that way, data from new surveys could be compared to data from this nearly three-decades-long time series. Unfortunately, NSB has discontinued its surveys, and it is not clear if the surveys will be restarted in the future. The 2001 and 2004 ITEA/Gallup polls on technological literacy might also provide content for a broad population survey. In some cases, rather than relying on earlier assessment instruments or surveys, assessment developers might consult with subject-matter experts in technology, the history of technology, and science, technology and society studies, as well as representatives of populations participating in the assessment and groups that are expected to make use of the results.

The dimensions of technological literacy must be approached from a different angle in the context of broad populations. For technology consumers, all three dimensions of technological literacy—knowledge, capability, and critical thinking and decision making—should be assessed. Measuring attitudes related to consumer issues is partly a marketing concern, and well-developed tools are available for assessing attitudes toward specific technologies and products. But consumers also have personal concerns that may not be tapped in a marketing survey. For example, manufacturers are interested in the factors that influence consumers to purchase a particular model of cell phone but probably do not include questions about consumers' concerns about the effects of using cell phones on the health of the user, traffic safety, and civility in public places.

> Consumers have personal concerns that may not be tapped in a marketing survey.

For policy-attentive audiences, assessing the knowledge and attitudinal components of technological literacy are straightforward, but assessing capability can be problematic. Individuals concerned about environmental damage from waste disposal, for example, need to know the causes and sources of the waste-related pollution and the technical feasibility of controlling or reducing it, but they do not need to have the technical competence to engage directly in pollution control.

At the cultural level, all individuals need general knowledge about technology and the social significance of technology to follow public policy discussions on energy, the environment, and biotechnology, for example. Citizens also need to have enough background information to be able to absorb new information and form reasoned opinions about technological issues. Levels of understanding for various broad populations may range from a general appreciation of the importance of technology to a deeper understanding based on historical examples.

Performance Levels

The concept of performance levels, which are derived largely from educational contexts, is difficult to apply to broad population surveys. Performance levels relevant to particular occupations or professions could be specified for particular segments of the workforce, but these are likely to be occupation-specific, rather than general categories.

Administration and Logistics

Surveys of broad populations and supplementary studies should be administered so that the results are as representative as possible of the general population. Truly representative samples would provide information about gender, ethnic, and geographic differences in technology-related knowledge, capabilities, and critical thinking and decision making. And surveys of broad populations could also provide data on public attitudes toward technology.

A number of measurement methods, strategies, and practices have been developed for studying broad populations. Deciding which of these to use will depend on the population of interest and the goals of the study.

Obstacles to Implementation

In recent decades, most measurements of all segments of the adult population have been conducted through large-scale sample surveys, mostly telephone samples and interviews. In addition, a solid body of research has been accumulated on the best methods of constructing questionnaires and analyzing their results. In the last decade, however, resistance to telephone-based surveys has been growing, and response rates are often unacceptably low. As a result, researchers of broad populations now rely increasingly on online panels, which raise questions about probability-based recruitment versus online participants' self-selection. Some researchers have turned to surveys of broad populations that are co-located, such as patrons of science museums, but these samples may be biased toward people familiar with both science and technology.

Another difficulty for survey designers is that some types of knowledge questions quickly lose currency because of rapid advancements in technology. This can make changes over time difficult to track.

Sample Assessment Items

For Technology Consumers

1. You have bought a new home entertainment system. The system has several large components, not including the speakers, as well as a number of connecting wires and plugs, batteries, and a remote-control device. When you unpack the system at home, you discover that the instruction manual for assembling it is missing. Which of the following best reflects your approach to this problem?

a. I have a good idea how systems like this work, so I would be able to assemble it without instructions or outside help.
b. I do not have experience with this exact type of system, but I would be comfortable trying to figure out how everything fits together through a process of trial and error.
c. I do not have experience with this type of system and would search the World Wide Web for a copy of the instruction manual or to get other online help.
d. I do not have experience with this type of system and would not feel comfortable searching the Web for help.

2. All technologies have consequences not intended by their designers, and some of these consequences are undesirable. Below is a list of consequences some people associate with cell phones. For each, please indicate the level of concern you have (no concern at all; a little concern; a moderate amount of concern; a lot of concern).

a. Possible negative health effects, including cancer.
b. Loss of enjoyment of quiet in public places, such as restaurants.
c. Car accidents caused by drivers using cell phones while on the road.
d. Possible theft of personal data by cell-phone hackers.

For Policy-Attentive Citizens

1. To what extent do you agree or disagree that the following applications of technology pose a risk to society? (Answer choices: completely agree; agree; neither agree nor disagree; disagree; completely agree; not sure.)[6]

a. The use of biotechnology in the production of foods—for example, to increase their protein content—makes them last longer, or enhance their flavor.

---

[6]This question and answers a and b are adapted from U.S. Environmental and Biotechnology Study (Pardo and Miller, 2003).

b. Cloning human cells to replace the damaged cells that are not fulfilling their function well.

c. The computerized collection and sorting of personal data by private companies or the government in order to catch terrorists.

d. The placement under the skin of small computer chips that enable medical personnel to retrieve your personal health information.

2. Please indicate for each of the following sentences the extent to which you believe it is absolutely true, probably true, probably false, or absolutely false. If you do not know about or are not sure about a specific question, check the "Not Sure" box.[7]

a. Antibiotics kill viruses as well as bacteria.

b. Ordinary tomatoes, the ones we normally eat, do not have genes, whereas genetically modified tomatoes do.

c. The greenhouse effect is caused by the use of carbon-based fuels, like gasoline.

d. All pesticides and chemical products used in agriculture cause cancer in humans.

For the General Public

1. Please indicate the extent to which you believe the following statements to be absolutely true, probably true, probably false, or absolutely false.[8]

a. Nuclear power plants destroy the ozone layer.

b. All radioactivity is produced by humans.

c. The U.S. government regulates the World Wide Web to ensure that the information people retrieve is factually correct.

d. Using a cordless phone while in the bathtub creates the possibility of being electrocuted.[9]

---

[7]This question and answers a, b, c, and d are adapted from U.S. Environmental and Biotechnology Study (Pardo and Miller, 2003).

[8]This question and answers a and b are adapted from U.S. Environmental and Biotechnology Study (Pardo and Miller, 2003).

[9]This answer adapted from ITEA, 2004b.

Case 5: Assessments for Visitors to Museums and Other Informal-Learning Institutions

Description and Rationale

Case 5 describes an assessment of technological literacy for visitors to a museum, science center, or other informal-learning institution, where participants set their own learning agendas and determine the duration and selection of content; this is called "free-choice learning." Some 60 million people are served by public science-technology centers in the United States every year (ASTC, 2004). This number is consistent with NSB survey data indicating that 61 percent of adult Americans visit an informal science institution (e.g., a zoo, aquarium, science center, natural history museum, or arboretum) at least once a year (NSB, 2000).

Typically, visitors are children attending as part of a family or school group (which often includes teachers) or adults attending alone or in groups without children. Because of the transient nature of the population of interest (visitors usually spend no more than a few hours in these institutions), the assessment would rely on sampling techniques, although focus-group-style assessments might also be used.

The principal rationale for conducting assessments in informal-education settings is to gain insights into the type and level of technological literacy among a unique (though not random) cross-section of the general public. In addition, because visitors to these facilities are often surrounded by and interact with three-dimensional objects representing aspects of the designed world, informal-learning locations present opportunities for performance-related assessments. The sheer volume of visitors, particularly at mid-sized and large institutions, provides an additional incentive.

Purpose

Organizations that provide informal-learning opportunities, including museums, book and magazine publishers, television stations, websites, and continuing-education programs offered by colleges and universities, all provide information about technology, but generally have limited knowledge of the level of understanding or interest of their intended audiences. For this diverse group of institutions and companies, assessments of technological knowledge and attitudes would provide a context for making programming and marketing decisions.

For example, a science center might want to involve members of the non-expert public in discussions of how using technology to enhance national security might affect privacy. For these discussions to be effective, the center would have to know the nature and extent of participants' understanding (and misunderstanding) of various technologies, such as the Internet and voice- and face-recognition software, as well as their grasp of the nature of technology (e.g., the concepts of trade-offs and unintended consequences). The center might also benefit from an assessment of attitudes about the topic. For instance, knowing that two-thirds of potential participants feel powerless to influence government decisions about deploying such technology, for instance, might influence the type of background information the center provides prior to a discussion.

In addition to planning tools, assessments could be used to determine what members of the public take away from their experiences—new knowledge and understanding (as well as, possibly, misunderstanding), new skills and confidence in design-related processes, and new or different concerns and questions about specific technologies or technology in general. These findings, in turn, could be used to adjust and improve existing or future programs, exhibits, or marketing.

Apart from the direct impact of assessments of technology literacy on individual institutions that want to attract more visitors and improve the quality of their outreach to the public, the assessments might be of wider interest. The formal education system in the United States evolved at a time when the body of knowledge—the set of facts, reasoning abilities, and hands-on skills that defined an "educated" person—was small. A decade or so of formal education was enough to prepare most people to use and understand the technologies they would encounter throughout their lives. Today, the pace of technological change has increased, and individuals are being called upon to make important technological decisions, including career changes required by new technologies, many times in their lives. For this reason, "lifelong learning," which can take place formally in settings like community colleges and the workplace, or informally through independent reading, visits to museums and science centers, or exposure to radio, television, and the Internet, has become critical to technological literacy.

But little is known about how well informal, or free-choice, learning promotes technological understanding. This information would

> Individuals are called upon to make important technological decisions many times in their lives.

be of interest not only to the institutions themselves but also to the publics they serve, funders, policy makers, and the education research community.

Content

The three dimensions of technological literacy, as described in *Technically Speaking*, could provide a reasonable starting point for determining content relevant to an assessment of this population. The ITEA standards also should be consulted, particularly standards related to the nature of technology. To a great extent, however, the content of the assessment would be determined by the specific technology or technology-related concerns at issue. That is, just as a student assessment should be aligned with relevant standards and curriculum, an assessment of visitors to an informal-education institution should be aligned with the subject matter and goals of the program or exhibit.

In situations where the assessment involves a hands-on or design component, assessment developers could use a rubric for judging design-process skills. The model developed by Custer et al. (2001) might be useful here.

Performance Levels

Assessments of visitors to informal-learning institutions would be most useful for identifying a spectrum of technological literacy rather than specific levels of literacy. Changes in the spectrum, for example, movement—up or down—of the entire curve or changes in the shape of the curve, would provide valuable information. Correlations among the three dimensions and with attitudes would be of special interest. Does a high level of knowledge correlate with critical thinking and decision making? with attitudes? How are capabilities related to knowledge and attitudes? Does literacy in one aspect of technology translate to literacy in other areas? These are just a few of the questions that could be answered.

Administration and Logistics

Many informal-learning institutions are open 300 days a year or more, including weekends; thus, there would be fewer constraints on content selection and assessment methodologies than for formal-education settings, such as classrooms, where time, space, and trained staff are all at a premium. Practically all testing methods would work for this population: interviews, multiple-choice questions, constructed-response items, performance items, and focus groups.

Assessments could also measure changes in visitors' understanding of technology or technology-related exhibits over time. Short-term understanding could be measured by pre- and post-visit surveys; long-term understanding might be measured by e-mail or telephone follow-up. A variety of methods could be used to enable museums and other institutions to compare the effects of different exhibit formats and content on specific measures of technological literacy (Miller, 2004b).

Many informal-learning institutions routinely conduct visitor surveys for demographic and marketing purposes, and many also conduct extensive cognitive and affective visitor assessments for front-end, formative, and summative evaluations of exhibitions (Taylor and Serrell, 1991). Some larger institutions even have staff members or consultants capable of performing assessments of the type that could gauge technological literacy, although they rarely have the funds to carry out such assessments.

Obstacles to Implementation

Obtaining a sample of visitors that represents the diversity—in income, education, and other factors—of the U.S. population as a whole would be difficult in the typical informal-learning setting. The population represented by visitors to these institutions is undoubtedly biased in favor of the science-attentive, as opposed to the science-"inattentive" (Miller, 1983b). In addition, compared to the population at large, patrons of science centers, zoos, and related institutions tend to have higher socio-economic parameters, although institutions in urban areas attract more diverse patrons. For example, at the New York Hall of Science, in Queens, 38 percent to 68 percent of family visitors are non-Caucasian (depending on the season), probably because of the location of the institution and the diversity of the staff (Morley and Associates, unpublished). In any case, assessments should be conducted in ways that take into account potential sample bias. Pre-surveys might be used to identify those biases.

Another potential obstacle to assessment in informal-learning institutions is the reluctance of visitors to take part in structured interviews, surveys, or focus groups. Given the relatively short duration of a typical visit, the desire of many patrons to move freely among exhibits of their choosing, and the fact that admission is usually paid, this reluctance

> Assessments should be conducted in ways that take into account potential sample bias.

is understandable. Offering incentives for participation, such as token gifts or free admission, may help to lower this barrier. Exhibit designs that build in opportunities for assessment might also be helpful. For example, assessment designers might consider using technologies that are portable (e.g., PDAs, electronic tablets) and can be programmed to select assessment items based on the visitor's characteristics and physical location in an exhibit space.

Sample Test Items[10]

Give an example of a type of technology you like.

Give an example of a type of technology you don't like.

On a scale of 1 to 100, how much do you think technology affects people's lives?

On a scale of 1 to 100, how much of a role do you think people play in shaping the technologies we have and use?

Give an example of how people like you and me shape technologies.

Imagine that you work for Coca Cola or Pepsi and you are part of the team that came up with a new 20-ounce bottle. What steps did you go through?

Imagine that you are an inventor, and a friend of yours asks you to think about an idea. What steps would you go through to work on this idea?

Do you ever do things that involve creating or designing something, testing it, modifying how you do it, evaluating how someone uses it, and considering the consequences? Give an example.

---

[10]Test items are adapted from a formative evaluation conducted for the Oregon Museum of Science and Industry by People, Places & Design Research, Northhampton, Mass. Used with permission.

References

AAAS (American Association for the Advancement of Science). 1993. Benchmarks for Science Literacy. Project 2061. New York: Oxford University Press.

AAAS. 1998. Blueprints for Reform: Science, Mathematics, and Technology Education. New York: Oxford University Press.

ASTC (Association of Science-Technology Centers). 2004. ASTC Sourcebook of Science Center Statistics 2004. Washington, D.C.: ASTC.

Broughman, S.P., and K.W. Pugh. 2004. Characteristics of Private Schools in the United States: Results from the 2001–2002 Private School Universe Study, Table 1. Available online at: *http://nces.ed.gov/pubs2005/2005305.pdf* (April 11, 2006).

Bybee, R.W. 1997. Achieving Scientific Literacy: From Purposes to Practices. Portsmouth, N.H.: Heinemann.

Custer, R.L., G. Valesey, and B.N. Burke. 2001. An assessment model for a design approach to technological problem solving. Journal of Technology Education 12(2): 5–20.

DoEd (U.S. Department of Education). 2003. The Nation's Report Card: Science 2000. NCES 2003-453. Institute of Education Sciences, National Center for Education Statistics. Washington, D.C.: DoEd.

Friedman, S., S. Dunwoody, and C. Rogers, eds. 1986. Scientists and Journalists: Reporting Science as News. New York: Free Press.

Friedman, S., S. Dunwoody, and C. Rogers. 1999. Communicating Uncertainty. Mahwah, N.J.: Lawrence Erlbaum Associates.

ITEA (International Technology Education Association). 2000. Standards for Technological Literacy: Content for the Study of Technology. Reston, Va.: ITEA.

ITEA. 2004a. Measuring Progress: A Guide to Assessing Students for Technological Literacy. Reston, Va.: ITEA.

ITEA. 2004b. The Second Installment of the ITEA/Gallup Poll and What It Reveals as to How Americans Think About Technology. A Report of the Second survey Conducted by the Gallup Organization for the International Technology Education Association. Available online at: *http://www.iteaconnect.org/TAA/PDFs/GallupPoll2004.pdf* (October 5, 2005).

Lehr, C., and M. Thurlow. 2003. Putting It All Together: Including Students with Disabilities in Assessment and Accountability Systems. NCEO Policy Directions, Number 16/October 2003. Available online at: *http://education.umn.edu/nceo/OnlinePubs/Policy16.htm* (February 23, 2006).

MCREL (Mid-Continent Research for Education and Learning). 2004. Content Knowledge, 4th ed. Available online at: *http://mcrel.org/standards-benchmarks/* (January 13, 2006).

Miller, J.D. 1983a. The American People and Science Policy: The Role of Public Attitudes in the Policy Process. New York: Pergamon Press.

Miller, J.D. 1983b. Scientific literacy: a conceptual and empirical review. Daedalus 112(2): 29–48.

Miller, J.D. 1986. Reaching the Attentive and Interested Publics for Science. Pp. 55–69 in Scientists and Journalists: Reporting Science as News, edited by S. Friedman, S. Dunwoody, and C. Rogers. New York: Free Press.

Miller, J.D. 1987. Scientific Literacy in the United States. Pp. 19–40 in Communicating Science to the Public, edited by D. Evered and M. O'Connor. London: John Wiley and Sons.

Miller, J.D. 1992. From Town Meeting to Nuclear Power: The Changing Nature of Citizenship and Democracy in the United States. Pp. 327–328 in The United States Constitution: Roots, Rights, and Responsibilities, edited by A.E.D. Howard. Washington, D.C.: Smithsonian Institution Press.

Miller, J.D. 1995. Scientific Literacy for Effective Citizenship. Pp. 185–204 in Science/Technology/Society as Reform in Science Education, edited by R.E. Yager. New York: State University of New York Press.

Miller, J.D. 1998. The measurement of civic scientific literacy. Public Understanding of Science 7: 1–21.

Miller, J.D. 2000. The Development of Civic Scientific Literacy in the United States. Pp. 21–47 in Science, Technology, and Society: A Sourcebook on Research and Practice, edited by D.D. Kumar, and D. Chubin. New York: Plenum Press.

Miller, J.D. 2004a. Public understanding of and attitudes toward scientific research: what we know and what we need to know. Public Understanding of Science 13: 273–294.

Miller, J.D. 2004b. The Evaluation of Adult Science Learning. ASP Conference Series, vol. 319. Washington, D.C.: National Aeronautics and Space Administration.

Miller, J.D., and L. Kimmel. 2001. Biomedical Communications: Purposes, Audiences, and Strategies. New York: Academic Press.

Miller, J.D., and R. Pardo. 2000. Civic Scientific Literacy and Attitude to Science and Technology: A Comparative Analysis of the European Union, the United States, Japan, and Canada. Pp. 81–129 in Between Understanding and Trust: The Public, Science, and Technology, edited by M. Dierkes and C. von Grote. Amsterdam: Harwood Academic Publishers.

Miller, J.D., R. Pardo, and F. Niwa. 1997. Public Perceptions of Science and Technology: A Comparative Study of the European Union, the United States, Japan, and Canada. Madrid: BBV Foundation.

Morley and Associates. Unpublished. Unpublished visitor survey for the New York Hall of Science, 2005.

NAE (National Academy of Engineering) and NRC (National Research Council). 2002. Technically Speaking: Why All Americans Need to Know More About Technology. Washington, D.C.: National Academy Press.

NRC (National Research Council). 1996. National Science Education Standards. Washington, D.C.: National Academy Press.

NRC. 1997. Educating One and All: Students with Disabilities and Standards-Based Reform, edited by L.M. McDonnell, M.J. McLaughlin, and P. Morison. Washington, D.C.: National Academy Press.

NRC. 1999a. Recommendations from High Stakes Testing for Tracking, Promotion, and Graduation, edited by J.P. Heubert and R.M. Hauser. Washington, D.C.: National Academy Press.

NRC. 1999b. Being Fluent with Information Technology. Washington, D.C.: National Academy Press.

NSB (National Science Board). 2000. Science and Engineering Indicators 2000, vol. 2. Arlington, Va.: NSB.

Pardo, R., and J.D. Miller. 2003. U.S. Environmental and Biotechnology Study, 2003. Unpublished questionnaire.

Shen, B.S.P. 1975. Science Literacy and the Public Understanding of Science. Pp. 44–52 in Communication of Scientific Information, edited by S.B. Day. New York: Karger.

Taylor, S., and B. Serrell. 1991. Try It!: Improving Exhibits Through Formative Evaluation. Washington, D.C.: Association of Science Technology Centers and New York: New York Hall of Science.

U.S. Census Bureau. 2005. Annual Estimates of the Population for the United States and States, and for Puerto Rico: April 1, 2000 to July 1, 2005 (NST-EST2005-01): Table 1. Available online at: *http://www.census.gov/popest/states/tables/NST-EST2005-01.xls* (April 11, 2006).

Young, B.A. 2003a. Public school student, staff, and graduate counts by state: School year 2001–02. Education Statistics Quarterly 5 (1): Table 2. Available online at: *http://nces.ed.gov/programs/quarterly/vol_5/5_2/q3_4_t1.asp#Table-2* (April 11, 2006).

Young, B.A. 2003b. Public school student, staff, and graduate counts by state: School year 2001–02. Education Statistics Quarterly 5 (1): Table 1. Available online at: *http://nces.ed.gov/programs/quarterly/vol_5/5_2/q3_4_t1.asp#Table-1* (April 11, 2006).

7
Computer-Based Assessment Methods

The committee believes that assessments of technological literacy would benefit from—may even require—innovative approaches, especially for the capability dimension, for which test takers must demonstrate iterative problem-solving techniques typical of a design process. Even with thoughtfully developed paper-and-pencil assessments, it would be extremely difficult to assess this dimension. An alternative approach would be to present test takers with hands-on laboratory exercises, but the costs and complexities of developing, administering, and "grading" a truly hands-on design or problem-solving activity for a large sample of individuals would be prohibitive.

Social scientists, public opinion polling organizations, and others interested in assessing what out-of-school experiences contribute to technological literacy have few tools at their disposal. In national-scale surveys, for example, it is customary to contact participants by telephone using various forms of random-digit dialing. However, response rates have dropped significantly recently because of the number of research surveys, the exponential increase in cell phone use, and other factors, raising concerns about the reliability and validity of survey data. Free-choice learning environments, such as museums and science centers, are also struggling to find ways of measuring attitudinal changes and learning as a result of exposure to exhibits and other programs.

The presentation strategies and analyses possible with computer-based methods would be, at best, impractical, and often, out of the question with traditional assessment methods. Computer-based methods could have several advantages over traditional methods. They could provide faster, more accurate scoring (Bahr and Bahr, 1997), reduce test-administration times (Shermis et al., 1996), and make possible relatively low-cost scaling to large numbers of test takers. They could also be designed to meet the needs of special populations, including people with physical disabilities and people from diverse cultural or linguistic backgrounds (Naglieri et al., 2004).

There are legitimate concerns about using computers in educational testing.

However, there are legitimate concerns about using computers in educational testing. A potential limitation, of course, is the lack of computer literacy of the test population. Test takers—children or adults—who do not have at least a basic familiarity with computers and computer keyboarding may not perform as well as those who have at least basic computer skills (Russell, 1999). In addition, requirements for computer memory and processing speeds, graphics quality, and bandwidth—for applications using the Internet—may pose significant cost and resource barriers.

Computer-based tests would be just as susceptible to cheating as traditional paper-and-pencil assessments, although the types of cheating and strategies for countering them may differ. For example, someone other than the registered examinee could take the test or help answer questions on an assessment administered remotely (online). To preclude this kind of cheating, authentication could be attempted using a biometric measure (e.g., a fingerprint or retina scan), or the test taker could be required to take a short, proctored confirmatory test (Segall, 2001).

It is important to keep in mind that although computer technology could potentially increase testing flexibility, authenticity, efficiency, and accuracy, computer-based assessments must still be subject to the same defensible standards as paper-and-pencil assessments, particularly if the results are used to make important decisions. The reference of choice is *Standards for Educational and Psychological Testing* (AERA et al., 1999).

The following discussion focuses on aspects of computer-based testing that offer significant potential benefits for the assessment of technological literacy.

Computer-Based Adaptive Assessments

Computer-based, flexi-level, branching, and stratified adaptive testing have been investigated for more than 30 years (Baker, 1989; Bunderson et al., 1989; Lord, 1971a,b,c; van der Linden, 1995; Weiss, 1983). Research has been focused mostly on using interactive (computer) technology to select, in real time, specific items to present to individual examinees based on responses to previous items. Incorrect responses evoke less difficult items in that dimension, whereas correct responses evoke increasingly difficult items until the standard error of estimate for that dimension oscillates regularly—within preset confidence levels—around a particular value.

Adaptive testing has been used by the U.S. Department of Defense in some high-profile areas. For example, a computerized version of the Armed Services Vocational Ability Test (ASVAB) has been administered to thousands of recruits since 1998. ASVAB now uses computers for item writing, item banking, test construction, test administration, test scoring, item and test analyses, and score reporting (Baker, 1989). Overall, research findings and experience suggest that tests using adaptive techniques are shorter, more precise, and more reliable than tests using other techniques (Weiss, 2004). Therefore, it is reasonable to expect that adaptive testing would be effective for assessments of technological literacy.

> Tests using adaptive techniques are shorter, more precise, and more reliable than tests using other techniques.

However, computer-based adaptive testing has some shortcomings. Because of the nature of the algorithms used to select successive test questions, computer-adaptive items are usually presented only once. Thus, test takers do not have an opportunity to review and modify responses, which could be a disadvantage to some test takers who might improve their scores by changing responses on a traditional paper-and-pencil test.

In theory, each person who takes a computer-adaptive test is presented with a unique subset of the total pool of test items, which would seem to make it very difficult for cheaters to beat the system by memorizing individual items. However, this assumption was challenged in the mid-1990s when significant cheating was uncovered on the Educational Testing Service (ETS) computer-adaptive Graduate Record Exam (Fair Test Examiner, 1997), causing the company to withdraw this version of the exam. ETS has since made a number of changes, including enlarging the item pool, and the online test is now back on the market.

The two main costs of computer-adaptive testing are (1) the software coding necessary to create an adaptive test environment and (2) the creation of items. Although the cost varies depending on the nature of the assessment, it is not unusual for an assessment developer to spend $250,000 for software coding (D. Fletcher, Institute for Defense Analyses, personal communication, February 27, 2006). Per-item development costs are about the same for paper-and-pencil and computer-adaptive tests, but two to four times as many items may be required to support a computerized assessment. Nevertheless, computerized adaptive tests, such as the Renaissance Learning Star Reading Test (*http://www.renlearn.com/starreading/*), are being used in some K–12 settings. Some firms (e.g., Microsoft) are also using adaptive testing to certify an individual's product knowledge.

Simulations

Rather than presenting a series of test items, even items adapted to an individual's responses, assessments might be improved by immersing the test taker in simulations of real-life situations. This idea is particularly appealing for assessments of technological literacy, which necessarily emphasize capability and critical thinking and decision making, in addition to basic knowledge.

With simulated environments, performance and competence can be assessed in situations that cannot be attempted in the real world. Aircraft can be crashed, bridges can be tested with heavy loads, expensive equipment can be ruined, and lives can be risked in simulated environments in ways that would be impractical, or unthinkable, in the real world. Simulated environments can also make the invisible visible, compress or expand time, and repeatedly reproduce events, situations, and decision points.

The military has long used simulations to assess the readiness of individuals and groups for military operations (Andrews and Bell, 2000; Fletcher, 1999; Fletcher and Chatelier, 2000; Pohlman and Fletcher, 1999). Industry also uses simulation-based assessments for everything from device maintenance and social role-playing to planning marketing campaigns (Aldrich, 2004). In formal education, simulations and computer-based modeling are being investigated as tools for improving learning in biology, chemistry, and physics (e.g., Concord Consortium, 2005; TELS, 2005; Thinkertools, 2005).

Simulation can be used in a variety of ways: (1) in design, to describe the behavior of a system that does not yet exist; (2) in analysis, to describe the behavior of an existing system under various operating conditions; (3) in training, to shape the behavior of individuals and groups and prepare them for situations they may encounter on the job; and (4) in entertainment, to provide computer games (Smith, 2000). The quality of a simulation depends on its purpose—the question(s) it is expected to answer—and the accuracy with which it represents system components that are relevant to this purpose.

A simulation can be used to situate individuals in the system it represents and then compare their judgments about the operation of the system with those of the simulation. Simulations might represent a system with sufficient accuracy to allow individuals and groups to try to understand and apply technology, without delving into the scientific basis of the system's operation.

Because simulation-based assessments have highly reactive and interactive capabilities, they can be more sophisticated and elaborate than paper-based tests and provide more comprehensive and more substantive measures of technological literacy. Simulations can not only provide opportunities for individuals or teams to demonstrate technological literacy through designing, building, and application capabilities, they can also review the results, assess the ability to correct errors (if any), apply probability techniques to infer understanding of actions, and "coach" and "supply hints" to improve partial solutions. One can imagine a number of simulated design-related tasks (Box 7-1) in which individuals could build and test their own systems and system components within a larger, simulated context that could assess their actions.

One concern about computer-based simulations is the cost of developing them. In some instances, the costs could even outweigh the value of using simulation in an assessment. But determining when simulation would be too expensive requires that one know the costs and benefits of assessment with and without simulation, and the committee was unable to find studies that address this issue.

Cost-benefit decisions would have to take into account the time-saving potential of so-called authoring tools (software designed to simplify the creation of simulations). A number of off-the-shelf products have been developed for this purpose, such as Macromedia Captivate

---

BOX 7-1   Sample Simulation Tasks for Assessing Technological Literacy

- Assemble a working system from components.
- Disassemble a working system and identify the purpose of each component.
- Redesign a working system to make it more ergonomic, more environmentally friendly, or more cost effective.
- Repair a nonworking or faulty system by replacing one or more components.
- Operate a system (or system of systems) to achieve a specified outcome.
- Observe a debate (portrayed by actors or animated figures) about a controversial new technology, choose a point of view, and defend it using information gathered from the Web.

(*http://www.macromedia.com/software/captivate*) and Vcommunicator Studio (*http://www.vcom3d.com/vstuidio.htm*). Other authoring tools have been developed with government funding by academic researchers (e.g., Munro and Pizzini, 1996; Pizzini and Munro, 1998).

One study describes the use of DIAG, a set of authoring tools developed by the Behavioral Technology Laboratories at the University of Southern California, to create a simulation-based instructional module for diagnosing faults in an aircraft power-distribution system (Towne, 1997). The module consists of 28 screen displays (including a fully operational front panel simulation), 13 operational circuit breakers, 11 connectors, 94 wires, and 21 other components that could be faulty. The system was capable of generating and diagnosing 19,110 fault conditions.

Using the authoring tool, Towne found that it required 22 person-days to develop the module with all of the control and logic necessary for its operation as an instructional system. Without DIAG, he estimated that the time required would be 168 days. Whether 22 days of a technician's time is a reasonable cost for the development of a computer-based simulation for assessing technological literacy depends on the uses of the simulation and the decisions it is intended to inform. In any case, this study suggests that it is reasonable to expect that authoring tools will have a substantial impact on the costs of developing simulations.

Despite increasing use of simulations by industry, the military, and educators, the design, development, and use of simulations specifically for assessments is rarely discussed in the technical literature. In addition, the prospect of assessment via simulation has raised questions about measurement that are just being articulated and addressed by assessment specialists. For instance, O'Neil and colleagues have conducted empirical studies of psychometric properties, such as reliability, validity, and precision (e.g., O'Neil et al., 1997a,b).

After reviewing the potential of using simulation for assessment, the committee identified several questions for researchers (Box 7-2). With simulations, individuals (or groups) may be immersed in a system (or situation) that reacts to their decisions and allows them to achieve their goals, or not—providing feedback on their success or failure. However, sometimes test takers may take correct actions for the wrong reasons—in other words, they may be lucky rather than competent. This could also happen, of course, in any design problem or laboratory-based exercise. Sometimes, if an incorrect decision is made early in the running of a simulation, all subsequent actions, even if correct, may lead to failure at

Use of simulations specifically for assessments is rarely discussed in the technical literature.

the end. Sometimes, an incorrect decision toward the end of a simulation may be inconsequential. In addition, simulations begin with a set of circumstances—a scenario. A change in any one of the circumstances could change the entire nature of the assessment.

Nevertheless, researchers are making progress in using simulations for assessing complex problem solving comparable to the skills required for technological literacy. For instance, one promising approach is based on evidence-centered design (ECD) (Mislevy et al., 2003). In this approach, capabilities are identified for a subject area and organized into a graphical framework. ECD then shows how to connect the responses of test takers working in a complex simulated environment to the framework. Bennett and colleagues (2003) have provided an example of how ECD might be used to assess scientific-inquiry skills in a simulated environment.

Simulations can also be used in networked configurations to assess individuals or groups at any time and anywhere from remote locations. Both the military and the computer-games industry have made major investments in networked simulation. In the military, the focus is on team performance, rather than individual performance. The members of crews, teams, and units are assumed to be proficient in their individual specialties (they are expected to know how to drive tanks, read maps, fly airplanes, fire weapons) before they begin networked simulation exercises (Alluisi, 1991). Because some aspects of technological literacy also involve group coordination and communication, networked simulation may be useful for assessing these competencies. However, as noted, development costs may be higher than for more traditional test methods.

Computer-Based and Web-Based Games

Games, especially games available over the World Wide Web, may also be useful for assessing technological literacy. Most technology-based games incorporate simulations of real and/or imagined systems. Although they emphasize entertainment over realism, well-designed games provide both realism and entertainment.

Some games are designed to be played by thousands of players. According to one estimate, there are some 5 million players of massive, multiplayer, on-line games (MMOGs) with at least 10,000 subscribers each (Woodcock, 2005). One might imagine an ongoing (continuous and unobtrusive) assessment of technological literacy based on an MMOG that collects data aggregated from the activities of hundreds of thousands of players who could contribute minimal personal data without compromising their privacy. Provisions would have to be put in place to ensure that participation was voluntary.

One example of a game that might be adapted to assess technological literacy is "Monkey Wrench Conspiracy" (available from *http://www.Games2train.com*). In this game, which is actually a set of training modules for new users of another company's computer-aided design/computer-aided manufacturing (CAD/CAM) design software, the player (i.e., trainee) becomes an intergalactic secret agent who has to save a space station from attack by using CAD software to build tools, repair weapons, and defeat booby traps. The 30 tasks to be performed are presented in order of difficulty and keyed to increasing levels of technological capability. Because the game is modular, modified or new tasks can be added easily; thus, the concept of technological literacy could evolve with the technology.

Another useful feature of computer games is their capacity for motivation. Great numbers of people are motivated to play games, perhaps even games intended to assess technological literacy, for extended periods of time, thereby increasing the reliability and accuracy of the assessments they could provide. A computer game that assesses technological literacy could be a national assessment instrument for identifiable segments of the population. If players allow their responses to be anonymously collected and pooled, a well designed game that taps into technological knowledge and capability could become an unobtrusive, continuous, self-motivating, and inexpensive source of diagnostic information on the levels of technological literacy of different segments of the national population.

Considerable research has been done to identify and describe gender differences in game-seeking and game-playing behavior, whether on a personal computer, video arcade console, or online. In absolute numbers, at least as many women as men play games, including online games, but women prefer different types of games and different types of interactions (Crusoe, 2005; Robar and Steele, 2004). Women prefer quizzes, trivia games, and board and contest games, whereas men prefer action games. Women tend to enjoy the social aspects of online gaming and relationship-building in games. In contrast, men prefer strategy games, military games, and games that involve fighting or shooting. Both men and women seem to be interested in simulations (e.g., The Sims), racing games (e.g., Need for Speed Underground), and role-playing games (e.g., Everquest).

> Women tend to enjoy the social aspects of online gaming.

Male-female differences in online game-playing behavior suggest that assessments that rely on computer technology may also be skewed by gender (i.e., sample bias). Other potential sources of sample bias include socioeconomic status and age. Lower income individuals, for example, may have relatively infrequent access to computers and computer-game software and therefore may not have experience or interest in operating computers and engaging in computer-based simulation. Similarly, older adults who have not grown up in the digital age—a demographic Prensky dubs "digital immigrants"—may have varying degrees of difficulty adapting to and using digital technology (Prensky, 2001). They may also simply have less interest in interacting with computers. Whether or not one accepts Prensky's characterization, assessment developers will have to ensure that the mode of assessment does not bias results based on test takers' computer literacy skills (Haertel and Wiley, 2003).

Electronic Portfolios

Artists, dancers, musicians, actors, and photographers have used portfolios to demonstrate their competency and show examples of their work. In formal education, portfolios have been used in K–12 and undergraduate classrooms, as well as schools of education (Carroll et al., 1996). Portfolios typically document student projects, often detailing the iterative steps in the production of a finished product. Portfolios can provide information for both formative and summative assessments, as well as an opportunity for making accurate measurements of performance and self-reflection.

Traditional paper-based portfolios, which may include writing, drawing, photos, and other visual information and which have been used for decades by U.S. educators, have several limitations. Most important, they require large amounts of physical storage space, and their contents can be difficult to maintain and share. With the introduction of computers and online communication into educational settings in the early 1990s, digital, or electronic, portfolios could be created (Georgi and Crowe, 1998). Electronic portfolios can be used for many purposes, including marketing or employment (to highlight competencies), accountability (to show attainment of standards), and self-reflection (to foster learning); these purposes may sometimes be at odds with one another (Barrett and Carney, 2005).

Electronic portfolios appear to be excellent tools for documenting and exploring the process of technological design.

To the committee's knowledge, electronic portfolios have not been used in the United States to assess technological literacy as defined in this report. However, electronic portfolios appear to be excellent tools for documenting and exploring the process of technological design. A number of companies produce off-the-shelf portfolio software (e.g., HyperStudio, FolioLive [McGraw Hill]), and customized software is being developed by universities and researchers in other settings (e.g, Open Source Portfolio Initiative, *http://www.osportfolio.org*). The question of whether existing software could be adapted for assessments of technological literacy is a subject for further inquiry.

Traditional, paper-based portfolios have been an essential component of the design and technology curriculum in the United Kingdom for documenting and assessing student projects. The portfolios of some 500,000 16-year-olds are reviewed and graded every year. Assembling a portfolio is a learning tool as much as an assessment tool, and students typically report that they learn more from their major project—which may occupy them for as long as eight months of their final year—than from anything else in their design and technology program (R. Kimbell, professor, Technology Education Research Unit, Goldsmiths College, London, personal communication, May 5, 2005).

Recently, the British government funded a research group at Goldsmiths College to develop an electronic-portfolio examination system to enable students to develop design projects digitally, submit them digitally (via a secure website), and have them assessed digitally. In addition to computers and CAD software, other technologies that might enrich electronic portfolios are being considered, such as digital pens that can store what has been written and drawn with them; personal digital assistants that can store task-related data; and speech-to-text software that can enable sharing and analysis of design discussions. If the prototype system is successful, the research team will expand the electronic-portfolio system for four other areas of the curriculum, English, science, and two cross-curricular subjects.

Electronic Questionnaires

Adaptive testing, simulations, games, and portfolios could also be used in informal-education settings, such as museums and science centers. For example, portable devices, such as PC tablets and palm computers, might be used in museums, where people move from place to place. A questionnaire presented via these technologies could include logic branching and dynamic graphics, allowing a respondent to use visual as well as verbal resources in thinking about the question (Miller, 2004).

Very short questionnaires, consisting of only one or two questions, could be delivered as text messages on cell phones, a technique that some marketing companies now use to test consumer reactions to potential new products or product-related advertising. At least one polling organization used a similar technique to gauge young voters' political leanings during the 2004 U.S. presidential election (Zogby International, 2004). Finally, considering that more than 70 percent of U.S. homes have Internet access (Duffy and Kirkley, 2004), informal-learning centers, survey researchers, and others interested in tapping into public knowledge and attitudes about technology could send follow-up questionnaires by e-mail or online. Several relatively inexpensive software packages are available for designing and conducting online surveys, and the resulting data usually cost less and are of higher quality than data from traditional printed questionnaires or telephone interviews.

References

AERA (American Educational Research Association), APA (American Psychological Association), and NCME (National Council on Measurement in Education). 1999. Standards for Educational and Psychological Testing. Washington, D.C.: AERA.

Aldrich, C. 2004. Simulations and the Future of Learning. San Francisco: Pfeiffer.

Alluisi, E.A. 1991. The development of technology for collective training: SIMNET, a case history. Human Factors 33(3): 343–362.

Andrews, D.H., and H.H. Bell. 2000. Simulation-Based Training. Pp. 357–384 in Training and Retraining: A Handbook for Business, Industry, Government, and the Military, edited by S. Tobias and J.D. Fletcher. New York: Macmillan Reference USA.

Bahr, M.W, and C.M. Bahr. 1997. Education assessment in the next millennium: contributions of technology. Preventing School Failure 4(Winter): 90–94.

Baker, F.B. 1989. Computer technology in test construction and processing. Pp. 409–428 in Educational Measurement, 3rd ed., edited by R.L. Linn. New York: Macmillan.

Barrett, H., and J. Carney. 2005. Conflicting paradigms and competing purposes in electronic portfolio development. Educational Assessment. Submitted for publication.

Bennett, R.E., F. Jenkins, H. Persky, and A. Weiss. 2003. Assessing complex problem-solving performances. Assessment in Education 10(3): 347–359.

Bunderson, C.V., D.K. Inouye, and J.B. Olson. 1989. The four generations of computerized educational measurement. Pp. 367–408 in Educational Measurement, 3rd ed., edited by R.L. Linn. New York: Macmillan.

Carroll, J., D. Potthoff, and T. Huber. 1996. Learning from three years of portfolio use in teacher education. Journal of Teacher Education 47(4): 253–262.

Concord Consortium. 2005. Molecular Logic Project. Available online at: *http://molo.concord.org/* (October 19, 2005).

Crusoe, D. 2005. A discussion of gender diversity in computer-based assessment. Available online at: *http://www.bitculture.org/storage/DHC_Gender_Div_EdDRvw0705.pdf* (December 23, 2005).

Duffy, T.M., and J.R. Kirkley. 2004. Learning Theory and Pedagogy Applied in Distanced Learning: The Case of Cardean University. Pp. 107–141 in Learner Centered Theory and Practice in Distance Education: Cases from Higher Education, edited by T.M. Duffy and J.R. Kirkley. Mahwah, N.J.: Lawrence Erlbaum Associates.

Fair Test Examiner. 1997. ETS and test cheating. Available online at: *http://www.fairtest.org/examarts/winter97/etscheat.htm* (January 4, 2006).

Fletcher, J.D. 1999. Using networked simulation to assess problem solving by tactical teams. Computers in Human Behavior 15(May/July): 375–402.

Fletcher, J.D., and P.R. Chatelier. 2000. Military Training. Pp. 267–288 in Training and Retraining: A Handbook for Business, Industry, Government, and the Military, edited by S. Tobias and J.D. Fletcher. New York: Macmillan.

Georgi, D., and J. Crowe. 1998. Digital portfolios: a confluence of portfolio assessment and technology. Teacher Education Quarterly 25(1): 73–84.

Haertel, E., and D. Wiley. 2003. Comparability issues when scores are produced under varying test conditions. Paper presented at the Validity and Accommodations: Psychometric and Policy Perspectives Conference, August 4–5, College Park, Maryland.

Lord, F.M. 1971a. Robbins-Monro procedures for tailored testing. Educational and Psychological Measurement 31: 3–31.

Lord, F.M. 1971b. A theoretical study of the measurement effectiveness of flexilevel tests. Educational and Psychological Measurement 31: 805–813.

Lord, F.M. 1971c. The self-scoring flexilevel test. Educational and Psychological Measurement 31: 147–151.

Miller, J. 2004. The Evaluation of Adult Science Learning. Pp. 26–34 in Proceedings of NASA Office of Space Science Education and Public Outreach Conference 2002. ASP Conference Series 319. Washington, D.C.: National Aeronautics and Space Administration.

Mislevy, R.J., R.G. Almond, and J.F. Lukas. 2003 A Brief Introduction to Evidence-Centered Design. RR-03-16. Princeton, N.J.: Educational Testing Service.

Munro, A., and Q.A. Pizzini. 1996. RIDES Reference Manual. Los Angeles, Calif.: Behavioral Technology Laboratories, University of Southern California.

Naglieri, J.A., F. Drascow, M. Schmidt, L. Handler, A. Prifitera, A. Margolis, and R. Velasquez. 2004. Psychological testing on the Internet: new problems, old issues. American Psychologist 59(3): 150–162.

O'Neil, H.F., K. Allred, and R.A. Dennis. 1997a. Validation of a Computer Simulation for Assessment of Interpersonal Skill. Pp. 229–254 in Workplace Readiness: Competencies and Assessment, edited by H.F. O'Neil. Mahwah, N.J.: Lawrence Erlbaum Associates.

O'Neil, H.F., G.K.W.K. Chung, and R.S. Brown. 1997b. Use of Networked Simulations as a Context to Measure Team Competencies. Pp. 411–452 in Workplace Readiness: Competencies and Assessment, edited by H.F. O'Neil. Mahwah, N.J.: Lawrence Erlbaum Associates.

Pizzini, Q.A., and A. Munro. 1998. VIVIDS Authoring for Virtual Environments. Los Angeles, Calif.: Behavioral Technology Laboratories, University of Southern California.

Pohlman, D.L., and J.D. Fletcher. 1999. Aviation Personnel Selection and Training. Pp. 277–308 in Handbook of Aviation Human Factors, edited by D.J. Garland, J.A. Wise, and V.D. Hopkin. Mahwah, N.J.: Lawrence Erlbaum Associates.

Prensky, M. 2001. Digital natives, digital immigrants. On the Horizon 9(5). Available online at: *http://www.marcprensky.com/writing/Prensky%20-%20Digital%20Natives,%20Digital%20Immigrants%20-%20Part1.pdf* (January 4, 2006).

Robar, J., and A. Steele. 2004. Females and Games. Computer and Video Game Industry Research Study. March 2004. Issaquah, Washington: AisA Group.

Russell, M. 1999. Testing on Computers: A Follow-up Study Comparing Performance on Computer and on Paper. Available online at: *http://epaa.asu.edu/epaa/v7n20/* (January 4, 2006).

Segall, D.O. 2001. ASVAB Testing via the Internet. Unpublished paper.

Shermis, M.D., P.M. Stemmer, and P.M. Webb. 1996. Computerized adaptive skill assessment in a statewide testing program. Journal of Research on Computing in Education 29(1): 49–67.

Smith, R.D. 2000. Simulation. Pp. 1578–1587 in Encyclopedia of Computer Science, 4th ed., edited by A. Ralston, E.D. Reilley, and D. Hemmendinger. New York: Grove's Dictionaries.

TELS (Technology Enhanced Learning in Science). 2005. Web-based inquiry science environment. Available online at: *http://wise.berkeley.edu/* (October 19, 2005).

Thinkertools. 2005. Force and motion. Available online at: *http://thinkertools. soe.berkeley.edu/Pages/force.html* (October 19, 2005).

Towne, D.M. 1997. An Intelligent Tutor for Diagnosing Faults in an Aircraft Power Distribution System. Technical Report 118. Los Angeles, Calif.: Behavioral Technology Laboratories, University of Southern California.

van der Linden, W.J. 1995. Advances in Computer Applications. Pp. 105–123 in International Perspectives on Academic Assessment, edited by T. Oakland and R.K. Hambleton. Boston: Kluwer Academic Publishers.

Weiss, D.J. 1983. Computer-Based Measurement of Intellectual Capabilities: Final Report. Minneapolis, Minn.: Computerized Adaptive Testing Laboratory, University of Minnesota.

Weiss, D.J. 2004. Computerized adaptive testing for effective and efficient measurement in counseling and education. Measurement and Evaluation in Counseling and Development 37(2): 70–84.

Woodcock, B.S. 2005. Total MMOG Active Subscriptions (Excluding Lineage, Lineage II, and Ragnorak Online). Available online at: *http://mmogchart.com/* (August 22, 2005).

Zogby International. 2004. Young Mobile Voters Pick Kerry over Bush 55% to 40%, Rock the Vote/Zogby Poll Reveals: National Text-Message Poll Breaks New Ground. Press release dated October 31, 2004. Available online at: *http://www.zogby.com/news/ReadNews.dbm?ID=919* (August 22, 2005).

8
Findings and
Recommendations

The overarching goal of assessing technological literacy is to provide an accurate picture of what Americans of all ages know and can do with respect to technology. After reviewing the literature related to assessment, cognition, and technological literacy; receiving input from a variety of stakeholders; and drawing on its own experiences and judgment, the committee developed the following general principles to guide the development of assessments of technological literacy for students, teachers, and out-of-school adults:

1. **Assessments should be designed with a clear purpose in mind.** The purpose must be clear to the developers of the assessment, as well as to test takers and the users of the results.

2. **Assessment developers should take into account research findings related to how children and adults learn, including how they learn about technology.** Insights into how conceptual understanding of technology develops and the mental processes involved in solving technological problems can help assessment designers construct appropriate items and tasks.

3. **The content of an assessment should be based on rigorously developed learning standards.** The knowledge and skills identified in learning standards reflect the judgments of technical experts and experienced educators about the development of technological literacy.

4. **Assessments should provide information about all three dimensions of technological literacy—knowledge, capabilities, and critical thinking and decision making.** Meaningful

conclusions about the state of technological literacy in the United States must reflect skills and knowledge in all three dimensions.

5. **Assessments should not reflect gender, culture, or socio-economic bias.** Because of the nature of technology, men and women, people from different cultures, and people from different economic backgrounds experience and value technology in different ways. Designers of assessments must take these differences into account to avoid including items and tasks that favor or disadvantage particular groups.

6. **Assessments should be accessible to people with mental or physical disabilities.** In keeping with federal and state laws and regulations, assessments of technological literacy must be designed, as much as possible, to allow individuals with mental or physical disabilities to participate.

In addition to these general guidelines, the committee developed findings and related recommendations in five categories: opportunities for assessment; research on learning; the use of innovative measurement techniques; framework development; and broadening the definition of technology. The numbering of the recommendations does not indicate prioritization. Although some recommendations will be easier to implement than others, the recommendations are interdependent, and the committee believes that all of them are necessary.

Opportunities for Assessment

General Findings

Based on the review of assessment instruments (Chapter 4 and Appendix E) and input from participants in a committee-sponsored workshop, the committee finds that the assessment of technological literacy is in its infancy. This is not surprising considering that most students still have no access to courses in school that are likely to encourage technological thinking. Although a majority of states have adopted the learning goals spelled out in the ITEA standards in one form or another, fewer than one-quarter require that students take coursework consistent with the standards in order to graduate (Meade and Dugger, 2004). With the notable exception of technology educators, few teachers currently have an incentive to learn about or demonstrate knowledge of technology as described in *Technically Speaking*. Finally, very little thought has been given to assessing the technological literacy or attitudes toward technology of out-of-school adults.

On a more positive note, the review of assessment instruments suggests that valid and reliable items can be developed that address one or more of the cognitive dimensions and all of the content domains of technological literacy. Items related to critical thinking and decision making may be the most challenging for assessment developers, and time and resource constraints will pose obstacles to the development of items to measure design-related capability. But both types of items can and should be developed.

The paucity of instruments for measuring technological literacy in informal-learning settings, such as museums, indicates a major area of opportunity. Adults and children learn about many things, including technology, through exposure to television, the Internet, movies, magazines, books, and other media, as well as through life experiences and self-study. Very few of the assessments seen by the committee attempt to document the effects of learning outside of a formal school structure or learning related to the use of specific technologies (Gee, 2003; Kasesniemi and Rautiainen, 2002; Valentine et al., 2000).

Until rigorously developed assessments of technological literacy become more prevalent in the United States, neither educators nor policy makers, business leaders, or the public at large will be able to gauge the ability of citizens to participate confidently and responsibly in our technology-dependent world.

The committee finds there are two main areas of opportunity for increasing the use of assessments of technological literacy: (1) the modification of existing assessments; and (2) the development of new assessments. Existing assessments in technology-related subject areas, particularly science, mathematics, and history (or social studies), could be modified by adding items, tasks, or survey questions for measuring technological literacy. The obvious benefit of this strategy is that it leverages validated assessment designs and existing implementation networks. This "plug-and-play" approach would also provide data about technological literacy relatively quickly.

The second area of opportunity is the development of new assessment instruments devoted entirely to technological literacy. This more ambitious course of action would require breaking new ground. The development of assessment instruments *de novo*, especially in an area like

> The committee finds there are two main areas of opportunity for increasing the use of assessments of technological literacy.

technology, which is largely outside the mainstream of formal education, would face significant hurdles, as noted in several case studies in Chapter 6. However, the potential benefits would also be significant, especially the prospect of realizing a comprehensive picture of Americans' understanding of and engagement in our technological world.

The two areas of opportunity just described are not mutually exclusive, and the committee recommends that both approaches be pursued simultaneously. As a practical matter, data gathered from early, integrative attempts to assess aspects of technological literacy would provide valuable input for comprehensive, stand-alone assessments, whether for students, teachers, or out-of-school adults. No matter which approach is taken, assessment items should be designed to encourage both higher order and design-related thinking, because questions and tasks that require the analysis and synthesis of information are more useful for measuring technological literacy than items that require the recall of information. And because design processes are at the heart of technology development, it makes sense that assessments of technological literacy provide opportunities for people to demonstrate design capability. Of course, test instruments and the specification of test items in assessments for students must be aligned with content standards and curriculum.

> Assessment items should be designed to encourage both higher order and design-related thinking.

The gaps in our understanding of attitudes toward technology are as wide as the gaps in our knowledge of what people know and can do with respect to technology. Attitudinal information for all three populations would benefit the developers of assessments and researchers. Assessments designed to measure attitudes toward technology must include all of the components of attitudes—cognition, affect, and a tendency toward action (cf. Box 2-3). Designers should attempt to address all aspects of these components and should specifically elicit positive/negative or favorable/unfavorable responses to particular aspects or objects of technology.

Findings and Recommendations for K–12 Students

There are a handful of established, thoughtfully developed national and international assessments to which technology-related items might be added. The National Assessment of Educational Progress (NAEP) samples achievement in reading, mathematics, writing, and science, among other subjects, in U.S. 5th-, 8th-, and 12th-graders. All states that receive Title I funds must take part in the NAEP assessments of mathematics and reading; participation in writing and science assessments is optional. Data from a subset of public schools participating in state NAEP assessments are combined to provide a representative national sample. NAEP results are reported on the national and state level and by region of the country, but not by school district, school, or individual student. Group statistics are broken down by gender, race/ethnicity, and a host of other variables to shed light on students' instructional experiences.

The most recent science-focused NAEP assessment was conducted in spring 2005. In late 2004, the agency hired WestEd, a regional education laboratory, to develop a new framework for a science assessment, which will be the basis of the next NAEP science test, in 2009. A draft of the framework was published for public comment in fall 2005 (NAGB, 2005). NAEP also occasionally conducts so-called special studies, usually small-scale projects to test new approaches, explore new content, or assess achievement in particular population groups.

Independent of NAEP, all states must assess the reading and mathematics achievement for all public-school students in grades 3 through 8, and at least once in grades 10 through 12, as part of the No Child Left Behind Act of 2001 (NCLB; P.L. 107-110). NCLB requires that individual and school-level results be reported. States are required to begin a similar testing regimen for science achievement in 2007.

NCLB heavily promotes the use of educational technology in schools. Among other provisions, the law requires that states make a determination of the "technology literacy" of all students by the end of grade 8, and language in the accompanying House report on the legislation notes the importance of students becoming "technologically literate." However, it is clear from the context of these references that the concept of technological literacy in these documents differs substantially from the concept described in *Technically Speaking* (NAE and NRC, 2002).

In early 2005, the Educational Testing Service released a new Information and Communication Technology (ICT) Literacy Assessment for college-age students that focuses on how well they understand, use, and make decisions about information technology (ETS, 2005).

The United States participates in two large-scale international assessments of K–12 students. The Trends in Mathematics and Science Study (TIMSS), based on science and mathematics curricula in participating countries, is given in grades 4, 8, and the last year of high school. TIMSS includes an analysis of frameworks and standards, a video analysis of teaching, and a review of textbooks.

The second international assessment, the Programme for International Student Assessment (PISA), is intended to gauge how well 15-year-old students apply and use what they have learned in and out of school in mathematics, reading, and science as an indication of the quality of potential entrants to the workforce. PISA is administered every three years, with the emphasis on one of the three subjects. The 2003 assessment, which was focused on mathematics, included a one-time cross-curricular measure of problem solving (OECD, 2004). Among other competencies, test items addressed students' ability to design solutions to practical problems under specified constraints and to troubleshoot everyday problems. The 2006 PISA assessment, which will be focused on science, will include a section called "Science and Technology in Society."

Recommendation 1. The National Assessment Governing Board, which oversees the National Assessment of Educational Progress (NAEP), should authorize special studies of the assessment of technological literacy as part of the 2009 NAEP mathematics and science assessments and the 2010 NAEP U.S. history assessment. The studies should explore the content connections between technology, science, mathematics, and U.S. history to determine the feasibility of adding technology-related items to future NAEP assessments in these subjects.

Recommendation 2. The U.S. Department of Education and National Science Foundation (NSF) should send a recommendation to the International Association for the Evaluation of Educational Achievement and the Trends in Mathematics and Science Study (TIMSS) governing board encouraging them to include technological literacy items in TIMSS assessments as a context for assessments of science and mathematics. The U.S. Department of Education and NSF should send a recommendation to the Organization for Economic Cooperation and Development and the governing board for the Programme for International Student Assessment (PISA) supporting the inclusion of technological literacy items as a cross-curricular competency.

The second area of opportunity for assessing technological literacy in the K–12 population is to create *de novo* instruments. This more ambitious course of action would face significant challenges but would also have significant potential benefits, such as providing a comprehensive picture of young Americans' understanding of and engagement in our technological world.

In spring 2005, the National Assessment Governing Board (NAGB), which oversees NAEP assessments, authorized a "probe study" of assessing technological literacy. Probe studies are small-scale research projects to determine the feasibility of developing new large-scale assessments under the NAEP umbrella. Among other things, the probe study of the assessment of technological literacy will look into the pros and cons of different assessment methods and collect considerable attitudinal data.

The NAGB probe study is a very encouraging development that suggests the possibility of collecting national sample-based data on technological literacy among U.S. K–12 students. However, the results of the study will not be known for many years. Because of the time required to develop a conceptual framework and conduct field tests of assessment items, the actual assessment will not take place until 2012. If NAGB then decides to add technological literacy to the subjects routinely assessed by NAEP, it could take another four years for a national test to be administered.

The committee believes that other efforts should be undertaken in the meantime to develop stand-alone assessments of technological literacy for K–12 students. For one thing, there is no guarantee that NAGB will ultimately decide to support a national test of technological literacy. Even if it does, however, the assessment methods, specific test items, and uses of assessment data are not likely to satisfy the needs or interests of all stakeholders.

Recommendation 3. The National Science Foundation should fund a number of sample-based studies of technological literacy in K–12 students. The studies should have different assessment designs and should assess different population subsets, based on geography, population density, socioeconomic status, and other factors. Decisions about the content of test items, the distribution of items among the three dimensions of technological literacy, and performance levels should be based on a detailed assessment framework.

Findings and Recommendations for K–12 Teachers

Technological literacy is especially important for teachers. In various forms, technology is integral to virtually every aspect of society. Therefore, no matter what the academic discipline, from history to art to

Technological literacy is especially important for teachers.

science, teachers should be able to discuss issues related to technology. For example, technology has been a critical factor in the economic and cultural development of the United States and is, therefore, critical to a comprehensive understanding of social and historical developments. Whereas science and mathematics are important in their own right, technology requires the application of scientific and mathematical principles to solve practical problems. Most discoveries in science would not have been possible without technological tools, such as microscopes, radiotelescopes, and genetic engineering. This basic understanding should be an aspect of teaching in every subject, and both students and teachers should have hands-on exposure to design processes that involve the use of tools and materials.

Anecdotally, the committee found that many teachers, particularly science teachers, do introduce technology-related concepts in their classrooms. However, very little information is available about the technological literacy of teachers. An assessment for prospective teachers of technology is offered through the Educational Testing Service Praxis series, and technology-related items are included in the Praxis tests given to pre-service science teachers. However, the committee believes that neither assessment adequately measures technological literacy. In addition, because Praxis tests are designed to assess individual performance, the results are not aggregated or made public. Thus, they cannot easily inform policies related to teacher education or curriculum development.

The committee recognizes that it would be difficult to persuade teachers to take part in assessments. Teachers and teachers' unions have traditionally opposed tests of knowledge or skills, except for the purposes of certification or licensing. However, since the passage of NCLB in 2001, the situation has changed somewhat. Provisions in NCLB related to teacher quality provide incentives to states to document that teachers are knowledgeable in the subjects they teach. By the end of the 2005–2006 school year, all states will be required to show that teachers of core subjects are "highly qualified" (DoEd, 2005),[1] and future teachers will have to

---

[1]Teachers are deemed "highly qualified" if they have a bachelor's degree, certification, or license from the state and can prove that they know the subject they teach. Teachers may satisfy the last requirement in several ways, including having majored or earned college credits equivalent to a major in the subject, having gained advanced certification from the state or a graduate degree, or having passed a state-developed test. Although the number of teachers who have opted for the testing option is not known, nearly every state offers tests in the core subjects (K. Walsh, president, National Council on Teacher Quality, personal communication, August 18, 2005).

meet the same requirements. (Even if NCLB is modified or abandoned completely by a future administration or Congress, it is likely that teacher competency related to information technology will still be required.)

Passing a competency test, such as those developed by Praxis or by the state, is one of several ways teachers can meet the quality mandate. Thus, given the relevance of technological understanding to a broad range of academic subjects and the current emphasis on teacher quality, NCLB provides an important opportunity for assessment at the state level.

Recommendation 4. When states determine whether teachers are "highly qualified" under the provisions of the No Child Left Behind Act (NCLB), they should ensure—to the extent possible—that assessments used for this purpose include items that measure technological literacy. This is especially important for science, mathematics, history, and social studies teachers, but it should also be considered for teachers of other subjects. In the review of state plans for compliance with NCLB, the U.S. Department of Education should consider the extent to which states have fulfilled this objective.

A different approach will be necessary to assess technological literacy among teachers at the national level. Because of financial, time, and logistical constraints, it will not be possible to administer the same battery of test items to every teacher in the United States. Thus, some type of sampling will be necessary. NAGB, which administers national student assessments, and other organizations use matrix sampling, in which participating individuals are presented with a subset of the total number of test items. By combining the results for a number of subsets, it is possible to construct a complete picture of performance.

One drawback of matrix sampling is that, because no individual answers all of the questions, individual scores cannot be reported. Thus, although matrix-sample results may reveal performance trends in certain subgroups—for example, all 3rd-grade teachers of science—it has no diagnostic value for individual teachers. In one sense, however, the absence of individual scores may be an advantage because it may alleviate fears that assessment results might be used by educational administrators to make pay or retention decisions.

Another form of sampling, census sampling, involves administering the same or comparable set of questions to a sample of people in a single group. With census sampling, individual scoring can be done, which is a significant advantage if the goal is to diagnose teacher's strengths and weaknesses. However, census sampling typically involves more limited coverage of subject matter than matrix sampling because fewer questions can be asked. In addition, because individual performance levels can be identified, some teachers may not want to participate. Their reluctance might be overcome by legal assurances that the results would not be used for determining individual rewards or punishments and/or by providing reasonable compensation for participation.

Recommendation 5. The National Science Foundation and U.S. Department of Education should fund the development and pilot testing of sample-based assessments of technological literacy among pre-service and in-service teachers of science, technology, English, social studies, and mathematics. These assessments should be informed by carefully developed assessment frameworks. The results should be disseminated to schools of education, curriculum developers, state boards of education, and other groups concerned with teacher preparation and teacher quality.

Findings and Recommendation for Out-of-School Adults

Very little information is available about technological literacy levels among American adults.

Very little information is available about technological literacy levels among American adults. As noted in the Introduction to this report, government, industry, the media, social science researchers, and other groups would all benefit from having more information about what out-of-school adults know and think about technology.

Some important data are provided by the 2001 and 2004 ITEA/Gallup polls, but they are limited in scope and treat the three dimensions of technological literacy unevenly, making it difficult to draw conclusions. NSF's biannual reports on public understanding of science and technology (S&T) provide some useful information, but NSF's efforts were focused on science and science literacy, rather than technology and technological literacy. In 2003, NSF discontinued funding for its longstanding survey of adult S&T literacy, which was published as part of the *Indicators* reports (see, for example, NSB, 2004). No other federal agencies with a role in education, technology research and development, or communicating with the public about technological issues have invested in efforts to document adults' understanding of technology.

Some of the questions from the NSF survey are being added to the 2005/2006 General Social Survey (GSS), another longstanding project now administered biennially by the National Opinion Research Center; other items from the NSF survey have been used by the Survey Research Center of the University of Michigan and other public opinion research groups (J. Miller, director, Center for Biomedical Communications, Northwestern University, personal communication, September 12, 2005). The GSS survey focuses mostly on national spending priorities, drinking behavior, marijuana use, crime and punishment, race relations, quality of life, confidence in institutions, and membership in voluntary associations (NORC, 2005). However, the survey periodically includes modules on new topics funded by outside sources, usually foundations or government agencies.

The National Household Education Surveys (NHES) Program, conducted by the National Center for Education Statistics, provides descriptive data on the educational activities of U.S. adults, children, and families. NHES, like GSS, also occasionally conducts one-time special studies. Since its inception in 1991, NHES has conducted three special studies, on civic involvement, household library use, and school safety and discipline (NCES, 2005).

Through the National Adult Literacy Survey, the United States assesses traditional literacy (i.e., written and spoken language competency) in adults. In the 1990s, the U.S. Department of Education, Educational Testing Service, and WestEd (a regional educational laboratory) participated in two International Adult Literacy Surveys (IALS), which surveyed prose and document literacy, as well as quantitative literacy. More recently, the United States and several other countries developed and administered a revamped international literacy assessment called the Adult Literacy and Lifeskills (ALL) Survey. Like IALS, ALL focuses on prose and document literacy, but also redefines quantitative literacy as numeracy, implying a broader range of activities, some of which might be relevant to assessing technological literacy (Lemke, 2004).

In addition, ALL measures a cross-curricular area of competency related to problem solving (OECD and Statistics Canada, 2005). The ITEA *Standards for Technological Literacy* suggest that all students should be familiar with problem solving, a distinguishing feature of the technological design process. Technological problem solving in adults might be manifested in concrete ways (e.g., determining possible reasons a flashlight does not work or a car does not start or a door sticks after heavy rain and then figuring out how to correct the problem).

Another consideration in assessing or surveying adults is defining the target population (e.g., technology consumers, people attentive to public policy, or the general population) and defining an appropriate purpose for an assessment of each (see Case 4 in Chapter 6). Technology consumers, for instance, may include adults and adolescents, who are major purchasers of technological products and services. Periodic surveys of consumers conducted by the University of Michigan Survey Research Center measure consumer understanding of selected technologies.

Recommendation 6. The International Technology Education Association should continue to conduct a poll on technological literacy every several years, adding items that address the three dimensions of technological literacy, in order to build a database that reflects changes over time in adult knowledge of and attitudes toward technology. In addition, the U.S. Department of Education, working with its international partners, should expand the problem-solving component of the Adult Literacy and Lifeskills Survey to include items relevant to the assessment of technological literacy. These items should be designed to gauge participants' general problem-solving capabilities in the context of familiar, relevant situations. Agencies that could benefit by knowing more about adult understanding of technology, such as the National Science Foundation, U.S. Department of Education, U.S. Department of Defense, and National Institutes of Health, should consider funding projects to develop and conduct studies of technological literacy. Finally, opportunities for integrating relevant knowledge and attitude measures into existing studies, such as the General Social Survey, the National Household Education Survey, and Surveys of Consumers, should be pursued.

> The research base on how people learn about technology is relatively immature.

Research on Learning

Based on a review of committee-commissioned surveys of the literature on learning related to technology (Petrina et al., 2004) and engineering (Waller, 2004), as well as the expert judgments of committee members, the committee finds that the research base on how people learn about technology, engineering, design, and related ideas is relatively immature. Most of the research—particularly related to engineering—relates to what people know or how knowledge varies by population, rather than *how* information is acquired, processed, and represented. Although researchers have turned up some important clues, the overall picture of how people come to understand and work with technology is far from clear. Based on the small number of published studies in this area, only a few graduate programs in engineering and technology education support research on how people learn.

The committee also finds that research on learning has traditionally been considered a public good and, therefore, has been supported by government agencies whose missions include the improvement of the U.S. education enterprise, rather than by the private sector. This is a trend that can be expected to continue.

A number of study designs, including those that use surveys, interviews, focus groups, and hands-on activities, are suitable for assessing some aspects of adult learning related to technology. Places where adults congregate for social, educational, or other reasons present interesting opportunities for data gathering, especially for pilot studies and measurement test beds. Exploratory studies with volunteer test takers could be an important part of this research, although more definitive studies would certainly require larger probability-based samples.

For all three populations—students, teachers, and out-of-school adults—it is important for assessment designers to know how mental structures, or schema, support problem solving in technology; the role of prior knowledge, including misconceptions, in understanding technology and design; how an understanding of core ideas in technology, such as systems and trade-offs, transfers to other knowledge domains; and how the social context (e.g., the classroom, home, or workplace) facilitates or hinders knowledge acquisition.

A number of specific research questions were suggested in the section on cognition in Chapter 4 of this report. Although that list is far from exhaustive, it provides a starting point for investigations in this area.

Recommendation 7. The National Science Foundation or U.S. Department of Education should fund a synthesis study focused on how children learn technological concepts. The study should draw on the findings of multidisciplinary research in mathematics learning, spatial reasoning, design thinking, and problem solving. The study should provide guidance on pedagogical, assessment, teacher education, and curricular issues of interest to educators at all levels, teacher-education providers and licensing bodies, education researchers, and federal and state education agencies.

Recommendation 8. The National Science Foundation (NSF) and U.S. Department of Education should support a research-capacity-building initiative related to the assessment of technological literacy. The initiative should focus on supporting graduate and postgraduate research related to how students and teachers learn technology and engineering concepts. Funding should be directed to academic centers of excellence in education research—including, but not limited to, NSF-funded centers for learning and teaching—whose missions and capabilities are aligned with the goal of this recommendation.

Recommendation 9. The National Science Foundation should take the lead in organizing an interagency federal research initiative to investigate technological learning in adults. Because adult learning is continuous, longitudinal studies should be encouraged. Informal-learning institutions that engage broad populations, such as museums and science centers, should be considered important venues for research on adult learning, particularly related to technological capability. To ensure that the perspectives of adults from a variety of cultural and socioeconomic backgrounds are included, studies should also involve community colleges, nonprofit community outreach programs, and other programs that engage diverse populations.

Innovative Measurement Techniques

The increasing speed, power, and ubiquity of computers in various configurations (e.g., desktops, laptops, personal digital assistants, e-tablets, and cell phones), combined with increasing access to the Internet, could support a variety of innovative approaches to assessment. Considerable work is already being done to develop software applications, including simulation authoring tools, that could be used by assessment developers to save time and money in the test design process.

Computer-based testing is particularly appealing for the assessment of technological literacy. As detailed in Chapter 7, computer-adaptive testing has the potential to assess student knowledge of technology quickly, reliably, and inexpensively. Simulation could be used as a safe

Computer-based testing is particularly appealing for the assessment of technological literacy.

and economical means of assessing more procedural, analytical, and abstract capabilities and skills. The use of Internet-based, massive-multiplayer online games to conduct assessments could be sufficiently motivating and inexpensive to engage very large numbers of individuals for extended periods of time.

At the same time, it is clear that more research and development will be necessary before computer-based assessments can be used with full confidence—and affordability—to assess technological literacy. For one thing, the formal, psychometric properties of simulation must be better understood. In addition, the cost of developing simulations *de novo* may be prohibitive. Nevertheless, the possibilities are tantalizing, especially the prospect of providing children and adults with authentic problem-solving and design challenges that map to the dimensions of technological literacy.

A potentially large number of organizations and individuals have a direct or indirect interest in how computers might be used to measure design and problem-solving capabilities, a key aspect of technological literacy. They include federal agencies (e.g., National Science Foundation, U.S. Department of Defense, U.S. Department of Labor), museums and science centers, private assessment-development companies (e.g., Educational Testing Service, ACT, McGraw Hill, Knowledge Networks, Harris Interactive), computer game and software firms, technology-intensive industries (e.g., computer hardware and software manufacturers, aerospace firms, makers of telemedicine and computer-assisted surgical systems), and university-based scientists and social scientists working in this area. The federal government could encourage research in this area (as it has in other areas of national interest) by bringing these organizations and individuals together.

Recommendation 10. The National Institute of Standards and Technology, which has a broad mandate to promote technology development and an extensive track record in organizing research conferences, should convene a major national meeting to explore the potential of innovative, computer-based techniques for assessing technological literacy in students, teachers, and out-of-school adults. The conference should be informed by research related to assessments of science inquiry and scientific reasoning and should consider how innovative assessment techniques compare with traditional methods.

Framework Development

An important and often necessary first step in the development of an assessment for technological literacy is the creation of a conceptual framework. Although a number of frameworks have been developed in other subjects, such as mathematics, science, and history, the committee found no frameworks for the domain of technology. Framework development requires resources and time but is essential for clarifying and organizing the content of an assessment. Ideally, rigorously developed frameworks should inform the development of both stand-alone assessments of technological literacy and assessments in other subjects that include technology-related questions. Even in the absence of a framework, however, the committee believes that the pursuit of integrative strategies for gaining information about technological literacy should continue.

The list of things one might know and be able to do with respect to technology is practically limitless. Even with the benefit of thoughtfully developed content standards, such as those produced by ITEA, creating a workable framework for the assessment of technological literacy will require narrowing the scope of the content. The authors of *Science for All Americans* (AAAS, 1990), whose argument for science literacy laid the groundwork for the AAAS and NRC science standards, addressed this problem directly. Their solution was to develop criteria (utility, social responsibility, intrinsic value of knowledge, philosophical value, and childhood enrichment) for determining the most important science content students should learn. Designers of a framework for an assessment of technological literacy will have to undertake a similar exercise to narrow and prioritize the content.

In Chapter 3, the committee proposed a matrix that could be helpful in designing a framework; however, the matrix is only one of a number of possible arrangements of content. No doubt the initial framework will require reworking as information is collected about what people know and can do with respect to technology. Reworking reflects a natural evolution and improvement in assessment design.

The committee's matrix relies heavily on frameworks designed to support assessments in student populations, rather than teachers and out-of-school adults. However, the committee believes that the proposed matrix would also be useful for the development of assessment frameworks for the other two populations. For out-of-school adults, rather than

> The list of things one might know and be able to do with respect to technology is practically limitless.

content standards designed for use in formal education, expectations for technological literacy could be based on what an informed member of the public (someone who has had exposure to informal-learning opportunities, including news media and museums and science centers) might be expected to know and do. Framework designers might also take into consideration educational background and work experience, both of which could affect performance in one or more dimensions of technological literacy.

Recommendation 11. Assessments of technological literacy in K–12 students, K–12 teachers, and out-of-school adults should be guided by rigorously developed assessment frameworks.

- **For K–12 students,** the National Assessment Governing Board, which has considerable experience in the development of assessment frameworks in other subjects, should commission the development of a framework to guide the development of national and state-level assessments of technological literacy.
- **For K–12 teachers,** the National Science Foundation and U.S. Department of Education, which both have programmatic interests in improving teacher quality, should fund research to develop a framework for an assessment of technological literacy in this population. The research should focus on (1) determining how the technological literacy needs of teachers differ from those of student populations and (2) strategies for implementing teacher assessments in a way that would provide useful information for both teachers and policy makers. The resulting framework would be a prerequisite for assessments of all teachers, including generalists and middle- and high-school subject-matter specialists.
- **For out-of-school adults,** the National Science Foundation and U.S. Department of Education, which both have programmatic activities that address adult literacy, should fund research to develop a framework for the assessment of technological literacy in this population. The research should focus on determining thresholds of technological literacy necessary for adults to make informed, everyday, technology-related decisions.

Definition of Technology

Based on data from ITEA's two Gallup polls on technological literacy (ITEA, 2001, 2004), input from the participants in the committee-sponsored workshop, and informal discussions with a variety of individuals knowledgeable about technological literacy, the committee finds that confusion about the word "technology" and the term "technological literacy" is one of the most serious challenges to improving technological literacy in the United States. Although resolving the confusion was not an explicit requirement of the committee's charge, the committee concluded that everyone interested in assessments of technological literacy should be sensitized to this issue.

> The confusion is fundamentally about the role of computers in our lives.

The confusion is fundamentally about the role of computers in our lives. There is considerable interest in the United States in measuring what adults and children know about and can do with computer technology. Some states, testing companies (e.g., ETS), and the federal government (through NCLB), among others, support the development of, or have developed assessments for measuring computer-related literacy. Standards for the use of information technology by K–12 students developed by the International Society for Technology in Education (ISTE, 1998) have been adopted or adapted by many states. In the K–12 arena, computer and other information technologies are now commonly referred to as "educational technologies," tools to aid learning.

Undoubtedly, people who live in a modern nation like the United States benefit by being able to use computer technologies. Thus, assessments of computer or information-technology literacy focused on application skills are important, particularly for students. But these assessments would be even more useful if they were expanded to address more enduring conceptions of technology, as discussed in *Technically Speaking* (NAE and NRC, 2002) and detailed in national educational standards for science (AAAS, 1993; NRC, 1996) and technology (ITEA, 2000). Policy makers would benefit from knowing not only the capabilities of certain populations in using computer technology, but also the abilities of citizens to think critically and make sensible decisions about technological development in a much broader sense.

Recommendation 12. The U.S. Department of Education, state education departments, private educational testing companies, and education-related accreditation organizations should broaden the definition of "technological literacy" to include not only the use of educational technologies (computers) but also the study of technology, as described in the International Technology Education Association *Standards for Technological Literacy* and the National Academy of Engineering and National Research Council report, *Technically Speaking*.

Conclusion

Although all of the issues addressed in the recommendations are important, some recommended actions are easier and less costly to implement—and more likely to have near-term results—than others. For example, unlike the creation of *de novo* assessments (Recommendations 3 and 5), the integration of technology-related items into existing assessments (Recommendations 1, 2, 4, and 6) would take advantage of existing instruments and a testing infrastructure.

In addition, many of the recommendations are interdependent. For instance, all assessments for technological literacy would benefit from the development of detailed assessment frameworks (Recommendation 11), and frameworks and assessments would improve as more becomes known about how adults and children learn technology- and engineering-related concepts (Recommendations 7, 8, and 9). This research would also inform efforts to exploit new techniques, such as simulation and gaming, for measuring what people know and can do with respect to technology (Recommendation 10). And these novel assessment tools have the potential to improve dramatically our ability to gauge technological literacy, particularly the capabilities dimension. As educators, policy makers, and the public at large begin to adopt a broader view of technology (Recommendation 12), the assessment of technological literacy would be recognized as not only important, but necessary.

The recommendations are addressed to a large number of entities, most of them government agencies (Table 8-1). The focus on the public sector is deliberate, because technological literacy—like traditional literacy, science literacy, civics, and numeracy—is considered a public good. In addition, improving and expanding the assessment of technological literacy will require broad-based, coordinated efforts by federal and state agencies with an interest or role in supporting science and engineering research, developing new technologies, maintaining and protecting the infrastructure, and training the nation's technical workforce. However, as noted in the Introduction, many nongovernmental

TABLE 8-1   Recommendations, by Target Population, Type of Action, and Actors

Recommendation	Target Population	Type of Action	Actor(s)
1	K–12 students	Integrate items into existing national assessment.	National Assessment Governing Board (NAGB)
2	K–12 students	Integrate items into existing international assessments.	U.S. Department of Education (DoEd), National Science Foundation (NSF)
3	K–12 students	Fund sample-based studies and pilot tests.	NSF
4	K–12 teachers	Integrate items into existing assessments for teacher qualifications.	States, DoEd
5	K–12 teachers	Fund development and pilot testing of sample-based assessments.	DoEd, NSF, States
6	Out-of-school adults	Encourage or fund the integration of items into existing assessments.	International Technology Education Association (ITEA), DoEd, National Institutes of Health (NIH), NSF
7	K–12 students	Fund a synthesis study on learning processes.	NSF, DoEd
8	K–12 students, K–12 teachers	Support capacity-building efforts in learning research.	NSF, DoEd
9	Out-of-school adults	Organize an interagency initiative in learning research.	NSF
10	K–12 students, K–12 teachers, Out-of-school adults	Convene a major national meeting to explore innovative assessment methods.	National Institute of Standards and Technology
11	K–12 students, K–12 teachers, Out-of-school adults	Develop frameworks for assessments in the three populations.	NAGB, NSF, DoEd
12	K–12 students, K–12 teachers, Out-of-school adults	Broaden the definitions of technology and technological literacy.	DoEd, state education departments, private educational testing companies, and education-related accreditation organizations

organizations will also benefit, directly or indirectly, from a more techno-logically literate citizenry. The committee hopes that these organizations will also become involved in the overall effort to promote assessment of technological literacy.

The impetus for technological literacy is a desire that all citizens be empowered to function confidently and productively in our technology-dependent society. A technologically literate public could engage in more-informed public dialogue on the pros and cons of technology-related developments, would provide a talent pool of techno-logically educated workers, and would contribute to the national science and engineering enterprise.

If we could assess technological knowledge, capability, and thinking skills in a rigorous and systematic way, we could track trends among students, teachers, and out-of-school adults. Reliable information would enable policy makers, educators, the business community, and others to take steps to improve the situation, if necessary. As a result, movement toward a more technologically literate society would be directed and purposeful, governed by data rather than anecdotal evidence and educated guesses. Over a period of many years, with considerable investment of human and financial resources, the benefits of technological literacy would be realized.

References

AAAS (American Association for the Advancement of Science). 1990. Science for All Americans. New York: Oxford University Press.

AAAS. 1993. Benchmarks for Science Literacy. Project 2061. New York: Oxford University Press.

DOEd (U.S. Department of Education). 2005. Fact Sheet: New No Child Left Behind Flexibility: Highly Qualified Teachers. Available online at: *http://www.ed.gov/nclb/methods/teachers/hqtflexibility.pdf* (January 22, 2005).

ETS (Educational Testing Service). 2005. ICT Literacy Assessment. Available online at: *http://www.ets.org/ictliteracy/* (September 9, 2005).

Gee, J.P. 2003. What Video Games Have to Teach Us About Learning and Literacy. New York: Palgrave.

ISTE (International Society for Technology in Education). 1998. National Education Technology Standards for Students. Eugene, Ore.: ISTE.

ITEA (International Technology Education Association). 2000. Standards for Technological Literacy: Content for the Study of Technology. Reston, Va.: ITEA.

ITEA. 2001. ITEA/Gallup Poll Reveals What Americans Think About Technology. A Report of the Survey Conducted by the Gallup Organization for the International Technology Education Association. Available online at: *http://www.iteaconnect.org/TAA/PDFs/Gallupreport.pdf* (October 5, 2005).

ITEA. 2004. The Second Installment of the ITEA/Gallup Poll and What It Reveals as to How Americans Think About Technology. A Report of the Second Survey Conducted by the Gallup Organization for the International Technology Education Association. Available online at: *http://www.iteaconnect.org/TAA/PDFs/GallupPoll2004.pdf* (October 5, 2005).

Kasesniemi, E., and P. Rautiainen. 2002. Mobile Culture of Children and Teenagers in Finland. Pp. 170–192 in Perpetual Contact: Mobile Communication, Private Talk, Public Performance, edited by J.E. Katz and M. Aakhus. Cambridge, U.K.: Cambridge University Press.

Lemke, M. 2004. Statement for the Assessing Technological Literacy Workshop, September 29, 2004. The National Academies, Washington, D.C. Unpublished.

Meade, S.D., and W.E. Dugger, Jr. 2004. Reporting on the status of technology education in the United States. Technology Teacher 63(October): 29–35.

NAE (National Academy of Engineering) and NRC (National Research Council). 2002. Technically Speaking: Why All Americans Need to Know More About Technology. Washington, D.C.: National Academy Press.

NAGB (National Assessment Governing Board). 2005. Science Framework for the 2009 National Assessment of Educational Progress. Draft, September 30, 2005. Available online at: *http://www.nagb.org/pubs/2005science_framework_dr.doc* (October 19, 2005).

NCES (National Center for Education Statistics). 2005. National Household Education Surveys Program. Survey Topics/Population. Available online at: *http://nces.ed.gov/nhes/surveytopics_special.asp* (January 24, 2005).

NORC (National Opinion Research Center). 2005. General Social Survey. Available online at: *http://www.norc.uchicago.edu/projects/gensoc.asp* (January 24, 2005).

NRC (National Research Council). 1996. National Science Education Standards. Washington, D.C.: National Academy Press.

NSB (National Science Board). 2004. Science and Technology: Public Attitudes and Understanding in Science and Engineering Indicators, 2004. Available online at: *http://www.nsf.gov/sbe/srs/seind04/c7/c7h.htm* (May 25, 2005).

OECD (Organisation for Economic Co-Operation and Development). 2004. Problem Solving for Tomorrow's World: First Measures of Cross-Curricular Competencies from PISA 2003. Programme for International Student Assessment. Available online at: *http://www.pisa.oecd.org/dataoecd/25/12/34009000.pdf* (January 21, 2005).

OECD and Statistics Canada. 2005. Learning a Living: First Results of the Adult Literacy and Lifeskills Survey. Available online at: *http://www.statcan.ca/english/freepub/89-603-XIE/2005001/pdf.htm* (October 19, 2005).

Petrina, S., F. Feng, and J. Kim. 2004. How We Learn (About, Through, and for Technology): A Review of Research. Paper commissioned by the National Research Council Committee on Assessing Technological Literacy. Unpublished.

Valentine, G., S.L. Holloway, and N. Bingham. 2000. Transforming Cyberspace: Children's Interventions in the New Public Sphere. Pp. 156–173 in Children's Geographies: Playing, Living, Learning, edited by L. Holloway and G. Valentine. London and New York: Routledge.

Waller, A. 2004. Final Report on a Literature Review of Research on How People Learn Engineering Concepts and Processes. Paper commissioned by the Committee on Assessing Technological Literacy. Unpublished.

APPENDIX A
Committee Biographies

ELSA GARMIRE, *chair*, the Sydney E. Junkins Professor of Engineering at Dartmouth College, is a member of the National Academy of Engineering (NAE) and the NAE Council. Professor Garmire was a member of the NAE and National Research Council (NRC) committees that conducted a technical review of the K–12 education standards for technological literacy developed by the International Technology Education Association. She was also the National Academies report review monitor for the 2002 NAE/NRC report, *Technically Speaking: Why All Americans Need to Know More About Technology*. At Dartmouth, she supported the Project for Teaching Engineering Problem Solving, a National Science Foundation (NSF)-funded summer institute to provide high school teachers with a framework for introducing engineering concepts into science, mathematics, and technology courses. Professor Garmire currently teaches two courses on technological literacy for non-engineers.

RODGER BYBEE, now executive director of the Biological Sciences Curriculum Study (BSCS), is the former executive director of the National Research Council (NRC) Center for Science, Mathematics, and Engineering Education (CSMEE), where he was a major participant in the development of the National Science Education Standards. From 1986 to 1995, as associate director of BSCS, he was principal investigator for four new National Science Foundation (NSF) programs: an elementary school program, Science for Life and Living: Integrating Science, Technology, and Health; a middle school program, Middle School Science and Technology; a high school biology program, Biological Science: A Human Approach; and a college program, Biological Perspectives.

During his tenure at BSCS, he was also principal investigator for programs to develop curriculum frameworks for teaching the history and nature of science and technology in biology classes in high schools, community colleges, and four-year colleges and to develop curricular reforms based on national standards. Dr. Bybee, who has been active in education for more than 30 years, has taught science at the elementary, junior high school, senior high school, and college levels. He was a co-principal investigator of the joint National Academy of Engineering/NRC project that resulted in the 2002 publication of *Technically Speaking: Why All Americans Need to Know More About Technology*.

RODNEY L. CUSTER is chair of the Department of Technology, Illinois State University, and president of the International Technology Education Association (ITEA) Council on Technology Teacher Education (CTTE). He was a member of the National Academy of Engineering (NAE)/National Research Council (NRC) Committee on Technological Literacy and led the secondary standards development team for the ITEA Technology for All Americans (TFAA) Project, which produced the Standards for Technological Literacy. Dr. Custer is head of a team working on the development of assessment standards for phase three of the TFAA Project. He has been editor of the *Journal of Industrial Teacher Education* and a member of the editorial boards of several other professional journals. He is the author of numerous articles on technological problem solving and issues related to technology and society and co-author with A. E. Weins of *Technology and the Quality of Life* (Glencoe/McGraw-Hill, 1996). Dr. Custer has been a program officer at the National Science Foundation (NSF) and a member of several NRC and NAE committees. He currently leads the technology teacher education component of the NSF-funded National Center for Engineering and Technology Education.

MARTHA N. CYR is director of K–12 outreach and an adjunct assistant professor in the Mechanical Engineering Department at Worcester Polytechnic Institute in Worcester, Massachusetts. She is a member of the Massachusetts Science and Mathematics Advisory Council and was an active participant in the development of the newly adopted statewide engineering curriculum frameworks. As director of outreach, she works with programs to incorporate hands-on projects that introduce engineering principles to students to motivate them and their teachers to continue studying mathematics and science in grades K–16. Dr. Cyr was a faculty advisor for the National Science Foundation model project for women and girls in which middle schools girls designed and built museum-quality, hands-on exhibits. She also coordinated a partnership with Prentice Hall for the revision of middle school science textbooks and is a member of a team that provides professional development in engineering design for K–12 teachers. Dr. Cyr received a B.S. in mechanical engineering from the University of New Hampshire in 1982 and an M.S. and Ph.D. in mechanical engineering from Worcester Polytechnic Institute in 1987 and 1997, respectively.

MARC J. DE VRIES is an assistant professor of philosophy and method-ology of technology, Eindhoven University of Technology, and an affiliate professor of reformational philosophy, Delft University of Technology, the Netherlands. Previously, he taught at a teacher training college for technology education and vocational technical education in Eindhoven. Dr. de Vries has published and made presentations in several countries on technology education, student assessment, and the philosophy of technol-ogy. He developed a 100-question survey, *Pupils' Attitudes Toward Tech-nology (PATT)*, which has been used in about 30 countries to measure student understanding of technological ideas. Since 1999, Dr. de Vries has been editor-in-chief of the *International Journal for Technology Educa-tion and Design*. He was co-organizer of 15 international PATT confer-ences and an advisor on technology education development and assess-ment for UNESCO and OECD. Dr. de Vries has worked with Dutch educational television to produce programs on technology and is coauthor of a number of textbooks for grades 7–9. He is also cofounder of the Dutch technology teachers association. His current research is focused on the nature of technological knowledge.

WILLIAM E. DUGGER JR. is director of the International Technol-ogy Education Association (ITEA) Technology for All Americans Project, which published *Standards for Technological Literacy: Content for the Study of Technology* (2000/2002) and *Advancing Excellence in Technological Lit-eracy: Student Assessment, Professional Development, and Program Standards* (2003). A Professor Emeritus at Virginia Polytechnic Institute and State University, Dr. Dugger was professor of education and program area leader for technology education in the College of Education from 1972 to 1994. From 1984 to 1985, he was president of ITEA, and from 1992 to 1998, he was a member of the Board of Directors of Phi Delta Kappa (PDK) and PDK District VIII representative. Dr. Dugger is also coauthor (with Allen Bame and Marc de Vries) of *Pupils' Attitudes Toward Technology—PATT-USA* (1989), the results of a survey of 10,000 U.S. middle and high school students. He is a past member of the National Research Council Committee on K–12 Science Education.

ARTHUR EISENKRAFT, Distinguished Professor of Science Education at the University of Massachusetts, Boston, taught high school science for 28 years. Dr. Eisenkraft is a recent past president of the National Science Teachers Association (NSTA) and has chaired a number of NSTA-sponsored competitions: Toshiba/NSTA Exploravision Awards (1991 to date); the Toyota TAPESTRY Grants (1990 to date); the Duracell/NSTA Scholarship Competitions (1984 to 2000); and the NYNEX Awards Program (1993 to 1995). From 1989 to 2000, he was a columnist and member of the advisory board of *Quantum*, a magazine for science and math students published by NSTA as a joint venture between the United States and Russia. Dr. Eisenkraft is director of Active Physics, a program to introduce physics instruction to all students. From 1986 to 1992, he was academic director of the U.S. team in the International Physics Olympiad, and in 1993, he was executive director of the event. He was a member of the curriculum working group that helped develop the National Science Education Standards and has been a member of several National Academies committees, including the Committee on Learning, Research, and Educational Practice. Dr. Eisenkraft is a recipient of the Presidential Award for Excellence in Science Teaching (1986) and the Disney Science Teacher of the Year Award (1991). He is a fellow of the American Association for the Advancement of Science and holds a patent for a laser vision-testing system based on Fourier optics.

J.D. FLETCHER is a member of the senior research staff at the Institute for Defense Analyses, where he specializes in personnel assessment, education, training, and human performance. A psychologist by training, Dr. Fletcher is a leading authority on technology-based instruction and performance assistance. He has held various university positions in psychology, computer science, and systems engineering and government positions in Navy and Army laboratories, the Defense Advanced Research Projects Agency, and the White House Office of Science and Technology Policy, where he helped develop national programs and policies for education and training. He has served on many science and technology panels for the Defense Science Board, Army Science Board, Naval Studies Board, Air Force Scientific Advisory Board, National Research Council, and North Atlantic Treaty Organization. He is the author of many articles, chapters, and technical reports on military and industrial training, personnel readiness and productivity, applications of technology in education and training, modeling and simulation, and human factors in computation. His research has led to the development of "intelligent" tutoring systems, networked desktop simulations, wearable voice-interactive performance aids, analyses of cognition in skill acquisition and maintenance, and analyses of the cost-effectiveness of instructional technology. He is the technical task leader for the Advanced Distributed Learning Initiative, which has produced globally adopted specifications for the development and management of sharable instructional objects.

ALAN J. FRIEDMAN has been the director and CEO of the New York Hall of Science since 1984. During his tenure, the Hall of Science has become a leading science-technology center recognized for its encouragement of new technologies, new models for teacher training, and the evaluation of informal science learning. The New York Hall of Science is also known for its commitment to providing services to the diverse population of the New York City area. In 1996, in recognition of Dr. Friedman's contributions, the American Association for the Advancement of Science (AAAS) awarded him the AAAS Award for Public Understanding of Science and Technology. In 2004, he received the Andrew W. Gemant Award from the American Institute of Physics for his contributions to the cultural, artistic, and humanistic dimensions of physics. Dr. Friedman is a AAAS Fellow and a New York Academy of Sciences Fellow. Before coming to New York, he was conseiller scientifique et muséologique for the Cité des Sciences et de l'Industrie, Paris, and director of astronomy and physics at the Lawrence Hall of Science, University of California, Berkeley, for 12 years. Dr. Friedman is coauthor of *Einstein as Myth and Muse* (Cambridge University Press, 1985) and the author or coauthor of 64 other publications.

RICHARD KIMBELL has taught design and technology and has been director of undergraduate and postgraduate programs of teacher education. Between 1985 and 1991, he directed the U.K. government-funded Assessment of Performance Unit Research Project in Design and

Technology. In 1990, he founded the Technology Education Research Unit (TERU) at Goldsmiths College, London, which runs a wide variety of externally funded research projects in design and technology and information technology, particularly as related to teaching, learning, and assessment. Dr. Kimbell is the author of three books, numerous contributions to edited collections, and reports commissioned by U.K. government departments, the U.S. Congress, UNESCO, and NATO. He has also written and presented television programs for the BBC and independent television stations, and he regularly lectures internationally. Dr. Kimbell was editor in chief of *DATA* from 1995 to 2005, and his latest book, *Assessing Technology: International Trends in Curriculum and Assessment*, was named outstanding publication of the year by the Council for Technology Teacher Education of the International Technology Education Association. He has been visiting professor at many international universities and is currently teaching at the Institute of Education in Stockholm.

JOSÉ P. MESTRE is professor of physics and educational psychology at the University of Illinois, Urbana-Champaign. His research interests include cognitive studies of problem solving in physics with a focus on the acquisition and use of knowledge by experts and novices. His recent work has been focused on the transfer of learning in science problem solving; the application of research findings to the design of instructional strategies that promote active learning in large physics classes; and the development of physics curricula that promote conceptual development through problem solving. He has been a member of the National Research Council Mathematical Sciences Education Board and Committee on Developments in the Science of Learning; the College Board Sciences Advisory Committee, SAT Committee, and Council on Academic Affairs; the Educational Testing Service Visiting Committee and Graduate Research Examination Technical Advisory Committee; the American Association of Physics Teachers Research in Physics Education Committee and the editorial board of *The Physics Teacher*; and the Expert Panel of the Federal Coordinating Council for Science, Engineering and Technology. Dr. Mestre has published numerous research and review articles on science learning and teaching and is coauthor or coeditor of 15 books.

JON D. MILLER is director of the Center for Biomedical Communication, a professor in the Feinberg School of Medicine, and a professor in the Department of Preventive Medicine at Northwestern University.

Trained as a political scientist, he brings his skills in survey research and quantitative analysis to the study of the public understanding of science and technology. For two decades, he has designed and conducted biennial national studies, *Science and Engineering Indicators*, of the public understanding of science and technology for the National Science Board. His framework for measuring scientific literacy and attitudes has been replicated in more than 40 countries. Professor Miller is also director of the Longitudinal Study of American Youth and director of the International Center for the Advancement of Scientific Literacy, both located at Northwestern University. He is the author of four books and more than 50 refereed articles and chapters in collected volumes. He is a member of the Committee on the Public Understanding of Science and Technology of the American Association for the Advancement of Science and a member of the editorial board of *Public Understanding of Science*.

SUSANNA HORNIG PRIEST, associate professor and research director in the College of Mass Communications and Information Studies, University of South Carolina (USC), Columbia, has degrees in linguistic anthropology and sociology, as well as a doctorate in communications. She is pursuing research on risk perception and social values related to public responses to emerging technologies (including biotechnology and nanotechnology) internationally in cooperation with Canadian, European, and other international colleagues. Dr. Priest has published more than 40 articles, books, and book chapters, primarily in these areas. She is also currently affiliated with the USC Nanotechnology Center, where she is working on public understanding and other social dimensions of emerging nanotechnologies. She teaches research methods and media theory at the doctoral level and a course on propaganda and public opinion for graduate and undergraduate students. Prior to joining the USC faculty, she was, for 15 years, a member of the faculty in the Department of Journalism at Texas A&M University, where she was director of the Science and Technology Policy and Ethics Center and the Science Journalism Master of Science Program.

SHARIF SHAKRANI, co-director of the Education Policy Research Center and professor of measurement and quantitative methods at Michigan State University, conducts research on educational policy and accountability focused on teaching and learning. He works with K–12 educators, researchers, and policy makers at the state and national levels on issues related to mathematics and science curriculum, assessment, and educational reform. He has a Ph.D. in educational research and measurement from Michigan State University and extensive knowledge and experience in testing, assessment, and psychometric issues at the national, state, and district levels. Dr. Shakrani was the deputy executive director of the National Assessment Governing Board, where he was in charge of addressing technical and policy issues related to the National Assessment of Educational Progress (NAEP). He has also been program director of design and analysis at the National Center for Education Statistics of the U.S. Department of Education and director of K–12 curriculum and assessment programs for the Michigan Department of Education.

JOHN D. STUART is senior vice president of education and global partners at Parametric Technology Corporation (PTC), a company that develops, markets, and supports software solutions to help manufacturing companies design and manage the global product development process. The 69 partners in the PTC global partner program include enterprise consulting partners, system integrators, and computer platform partners. The education program includes the sale of PTC's University Plus engineering design and PLM enterprise software to more than 1,250 colleges and universities worldwide and the marketing and distribution of PTC's Design and Technology Program for middle schools and high schools worldwide. More than 15,000,000 students and 45,000 teachers currently participate in the program. In Mr. Stuart's 13 years with PTC, he has held several positions in sales and marketing management. Prior to joining PTC, he was assistant vice president of sales at Centel Information Systems (an IBM business partner) for 11 years and a sales manager for Texas Instruments Digital Systems Group. He is currently a member of the board of directors of the Greater Boston Aid to the Blind, University of Massachusetts Industry Advisory Board, and K–12 Advisory Board of the American Society of Engineering Education. He earned a degree in finance from the University of Illinois.

MARY E. YAKIMOWSKI-SREBNICK was director of assessment at the Council of Chief State School Officers and chief of educational accountability for the Division of Research, Evaluation, and Accountability for the Baltimore City Public School System, where she was responsible for student assessment, program evaluation, institutional research, and shared planning and accountability functions. She also facilitated the implementation of the No Child Left Behind Act of 2001. During Dr. Yakimowski-Srebnick's 20 years of experience in educational research and assessment, she has been director of the Department of Assessment and Instructional Support for the Hampton City School System in Virginia and president of the National Association of Test Directors, Directors of Research and Evaluation, and Connecticut Testing Network. She is currently vice president for Division H and past secretary of the American Educational Research Association (AERA) and has received numerous AERA Division H Outstanding Publication Competition Awards in district assessment reporting, institutional research, policy and planning, management studies, and training materials. She is cochair and committee member for many doctoral students, many from the Educational Leadership and Policy Studies Department at Virginia Polytechnic Institute and State University.

APPENDIX B
Technology-Related Standards and Benchmarks in the National Science Education Standards,[1] Benchmarks for Science Literacy,[2] and Standards for Technological Literacy[3]

National Science Education Standards

Standards Related to "Science and Technology"

Standard E1: Abilities of Technological Design

Benchmarks for Grades K–4

Identify a simple problem. In problem identification, children should develop the ability to explain a problem in their own words and identify a specific task and solution related to the problem.

[1]National Research Council. 1996. National Science Education Standards. Washington, D.C.: National Academy Press.

[2]American Association for the Advancement of Science. 1993. Benchmarks for Science Literacy. New York: Oxford University Press. Reprinted with permission.

[3]International Technology Education Association. 2002. Standards for Technological Literacy: Content for the Study of Technology. Reston, Va.: ITEA. Reprinted with permission.

Propose a solution. Students should make proposals to build something or get something to work better; they should be able to describe and communicate their ideas. Students should recognize that designing a solution might have constraints, such as cost, materials, time, space, or safety.

Implementing proposed solutions. Children should develop abilities to work individually and collaboratively and to use suitable tools, techniques, and quantitative measurements when appropriate. Students should demonstrate the ability to balance simple constraints in problem solving.

Evaluate a product or design. Students should evaluate their own results or solutions to problems, as well as those of other children, by considering how well a product or design met the challenge to solve a problem. When possible, students should use measurements and include constraints and other criteria in their evaluations. They should modify designs based on the results of evaluations.

Benchmarks for Grades 5–8

Identify appropriate problems for technological design. Students should develop their abilities by identifying a specified need, considering its various aspects, and talking to different potential users or beneficiaries. They should appreciate that for some needs, the cultural backgrounds and beliefs of different groups can affect the criteria for a suitable product.

Design a solution or product. Students should make and compare different proposals in the light of the criteria they have selected. They must consider constraints—such as cost, time, trade-offs, and materials needed—and communicate ideas with drawings and simple models.

Implement a proposed design. Students should organize materials and other resources, plan their work, make good use of group collaboration where appropriate, choose suitable tools and techniques, and work with appropriate measurement methods to ensure adequate accuracy.

Evaluate completed technological designs or products. Students should use criteria relevant to the original purpose or need, consider a variety of factors that might affect acceptability and suitability for intended users or beneficiaries, and develop measures of quality with respect to such criteria and factors; they should also suggest improvement and, for their own products, try proposed modifications.

Communicate the process of technological design. Students should review and describe any completed piece of work and identify the stages of problem identification, solution design, implementation, and evaluation.

Benchmarks for Grades 9–12

Identify a problem or design an opportunity. Students should be able to identify new problems or needs and to change and improve current technological designs.

Propose designs and choose between alternative solutions. Students should demonstrate thoughtful planning for a piece of technology or technique. Students should be introduced to the roles of models and simulations in these processes.

Implement a proposed solution. A variety of skills can be needed in proposing a solution depending on the type of technology that is involved. The construction of artifacts can require the skills of cutting, shaping, treating, and joining common materials—such as wood, metal, plastics, and textiles. Solutions can also be implemented using computer software.

Evaluate the solution and its consequences. Students should test any solution against the needs and criteria it was designed to meet. At this stage, new criteria not originally considered may be reviewed.

Communicate the problem, process, and solution. Students should present their results to students, teachers, and others in a variety of ways, such as orally, in writing, and in other forms—including models, diagrams, and demonstrations.

Standard E2: Understanding about Science and Technology

Benchmarks for Grades K–4

- People have always had questions about their world. Science is one way of answering questions and explaining the natural world.
- People have always had problems and invented tools and techniques (ways of doing something) to solve problems. Trying to determine the effects of solutions helps people avoid some new problems.
- Scientists and engineers often work in teams with different individuals doing different things that contribute to the results. This understanding focuses primarily on teams working together and, secondarily, on the combination of scientist and engineer teams.
- Women and men of all ages, backgrounds, and groups engage in a variety of scientific and technological work.
- Tools help scientists make better observations, measurements, and equipment for investigations. They help scientists see, measure, and do things that they could not otherwise see, measure, and do.

Benchmarks for Grades 5–8

- Scientific inquiry and technological design have similarities and differences. Scientists propose explanations for questions about the natural world, and engineers propose solutions relating to human problems, needs, and aspirations. Technological solutions are temporary; technologies exist within nature and so they cannot contravene physical or biological principles; technological solutions have side effects; and technologies cost, carry risks, and provide benefits.
- Many different people in different cultures have made and continue to make contributions to science and technology.
- Science and technology are reciprocal. Science helps drive technology, as it addresses questions that demand more sophisticated instruments and provides principles for better instrumentation and technique. Technology is essential to science, because it provides instruments and techniques that enable observations of objects and phenomena that are otherwise unobservable due to factors such as quantity, distance, location, size, and speed. Technology also provides tools for investigations, inquiry, and analysis.

- Perfectly designed solutions do not exist. All technology solutions have trade-offs, such as safety, cost, efficiency, and back-up systems to provide safety. Risk is part of living in a highly technological world. Reducing risk often results in new technology.
- Technological designs have constraints. Some constraints are unavoidable, for example, properties of materials, or effects of weather and friction; other constraints limit choices in the design, for example, environmental protection, human safety, and aesthetics.
- Technological solutions have intended benefits and unintended consequences. Some consequences can be predicted, others cannot.

Benchmarks for Grades 9–12

- Scientists in different disciplines ask different questions, use different methods of investigation, and accept different types of evidence to support their explanations. Many scientific investigations require the contributions of individuals from different disciplines, including engineering. New disciplines of science, such as geophysics and biochemistry often emerge at the interface of two older disciplines.
- Science often advances with the introduction of new technologies. Solving technological problems often results in new scientific knowledge. New technologies often extend the current levels of scientific understanding and introduce new areas of research.
- Creativity, imagination and a good knowledge base are all required in the work of science and engineering.
- Science and technology are pursued for different purposes. Scientific inquiry is driven by the desire to understand the natural world, and technological design is driven by the need to meet human needs and solve human problems. Technology, by its nature, has a more direct effect on society than science because its purpose is to solve human problems, help humans adapt, and fulfill human aspirations. Technological solutions may create new problems. Science, by its nature, answers questions that may or may not directly influence humans. Sometimes scientific advances challenge people's beliefs and practical explanations concerning various aspects of the world.
- Technological knowledge is often not made public because of patents and the financial potential of the idea or invention. Scientific knowledge is made public through presentations at professional meetings and publications in scientific journals.

Standard E3: Abilities to Distinguish Between Natural Objects and Objects Made by Humans

Benchmarks for Grades K–4

- Some objects occur in nature; others have been designed and made by people to solve human problems and enhance the quality of life.
- Objects can be categorized into two groups, natural and designed.

Benchmarks for Science Literacy

Standards Related to "the Nature of Technology"

Standard 3A: Technology and Science

Benchmarks for Grades K–2

By the end of the 2nd grade, students should know that:
- Tools are used to do things better or more easily and to do some things that could not otherwise be done at all. In technology, tools are used to observe, measure, and make things.
- When trying to build something or to get something to work better, it usually helps to follow directions if there are any, or to ask someone who has done it before for suggestions.

Benchmarks for Grades 3–5

By the end of the 5th grade, students should know that:
- Throughout all of history, people everywhere have invented and used tools. Most tools of today are different from those of the past, but many are modifications of very ancient tools.
- Technology enables scientists and others to observe things that are too small or too far away to be seen without them and to study the motion of objects that are moving very rapidly or are hardly moving at all.
- Measuring instruments can be used to gather accurate information for making scientific comparisons of objects and events and for designing and constructing things that will work properly.
- Technology extends the ability of people to change the world: to cut, shape, or put together materials; to move things from one place to

another; and to reach farther with their hands, voices, senses, and minds. The changes may be for survival needs such as food, shelter, and defense, for communication and transportation, or to gain knowledge and express ideas.

Benchmarks for Grades 6–8

By the end of the 8th grade, students should know that:
- In earlier times, the accumulated information and techniques of each generation of workers were taught on the job directly to the next generation of workers. Today the knowledge base for technology can be found as well in libraries of print and electronic resources and is often taught in the classroom.
- Technology is essential to science for such purposes as access to outer space and other remote locations, sample collection and treatment, measurement, data collections and storage, computation, and communication of information.
- Engineers, architects, and others who engage in design and technology use scientific knowledge to solve practical problems. But they usually have to take human values and limitations into account as well.

Benchmarks for Grades 9–12

By the end of the 12th grade, students should know that:
- Technological problems often create a demand for new scientific knowledge, and new technologies make it possible for scientists to extend their research in new ways or to undertake entirely new lines of research. The very availability of new technology itself often sparks scientific advances.
- Mathematics, creativity, logic, and originality are all needed to improve technology.
- Technology usually affects society more directly than science because it solves practical problems and serves human needs (and may create new problems and needs). In contrast, science affects society mainly by stimulating and satisfying people's curiosity and occasionally by enlarging or challenging their view of what the world is like.

Standard 3B: Design and Systems

Benchmark for Grades K–2

By the end of the 2nd grade, students should know that:
- People may not be able to actually make or do everything that they can design.

Benchmarks for Grades 3–5

By the end of the 5th grade, students should know that:
- There is no perfect design. Designs that are best in one respect (safety or ease of use, for example) may be inferior in other ways (cost or appearance). Usually some features must be sacrificed to get others. How such trade-offs are received depends upon which features are emphasized and which are down-played.
- Even a good design may fail. Sometimes steps can be taken ahead of time to reduce the likelihood of failure, but it cannot be entirely eliminated.
- The solution to one problem may create other problems.

Benchmarks for Grades 6–8

By the end of the 8th grade, students should know that:
- Design usually requires taking constraints into account. Some constraints, such as gravity or the properties of the materials to be used, are unavoidable. Other constraints, including economic, political, social, ethical, and aesthetic ones, limit choices.
- All technologies have effects other than those intended by the design, some of which may have been predictable and some not. In either case, these side effects may turn out to be unacceptable to some of the population and therefore lead to conflict between groups.
- Almost all control systems have inputs, outputs, and feedback. The essence of control is comparing information about what is happening to what people want to happen and then making appropriate adjustments. This procedure requires sensing information, processing it, and making changes. In almost all modern machines, microprocessors serve as centers of performance control.

- Systems fail because they have faulty or poorly matched parts, are used in ways that exceed what was intended by the design, or were poorly designed to begin with. The most common ways to prevent failure are pretesting parts and procedures, overdesign, and redundancy.

Benchmarks for Grades 9–12

By the end of the 12th grade, students should know that:
- In designing a device or process, thought should be given to how it will be manufactured, operated, maintained, replaced, and disposed of and who will sell, operate, and take care of it. The costs associated with these functions may introduce yet more constraints on the design.
- The value of any given technology may be different for different groups of people and at different points in time.
- Complex systems have layers of controls. Some controls operate particular parts of the system and some control other controls. Even fully automatic systems require human control at some point.
- Risk analysis is used to minimize the likelihood of unwanted side effects of a new technology. The public perception of risk may depend, however, on psychological factors as well as scientific ones.
- The more parts and connections a system has, the more ways it can go wrong. Complex systems usually have components to detect, back up, bypass, or compensate for minor failures.
- To reduce the chance of system failure, performance testing is often conducted using small-scale models, computer simulations, analogous systems, or just the parts of the system thought to be least reliable.

Standard 3C: Issues in Technology

Benchmarks for Grades K–2

By the end of the 2nd grade, students should know that:
- People, alone or in groups, are always inventing new ways to solve problems and get work done. The tools and ways of doing things that people have invented affect all aspects of life.
- When a group of people wants to build something or try something new, they should try to figure out ahead of time how it might affect other people.

Benchmark for Grades 3–5

By the end of the 5th grade, students should know that:
- Technology has been part of life on the earth since the advent of the human species. Like language, ritual, commerce, and the arts, technology is an intrinsic part of human culture, and it both shapes society and is shaped by it. The technology available to people greatly influences what their lives are like.
- Any invention is likely to lead to other inventions. Once an invention exists, people are likely to think up ways of using it that were never imagined at first.
- Transportation, communications, nutrition, sanitation, health care, entertainment, and other technologies give large numbers of people today the goods and services that once were luxuries enjoyed only by the wealthy. These benefits are not equally available to everyone.
- Scientific laws, engineering principles, properties of materials, and construction techniques must be taken into account in designing engineering solutions to problems. Other factors, such as cost, safety, appearance, environmental impact, and what will happen if the solution fails also must be considered.
- Technologies often have drawbacks as well as benefits. A technology that helps some people or organisms may hurt others—either deliberately (as weapons can) or inadvertently (as pesticides can). When harm occurs or seems likely, choices have to be made or new solutions found.
- Because of their ability to invent tools and processes, people have an enormous effect on the lives of other living things.

Benchmarks for Grades 6–8

By the end of the 8th grade, students should know that:
- The human ability to shape the future comes from a capacity for generating knowledge and developing new technologies—and for communicating these ideas to others.
- Technology cannot always provide successful solutions for problems or fulfill every human need.
- Throughout history, people have carried out impressive technological feats, some of which would be hard to duplicate today even with modern tools. The purposes served by these achievements have sometimes been practical, sometimes ceremonial.

- Technology has strongly influenced the course of history and continues to do so. It is largely responsible for the great revolutions in agriculture, manufacturing, sanitation and medicine, warfare, transportation, information processing, and communications that have radically changed how people live.
- New technologies increase some risks and decrease others. Some of the same technologies that have improved the length and quality of life for many people have also brought new risks.
- Rarely are technology issues simple and one-sided. Relevant facts alone, even when known and available, usually do not settle matters entirely in favor of one side or another. That is because the contending groups may have different values and priorities. They may stand to gain or lose in different degrees, or may make very different predictions about what the future consequences of the proposed action will be.
- Societies influence what aspects of technology are developed and how these are used. People control technology (as well as science) and are responsible for its effects.

Benchmarks for Grades 9–12

By the end of the 12th grade, students should know that:

- Social and economic forces strongly influence which technologies will be developed and used. Which will prevail is affected by many factors, such as personal values, consumer acceptance, patent laws, the availability of risk capital, the federal budget, local and national regulations, media attention, economic competition, and tax incentives.
- Technological knowledge is not always as freely shared as scientific knowledge unrelated to technology. Some scientists and engineers are comfortable working in situations in which some secrecy is required, but others prefer not to do so. It is generally regarded as a matter of individual choice and ethics, not one of professional ethics.
- In deciding on proposals to introduce new technologies or to curtail existing ones, some key questions arise concerning alternatives, risks, costs, and benefits. What alternative ways are there to achieve the same ends, and how do the alternatives compare to the plan being put forward? Who benefits and who suffers? What are the financial and social costs, do they change over time, and who bears them? What are the risks associated with using (or not using) the new technology, how serious are they, and who is in jeopardy? What human, material, and

energy resources will be needed to build, install, operate, maintain, and replace the new technology, and where will they come from? How will the new technology and its waste products be disposed of and at what costs?

- The human species has a major impact on other species in many ways: reducing the amount of the earth's surface available to those other species, interfering with their food sources, changing the temperature and chemical composition of their habitats, introducing foreign species into their ecosystems, and altering organisms directly through selective breeding and genetic engineering.
- Human inventiveness has brought new risks as well as improvements to human existence.

Standards Related To "The Designed World"

Standard 8A: Agriculture

Benchmarks for Grades K–2

By the end of the 2nd grade, students should know that:
- Most food comes from farms either directly as crops or as the animals that eat the crops. To grow well, plants need enough warmth, light, and water. Crops also must be protected from weeds and pests that can harm them.
- Part of a crop may be lost to pests or spoilage.
- A crop that is fine when harvested may spoil before it gets to consumers.
- Machines improve what people get from crops by helping in planting and harvesting, in keeping food fresh by packaging and cooling, and in moving it long distances from where it is grown to where people live.

Benchmarks for Grades 3–5

By the end of the 5th grade, students should know that:
- Some plant varieties and animal breeds have more desirable characteristics than others, but some may be more difficult or costly to grow. The kinds of crops that can grow in an area depend on the climate and soil. Irrigation and fertilizers can help crops grow in places where there is too little water or the soil is poor.

- The damage to crops caused by rodents, weeds, and insects can be reduced by using poisons, but their use may harm other plants or animals as well, and pests tend to develop resistance to poisons.
- Heating, salting, smoking, drying, cooling, and airtight packaging are ways to slow down the spoiling of food by microscopic organisms. These methods make it possible for food to be stored for long intervals before being used.
- Modern technology has increased the efficiency of agriculture so that fewer people are needed to work on farms than ever before.
- Places too cold or dry to grow certain crops can obtain food from places with more suitable climates. Much of the food eaten by Americans comes from other parts of the country and other places in the world.

Benchmarks for Grades 6–8

By the end of the 8th grade, students should know that:
- Early in human history, there was an agricultural revolution in which people changed from hunting and gathering to farming. This allowed changes in the division of labor between men and women and between children and adults, and the development of new patterns of government.
- People control the characteristics of plants and animals they raise by selective breeding and by preserving varieties of seeds (old and new) to use if growing conditions change.
- In agriculture, as in all technologies, there are always trade-offs to be made. Getting food from many different places makes people less dependent on weather in any one place, yet more dependent on transportation and communication among far-flung markets. Specializing in one crop may risk disaster if changes in weather or increases in pest populations wipe out the crop. Also, the soil may be exhausted of some nutrients, which can be replenished by rotating the right crops.
- Many people work to bring food, fiber, and fuel to U.S. markets. With improved technology, only a small fraction of workers in the U.S. actually plant and harvest the products that people use. Most workers are engaged in processing, packaging, transporting, and selling what is produced.

By the end of the 12th grade, students should know that:
- New varieties of farm plants and animals have been engineered by manipulating their genetic instructions to produce new characteristics.
- Government sometimes intervenes in matching agricultural supply to demand in an attempt to ensure a stable, high-quality, and inexpensive food supply. Regulations are often also designed to protect farmers from abrupt changes in farming conditions and from competition by farmers in other countries.
- Agricultural technology requires trade-offs between increased production and environmental harm and between efficient production and social values. In the past century, agricultural technology led to a huge shift of population from farms to cities and a great change in how people live and work.

Standard 8B: Materials and Manufacturing

Benchmarks for Grades K–2

By the end of the 2nd grade, students should know that:
- Some kinds of materials are better than others for making any particular thing. Materials that are better in some ways (such as stronger or cheaper) may be worse in other ways (heavier or harder to cut).
- Several steps are usually involved in making things.
- Tools are used to help make things, and some things cannot be made at all without tools. Each kind of tool has a special purpose.
- Some materials can be used over again.

Benchmarks for Grades 3–5

By the end of the 5th grade, students should know that:
- Naturally occurring materials such as wood, clay, cotton, and animal skins may be processed or combined with other materials to change their properties.
- Through science and technology, a wide variety of materials that do not appear in nature at all have become available, ranking from steel to nylon to liquid crystals.
- Discarded products contribute to the problem of waste disposal. Some-

times it is possible to use the materials in them to make new products, but materials differ widely in the ease with which they can be recycled.

- Through mass production, the time required to make a product and its cost can be greatly reduced. Although many things are still made by hand in some parts of the world, almost everything in the most technologically developed countries is not produced using automatic machines. Even automatic machines require human supervision.

Benchmarks for Grades 6–8

By the end of the 8th grade, students should know that:

- The choice of materials for a job depends on their properties and on how they interact with other materials. Similarly, the usefulness of some manufactured parts of an object depends on how well they fit together with the other parts.
- Manufacturing usually involves a series of steps, such as designing a product, obtaining and preparing raw materials, processing the materials mechanically or chemically, and assembling, testing, inspecting, and packaging. The sequence of these steps is also often important.
- Modern technology reduces manufacturing costs, produces more uniform products, and creates new synthetic materials that can help reduce the depletion of some natural resources.
- Automation, including the use of robots, has changed the nature of work in most fields, including manufacturing. As a result, high-skill, high-knowledge jobs in engineering, computer programming, quality control, supervision, and maintenance are replacing many routine manual-labor jobs. Workers therefore need better learning skills and flexibility to take on new and rapidly changing jobs.

Benchmarks for Grades 9–12

By the end of the 12th grade, students should know that:

- Manufacturing processes have been changed by improved tools and techniques based on more thorough scientific understanding, increases in the forces that can be applied and the temperatures that can be reached, and the availability of electronic controls that make operations occur more rapidly and consistently.
- Waste management includes considerations of quantity, safety, degradability, and cost. It requires social and technological innovations,

because waste-disposal problems are political and economic as well as technical.

- Scientific research identifies new materials and new uses of known materials.
- Increased knowledge of the molecular structure of materials helps in the design and synthesis of new materials for special purposes.

Standard 8C: Energy Sources and Use

Benchmarks for Grades K–2

By the end of the 2nd grade, students should know that:

- People can save money by turning off machines when they are not using them.
- People burn fuels such as wood, oil, coal, or natural gas, or use electricity to cook their food and warm their houses.

Benchmarks for Grades 3–5

By the end of the 5th grade, students should know that:

- Moving air and water can be used to run machines.
- The sun is the main source of energy for people and they use it in various ways. The energy in fossil fuels, such as oil and coal comes from the sun indirectly, because the fuels come from plants that grew long ago.
- Some energy sources cost less than others and some cause less pollution than others.
- People try to conserve energy in order to slow down the depletion of energy resources and/or to save money.

Benchmarks for Grades 6–8

By the end of the 8th grade, students should know that:

- Energy can change from one form to another, although in the process some energy is always converted to heat. Some systems transform energy with less loss of heat than others.
- Different ways of obtaining, transforming, and distributing energy have different environmental consequences.

- In many instances, manufacturing and other technological activities are performed at a site close to an energy source. Some forms of energy are transported easily, others are not.
- Electrical energy can be produced from a variety of energy sources and can be transformed into almost any other form of energy. Moreover, electricity is used to distribute energy quickly and conveniently to distant locations.
- Energy from the sun (and the wind and water energy derived from it) is available indefinitely. Because the flow of energy is weak and variable, very large collection systems are needed. Other sources don't renew or renew only slowly.
- Different parts of the world have different amounts and kinds of energy resources to use and use them for different purposes.

Benchmarks for Grades 9–12

By the end of the 12th grade, students should know that:
- A central factor in technological change has been how hot a fire could be made. The discovery of new fuels, the design of better ovens and furnaces, and the forced delivery of air or pure oxygen have progressively increased the available temperature. Lasers are a new tool for focusing radiation energy with great intensity and control.
- At present, all fuels have advantages and disadvantages so that society must consider the trade-offs among them.
- Nuclear reactions release energy without the combustion products of burning fuels, but the radioactivity of fuels and by-products poses other risks, which may last for thousands of years.
- Industrialization brings an increased demand for and use of energy. Such usage contributes to the high standard of living in the industrially developing nations but also leads to more rapid depletion of the earth's energy resources and to environmental risks associated with the use of fossil and nuclear fuels.
- Decisions to slow the depletion of energy sources through efficient technology can be made at many levels, from personal to national, and they always involve trade-offs of economic costs and social costs.

Standard 8D: Communication

Benchmarks for Grades K–2

By the end of the 2nd grade, students should know that:
- Information can be sent and received in many different ways. Some allow answering back and some do not. Each way has advantages and disadvantages.
- Devices can be used to send and receive messages quickly and clearly.

Benchmarks for Grades 3–5

By the end of the 5th grade, students should know that:
- People have always tried to communicate with one another. Signed and spoken language was one of the first inventions. Early forms of recording messages used markings on materials such as wood or stone.
- Communication involves coding and decoding information. In any language, both the sender and the receiver have to know the same code, which means that secret codes can be used to keep communication private.
- People have invented devices, such as paper and ink, engraved plastic disks, and magnetic tapes, for recording information. These devices enable great amounts of information to be stored and retrieved—and be sent to one or many other people or places.
- Communication technologies make it possible to send and receive information more and more reliably, quickly, and cheaply over long distances.

Benchmarks for Grades 6–8

By the end of the 8th grade, students should know that:
- Errors can occur in coding, transmitting, or decoding information, and some means of checking for accuracy is needed. Repeating the message is a frequently used method.
- Information can be carried by many media, including sound, light, and objects. In this century, the ability to code information as electric currents in wires, electromagnetic waves in space, and light in glass fibers has made communication millions of times faster than is possible by mail or sound.

Benchmarks for Grades 9–12

By the end of the 12th grade, students should know that:
- Almost any information can be transformed into electrical signals. A weak electrical signal can be used to shape a stronger one, which can control other signals of light, sound, mechanical devices, or radio waves.
- The quality of communication is determined by the strength of the signal in relation to the noise that tends to obscure it. Communication errors can be reduced by boosting and focusing signals, shielding the signal from internal and external noise, and repeating information, but all of these increase costs. Digital coding of information (using only 1s and 0s) makes possible more reliable transmission of information.
- As technologies that provide privacy in communication improve, so do those for invading privacy.

Standard 8E: Information Processing

Benchmarks for Grades K–2

By the end of the 2nd grade, students should know that:
- There are different ways to store things so they can be easily found later.
- Letters and numbers can be used to put things in a useful order.

Benchmarks for Grades 3–5

By the end of the 5th grade, students should know that:
- Computers are controlled partly by how they are wired and partly by special instructions called programs that are entered into a computer's memory. Some programs stay permanently in the machine but most are coded on disks and transferred into and out of the computer to suit the user.
- Computers can be programmed to store, retrieve, and perform operations on information. These operations include mathematical calculations, word processing, diagram drawing, and the modeling of complex events.
- Mistakes can occur when people enter programs or data into a computer. Computers themselves can make errors in information processing because of defects in their hardware or software.

Benchmarks for Grades 6–8

By the end of the 8th grade, students should know that:
- Most computers use digital codes containing only two symbols, 0 and 1, to perform all operations. Continuous signals must be transformed into digital codes before they can be processed by a computer.
- What use can be made of a large collection of information depends upon how it is organized. One of the values of computers is that they are able, on command, to reorganize information in a variety of ways, thereby enabling people to make more and better uses of the collection.
- Computer control of mechanical systems can be much quicker than human control. In situations where events happen faster than people can react, there is little choice but to rely on computers. Most complex systems still require human oversight, however, to make certain kinds of judgments about the readiness of the parts of the system (including the computers) and the system as a whole to operate properly, to react to unexpected failures, and to evaluate how well the system is serving its intended purposes.
- An increasing number of people work at jobs that involve processing or distributing information. Because computers can do these tasks faster and more reliably, they have become standard tools both in the workplace and at home.

Benchmarks for Grades 9–12

By the end of the 12th grade, students should know that:
- Computer modeling explores the logical consequences of a set of instructions and a set of data. The instructions and data input of a computer model try to represent the real world so the computer can show what would actually happen. In this way, computers assist people in making decisions by simulating the consequences of different possible decisions.
- Redundancy can reduce errors in storing or processing information but increase costs.
- Miniaturization of information-processing hardware can increase processing speed and portability, reduce energy use, and lower cost. Miniaturization is made possible through higher-purity materials and more precise fabrication technology.

Standard 8F: Health Technology

Benchmarks for Grades K–2

By the end of the 2nd grade, students should know that:
- Vaccinations and other scientific treatments protect people from getting certain diseases, and different kinds of medicines may help those who do become sick to recover.

Benchmarks for Grades 3–5

By the end of the 5th grade, students should know that:
- There are normal ranges for body measurements—including temperature, heart rate, and what is in the blood and urine—that help to tell when people are well. Tools, such as thermometers and x-ray machines, provide us clues about what is happening inside the body.
- Technology has made it possible to repair and sometimes replace some body parts.

Benchmarks for Grades 6–8

By the end of the 8th grade, students should know that:
- Sanitation measures such as the use of sewers, landfills, quarantines, and safe food handling are important in controlling the spread of organisms that cause disease. Improving sanitation to prevent disease has contributed more to saving human life than any advance in medical treatment.
- The ability to measure the level of substances in body fluids has made it possible for physicians to make comparisons with normal levels, make very sophisticated diagnoses, and monitor the effects of the treatments they prescribe.
- It is becoming increasingly possible to manufacture chemical substances such as insulin and hormones that are normally found in the body. They can be used by individuals whose own bodies cannot produce the amounts required for good health.

Benchmarks for Grades 9–12

By the end of the 12th grade, students should know that:
- Owing to the large amount of information that computers can process,

they are playing an increasingly larger role in medicine. They are used to analyze data and to keep track of diagnostic information about individuals and statistical information on the distribution and spread of various maladies in populations.

- Almost all body substances and functions have daily or longer cycles. These cycles often need to be taken into account in interpreting normal ranges for body measurements, detecting disease, and planning treatment of illness. Computers aid in detecting, analyzing, and monitoring these cycles.

- Knowledge of genetics is opening whole fields of health care. In diagnosis, mapping of genetic instructions in cells makes it possible to detect defective genes that may lead to poor health. In treatment, substances from genetically engineered organisms may reduce the cost and side effects of replacing missing body chemicals.

- Inoculations use weakened germs (or parts of them) to stimulate the body's immune system to react. This reaction prepares the body to fight subsequent invasions by actual germs of that type. Some inoculations last for life.

- Knowledge of molecular structure and interactions aids in synthesizing new drugs and predicting their effects.

- The diagnosis and treatment of mental disorders are improving, but not as rapidly as for physical health. Techniques for detecting and diagnosing these disorders include observation of behavior, in-depth interviews, and measurements of body chemistry. Treatments range from discussing problems to affecting the brain directly with chemicals, electric shock, or surgery.

- Biotechnology has contributed to health improvement in many ways, but its cost and application have led to a variety of controversial social and ethical issues.

Standards for Technological Literacy

Standards Related to "the Nature of Technology"

Standard 1: The Characteristics and Scope of Technology.

Benchmarks for Grades K–2

- The natural world and human-made world are different.
- All people use tools and techniques to help them do things.

Benchmarks for Grades 3–5

- Things that are found in nature differ from things that are human-made in how they are produced and used.
- Tools, materials, and skills are used to make things and carry out tasks.
- Creative thinking and economic and cultural influences shape technological development.

Benchmarks for Grades 6–8

- New products and systems can be developed to solve problems or to help do things that could not be done without the help of technology.
- The development of technology is a human activity and is the result of individual and collective needs and the ability to be creative.
- Technology is closely linked to creativity, which has resulted in innovation.
- Corporations can often create demand for a product by bringing it onto the market and advertising it.

Benchmarks for Grades 9–12

- The nature and development of technological knowledge and processes are functions of the setting.
- The rate of technological development and diffusion is increasing rapidly.
- Inventions and innovations are the results of specific, goal-directed research.
- Most development of technologies these days is driven by the profit motive and the market.

Standard 2: The Core Concepts of Technology

Benchmarks for Grades K–2

- Some systems are found in nature, and some are made by humans.
- Systems have parts or components that work together to accomplish a goal.
- Tools are simple objects that help humans complete tasks.
- Different materials are used in making things.
- People plan in order to get things done.

Benchmarks for Grades 3–5

- A subsystem is a system that operates as a part of another system.
- When parts of a system are missing, it may not work as planned.
- Resources are the things needed to get a job done, such as tools and machines, materials, information, energy, people, capital, and time.
- Tools are used to design, make, use, and assess technology.
- Materials have many different properties.
- Tools and machines extend human capabilities, such as holding, lifting, carrying, fastening, separating, and computing.
- Requirements are the limits to designing or making a product or system.

Benchmarks for Grades 6–8

- Technological systems include input, processes, output, and at times, feedback.
- Systems thinking involves considering how every part relates to others.
- An open-loop system has no feedback path and requires human intervention, while a closed-loop system uses feedback.
- Technological systems can be connected to one another.
- Malfunctions of any part of a system may affect the function and quality of the system.
- Requirements are the parameters placed on the development of a product or system.
- Trade-off is a decision process recognizing the need for careful compromises among competing factors.
- Different technologies involve different sets of processes.

- Maintenance is the process of inspecting and servicing a product or system on a regular basis in order for it to continue functioning properly, to extend its life, or to upgrade its quality.
- Controls are mechanisms or particular steps that people perform using information about the system that causes systems to change.

Benchmarks for Grades 9–12

- Systems thinking applies logic and creativity with appropriate compromises in complex real-life problems.
- Systems, which are the building blocks of technology, are embedded within larger technological, social, and environmental systems.
- The stability of a technological system is influenced by all of the components in the system, especially those in the feedback loop.
- Selecting resources involves trade-offs between competing values, such as availability, cost, desirability, and waste.
- Requirements involve the identification of the criteria and constraints of a product or system and the determination of how they affect the final design and development.
- Optimization is an ongoing process or methodology of designing or making a product and is dependent on criteria and constraints.
- New technologies create new processes.
- Quality control is a planned process to ensure that a product, service, or system meets established criteria.
- Management is the process of planning, organizing, and controlling work.
- Complex systems have many layers of controls and feedback loops to provide information.

Standard 3: The Relationships Among Technologies and the Connections Between Technology and Other Fields of Study

Benchmarks for Grades K–2

- The study of technology uses many of the same ideas and skills as other subjects.

Benchmarks for Grades 3–5

- Technologies are often combined.
- Various relationships exist between technology and other fields of study.

Benchmarks for Grades 6–8

- Technological systems often interact with one another.
- A product, system, or environment developed for one setting may be applied to another setting.
- Knowledge gained from other fields of study has a direct effect on the development of technological products and systems.

Benchmarks for Grades 9–12

- Technology transfer occurs when a new user applies an existing innovation developed for one purpose in a different function.
- Technological innovation often results when ideas, knowledge, or skills are shared within a technology, among technologies, or across other fields.
- Technological ideas are sometimes protected through the process of patenting.
- Technological progress promotes the advancement of science and mathematics.

Standards Related to Technology and Society

Standard 4: The Cultural, Social, Economic, and Political Effects of Technology.

Benchmarks for Grades K–2

- The use of tools and machines can be helpful or harmful.

Benchmarks for Grades 3–5

- When using technology, results can be good or bad.
- The use of technology can have unintended consequences.

Benchmarks for Grades 6–8

- The use of technology affects humans in various ways, including their safety, comfort, choices, and attitudes about technology's development and use.
- Technology, by itself, is neither good nor bad, but decisions about the use of products and systems can result in desirable or undesirable consequences.
- The development and use of technology poses ethical issues.
- Economic, political, and cultural issues are influenced by the development and use of technology.

Benchmarks for Grades 9–12

- Changes caused by the use of technology can range from gradual to rapid and from subtle to obvious.
- Making decisions about the use of technology involves weighing the trade-offs between the positive and negative effects.
- Ethical considerations are important in the development, selection, and use of technologies.
- The transfer of a technology from one society to another can cause cultural, social, economic, and political changes affecting both societies to varying degrees.

Standard 5: The Effects of Technology on the Environment

Benchmarks for Grades K–2

- Some materials can be reused and/or recycled.

Benchmarks for Grades 3–5

- Waste must be appropriately recycled or disposed of to prevent unnecessary harm to the environment.
- The use of technology affects the environment in good and bad ways.

Benchmarks for Grades 6–8

- The management of waste produced by technological systems is an important societal issue.
- Technologies can be used to repair damage caused by natural disasters and to break down waste from the use of various products and systems.
- Decisions to develop and use technologies often put environmental and economic concerns in direct competition with one another.

Benchmarks for Grades 9–12

- Humans can devise technologies to conserve water, soil, and energy through such techniques as reusing, reducing, and recycling.
- When new technologies are developed to reduce the use of resources, considerations of trade-offs are important.
- With the aid of technology, various aspects of the environment can be monitored to provide information for decision-making.
- The alignment of technological processes with natural processes maximizes performance and reduces negative impacts on the environment.
- Humans devise technologies to reduce the negative consequences of other technologies.
- Decisions regarding the implementation of technologies involve the weighing of trade-offs between predicted positive and negative effects on the environment.

Standard 6: The Role of Society in the Development and Use of Technology

Benchmarks for Grades K–2

- Products are made to meet individual needs and wants.

Benchmarks for Grades 3–5

- Because people's needs and wants change, new technologies are developed, and old ones are improved to meet those changes.
- Individual, family, community, and economic concerns may expand or limit the development of technologies.

Benchmarks for Grades 6–8

- Throughout history, new technologies have resulted from the demands, values, and interests of individuals, businesses, industries, and societies.
- The use of inventions and innovations has led to changes in society and the creation of new needs and wants.
- Social and cultural priorities and values are reflected in technological devices.
- Meeting societal expectations is the driving force behind the acceptance and use of products and systems.

Benchmarks for Grades 9–12

- Different cultures develop their own technologies to satisfy their individual and shared needs, wants, and values.
- The decision whether to develop a technology is influenced by societal opinions and demands, in addition to corporate cultures.
- A number of different factors, such as advertising, the strength of the economy, the goals of a company, and the latest fads contribute to shaping the design of and demand for various technologies.

Standard 7: The Influence of Technology on History

Benchmarks for Grades K–2

- The way people live and work has changed throughout history because of technology.

Benchmark for Grades 3–5

- People have made tools to provide food, to make clothing, and to protect themselves.

Benchmarks for Grades 6–8

- Many inventions and innovations have evolved using slow and methodical processes of tests and refinements.
- The specialization of function has been at the heart of many technological improvements.

- The design and construction of structures for service or convenience have evolved from the development of techniques for measurement, controlling systems, and the understanding of spatial relationships.
- In the past, an invention or innovation was not usually developed with the knowledge of science.

Benchmarks for Grades 9–12

- Most technological development has been evolutionary, the result of a series of refinements to a basic invention.
- The evolution of civilization has been directly affected by, and has in turn affected, the development and use of tools and materials.
- Throughout history, technology has been a powerful force in reshaping the social, cultural, political, and economic landscape.
- Early in the history of technology, the development of many tools and machines was based not on scientific knowledge but on technological know-how.
- The Iron Age was defined by the use of iron and steel as the primary materials for tools.
- The Middle Ages saw the development of many technological devices that produced long-lasting effects on technology and society.
- The Renaissance, a time of rebirth of the arts and humanities, was also an important development in the history of technology.
- The Industrial Revolution saw the development of continuous manufacturing, sophisticated transportation and communication systems, advanced construction practices, and improved education and leisure time.
- The Information Age places emphasis on the processing and exchange of information.

Standards Related to Design

Standard 8: The Attributes of Design

Benchmarks for Grades K–2

- Everyone can design solutions to a problem.
- Design is a creative process.

Benchmarks for Grades 3–5

- The design process is a purposeful method of planning practical solutions to problems.
- Requirements for a design include such factors as the desired elements and features of a product or system or the limits that are placed on the design.

Benchmarks for Grades 6–8

- Design is a creative planning process that leads to useful products and systems.
- There is no perfect design.
- Requirements for design are made up of criteria and constraints.

Benchmarks for Grades 9–12

- The design process includes defining a problem, brainstorming, researching and generating ideas, identifying criteria and specifying constraints, exploring possibilities, selecting an approach, developing a design proposal, making a model or prototype, testing and evaluating the design using specifications, refining the design, creating or making it, and communicating processes and results.
- Design problems are seldom presented in a clearly defined form.
- The design needs to be continually checked and critiqued, and the ideas of the design must be redefined and improved.
- Requirements of a design, such as criteria, constraints, and efficiency, sometimes compete with each other.

Standard 9: Engineering Design

Benchmarks for Grades K–2

- The engineering design process includes identifying a problem, looking for ideas, developing solutions, and sharing solutions with others.
- Expressing ideas to others verbally and through sketches and models is an important part of the design process.

- The engineering design process involves defining a problem, generating ideas, selecting a solution, testing the solution(s), making the item, evaluating it, and presenting the results.
- When designing an object, it is important to be creative and consider all ideas.
- Models are used to communicate and test design ideas and processes.

Benchmarks for Grades 6–8

- Design involves a set of steps, which can be performed in different sequences and repeated as needed.
- Brainstorming is a group problem-solving design process in which each person in the group presents his or her ideas in an open forum.
- Modeling, testing, evaluating, and modifying are used to transform ideas into practical solutions.

Benchmarks for Grades 9–12

- Established design principles are used to evaluate existing designs, to collect data, and to guide the design process.
- Engineering design is influenced by personal characteristics, such as creativity, resourcefulness, and the ability to visualize and think abstractly.
- A prototype is a working model used to test a design concept by making actual observations and necessary adjustments.
- The process of engineering design takes into account a number of factors.

Standard 10: The Role of Troubleshooting, Research and Development, Invention and Innovation, and Experimentation in Problem Solving

Benchmarks for Grades K–2

- Asking questions and making observations helps a person to figure out how things work.

- All products and systems are subject to failure. Many products and systems, however, can be fixed.

Benchmarks for Grades 3–5

- Troubleshooting is a way of finding out why something does not work so that it can be fixed.
- Invention and innovation are creative ways to turn ideas into real things.
- The process of experimentation, which is common in science, can also be used to solve technological problems.

Benchmarks for Grades 6–8

- Troubleshooting is a problem-solving method used to identify the cause of a malfunction in a technological system.
- Invention is a process of turning ideas and imagination into devices and systems. Innovation is the process of modifying an existing product or system to improve it.
- Some technological problems are best solved through experimentation.

Benchmarks for Grades 9–12

- Research and development is a specific problem-solving approach that is used intensively in business and industry to prepare devices and systems for the marketplace.
- Technological problems must be researched before they can be solved.
- Not all problems are technological, and not every problem can be solved using technology.
- Many technological problems require a multidisciplinary approach.

Standards Related to Abilities for a Technological World

Standard 11: Apply the Design Process

Benchmarks for Grades K–2

- Brainstorm people's needs and wants and pick some problems that can be solved through the design process.

- Build or construct an object using the design process.
- Investigate how things are made and how they can be improved.

Benchmarks for Grades 3–5

- Identify and collect information about everyday problems that can be solved by technology, and generate ideas and requirements for solving a problem.
- The process of designing involves presenting some possible solutions in visual form and then selecting the best solution(s) from many.
- Test and evaluate the solutions for the design problem.
- Improve the design solutions.

Benchmarks for Grades 6–8

- Apply a design process to solve problems in and beyond the laboratory-classroom.
- Specify criteria and constraints for the design.
- Make two-dimensional and three-dimensional representations of the designed solution.
- Test and evaluate the design in relation to pre-established requirements, such as criteria and constraints, and refine as needed.
- Make a product or system and document the solution.

Benchmarks Grades 9–12

- Identify the design problem to solve and decide whether or not to address it.
- Identify criteria and constraints and determine how these will affect the design process.
- Refine a design by using prototypes and modeling to ensure quality, efficiency, and productivity of the final product.
- Evaluate the design solution using conceptual, physical, and math-ematical models at various intervals of the design process in order to check for proper design and to note areas where improvements are needed.
- Develop and produce a product or system using a design process.
- Evaluate final solutions and communicate observation, processes, and

results of the entire design process, using verbal, graphic, quantitative, virtual, and written means, in addition to three-dimensional models.

Standard 12: Use and Maintain Technological Products and Systems

Benchmarks for Grades K–2

- Discover how things work.
- Use hand tools correctly and safely and be able to name them correctly.
- Recognize and use everyday symbols.

Benchmarks for Grades 3–5

- Follow step-by-step directions to assemble a product.
- Select and safely use tools, products, and systems for specific tasks.
- Use computers to access and organize information.
- Use common symbols, such as numbers and words, to communicate key ideas.

Benchmarks for Grades 6–8

- Use information provided in manuals, protocols, or by experienced people to see and understand how things work.
- Use tools, materials, and machines safely to diagnose, adjust, and repair systems.
- Use computers and calculators in various applications.
- Operate and maintain systems in order to achieve a given purpose.

Benchmarks for Grades 9–12

- Document processes and procedures and communicate them to different audiences using appropriate oral and written techniques.
- Diagnose a system that is malfunctioning and use tools, materials, machines, and knowledge to repair it.
- Troubleshoot, analyze, and maintain systems to ensure safe and proper function and precision.
- Operate systems so that they function in the way they were designed.

- Use computers and calculators to access, retrieve, organize, process, maintain, interpret, and evaluate data and information in order to communicate.

Standard 13: Assess the Impact of Products and Systems

Benchmarks for Grades K–2

- Collect information about everyday products and systems by asking questions.
- Determine if the human use of a product or system creates positive or negative results.

Benchmarks for Grades 3–5

- Compare, contrast, and classify collected information in order to identify patterns.
- Investigate and assess the influence of a specific technology on the individual, family, community, and environment.
- Examine the trade-offs of using a product or system and decide when it could be used.

Benchmarks for Grades 6–8

- Design and use instruments to gather data.
- Use data collected to analyze and interpret trends in order to identify the positive and negative effects of a technology.
- Identify trends and monitor potential consequences of technological development.
- Interpret and evaluate the accuracy of the information obtained and determine if it is useful.

Benchmarks for Grades 9–12

- Collect information and evaluate its quality.
- Synthesize data, analyze trends, and draw conclusions regarding the effect of technology on the individual, society, and environment.

- Use assessment techniques, such as trend analysis and experimentation, to make decisions about the future development of technology.
- Design forecasting techniques to evaluate the results of altering natural systems.

Standards Related to the Design World

Standard 14: Medical Technologies

Benchmarks for Grades K–2

- Vaccinations protect people from getting certain diseases.
- Medicine helps people who are sick to get better.
- There are many products designed specifically to help people take care of themselves.

Benchmarks for Grades 3–5

- Vaccines are designed to prevent diseases from developing and spreading; medicines are designed to relieve symptoms and stop diseases from developing.
- Technological advances have made it possible to create new devices, to repair or replace certain parts of the body, and to provide a means for mobility.
- Many tools and devices have been designed to help provide clues about health and to provide a safe environment.

Benchmarks for Grades 6–8

- Advances and innovations in medical technologies are used to improve healthcare.
- Sanitation processes used in the disposal of medical products help to protect people from harmful organisms and disease, and shape the ethics of medical safety.
- The vaccines developed for use in immunization require specialized technologies to support environments in which a sufficient amount of vaccines is produced.
- Genetic engineering involves modifying the structure of DNA to produce novel genetic make-ups.

- Medical technologies include prevention and rehabilitation, vaccines and pharmaceuticals, medical and surgical procedures, genetic engineering, and the systems within which health is protected and maintained.
- Telemedicine reflects the convergence of technological advances in a number of fields, including medicine, telecommunications, virtual presence, computer engineering, informatics, artificial intelligence, robotics, materials science, and perceptual psychology.
- The sciences of biochemistry and molecular biology have made it possible to manipulate the genetic information found in living creatures.

Standard 15: Agricultural and Related Biotechnologies

Benchmarks for Grades K–2

- The use of technologies in agriculture makes it possible for food to be available year round and to conserve resources.
- There are many different tools necessary to control and make up the parts of an ecosystem.

Benchmarks for Grades 3–5

- Artificial ecosystems are human-made environments that are designed to function as a unit and are comprised of humans, plants, and animals.
- Most agricultural waste can be recycled.
- Many processes used in agriculture require different procedures, products, or systems.

Benchmarks for Grades 6–8

- Technological advances in agriculture directly affect the time and number of people required to produce food for a large population.
- A wide range of specialized equipment and practices is used to improve the production of food, fiber, fuel, and other useful products and in the care of animals.
- Biotechnology applies the principles of biology to create commercial products or processes.

- Artificial ecosystems are human-made complexes that replicate some aspects of the natural environment.
- The development of refrigeration, freezing, dehydration, preservation, and irradiation provide long-term storage of food and reduce the health risks caused by tainted food.

Benchmarks for Grades 9–12

- Agriculture includes a combination of businesses that use a wide array of products and systems to produce, process, and distribute food, fiber, fuel, chemical, and other useful products.
- Biotechnology has applications in such areas as agriculture, pharmaceuticals, food and beverages, medicine, energy, the environment, and genetic engineering.
- Conservation is the process of controlling soil erosion, reducing sediment in waterways, conserving water, and improving water quality.
- The engineering design and management of agricultural systems require knowledge of artificial ecosystems and the effects of technological development on flora and fauna.

Standard 16: Energy and Power Technologies

Benchmarks for Grades K–2

- Energy comes in many forms.
- Energy should not be wasted.

Benchmarks for Grades 3–5

- Energy comes in different forms.
- Tools, machines, products, and systems use energy in order to do work.

Benchmarks for Grades 6–8

- Energy is the capacity to do work.
- Energy can be used to do work, using many processes.
- Power is the rate at which energy is converted from one form to another or transferred from one place to another, or the rate at which work is done.

- Power systems are used to drive and provide propulsion to other technological products and systems.
- Much of the energy used in our environment is not used efficiently.

Benchmarks for Grades 9–12

- Energy cannot be created nor destroyed; however, it can be converted from one form to another.
- Energy can be grouped into major forms: thermal, radiant, electrical, mechanical, chemical, nuclear, and others.
- It is impossible to build an engine to perform work that does not exhaust thermal energy to the surroundings.
- Energy resources can be renewable or nonrenewable.
- Power systems must have a source of energy, a process, and loads.

Standard 17: Information and Communication Technologies

Benchmarks for Grades K–2

- Information is data that has been organized.
- Technology enables people to communicate by sending and receiving information over a distance.
- People use symbols when they communicate by technology.

Benchmarks for Grades 3–5

- The processing of information through the use of technology can be used to help humans make decisions and solve problems.
- Information can be acquired and sent through a variety of technological sources, including print and electronic media.
- Communication technology is the transfer of messages among people and/or machines over distances through the use of technology.
- Letters, characters, icons, and signs are symbols that represent ideas, quantities, elements, and operations.

Benchmarks for Grades 6–8

- Information and communication systems allow information to be transferred from human to human, human to machine, and machine to human.

- Communication systems are made up of a source, encoder, transmitter, receiver, decoder, and destination.
- The design of a message is influenced by such factors as intended audience, medium, purpose, and the nature of the message.
- The use of symbols, measurements, and drawings promotes a clear communication by providing a common language to express ideas.

Benchmarks for Grades 9–12

- Information and communication technologies include the inputs, processes, and outputs associated with sending and receiving information.
- Information and communication systems allow information to be transferred from human to human, human to machine, machine to human, and machine to machine.
- Information and communication systems can be used to inform, persuade, entertain, control, manage, and educate.
- Communication systems are made up of source, encoder, transmitter, receiver, decoder, storage, retrieval, and destination.
- There are many ways to communicate information, such as graphic and electronic means.
- Technological knowledge and processes are communicated using symbols, measurement, conventions, icons, graphic images, and languages that incorporate a variety of visual, auditory, and tactile stimuli.

Standard 18: Transportation Technologies

Benchmarks for Grades K–2
- A transportation system has many parts that work together to help people travel.
- Vehicles move people or goods from one place to another in water, air or space, and on land.
- Transportation vehicles need to be cared for to prolong their use.

Benchmarks for Grades 3–5

- The use of transportation allows people and goods to be moved from place to place.

- A transportation system may lose efficiency or fail if one part is missing or malfunctioning or if a subsystem is not working.

Benchmarks for Grades 6–8

- Transporting people and goods involves a combination of individuals and vehicles.
- Transportation vehicles are made up of subsystems, such as structural propulsion, suspension, guidance, control, and support, that must function together for a system to work effectively.
- Governmental regulations often influence the design and operation of transportation systems.
- Processes, such as receiving, holding, storing, loading, moving, unloading, delivering, evaluating, marketing, managing, communicating, and using conventions are necessary for the entire transportation system to operate efficiently.

Benchmarks for Grades 9–12

- Transportation plays a vital role in the operation of other technologies, such as manufacturing, construction, communication, health and safety, and agriculture.
- Intermodalism is the use of different modes of transportation, such as highways, railways, and waterways as part of an interconnected system that can move people and goods easily from one mode to another.
- Transportation services and methods have led to a population that is regularly on the move.
- The design of intelligent and non-intelligent transportation systems depends on many processes and innovative techniques.

Standard 19: Manufacturing Technologies

Benchmarks for Grades K–2

- Manufacturing systems produce products in quantity.
- Manufactured products are designed.

Benchmarks for Grades 3–5

- Processing systems convert natural materials into products
- Manufacturing processes include designing products, gathering resources, and using tools to separate, form, and combine materials in order to produce products.
- Manufacturing enterprises exist because of a consumption of goods.

Benchmarks for Grades 6–8

- Manufacturing systems use mechanical processes that change the form of materials through the processes of separating, forming, combining, and conditioning them.
- Manufactured goods may be classified as durable and non-durable.
- The manufacturing process includes the designing, development, making, and servicing of products and systems.
- Chemical technologies are used to modify or alter chemical substances.
- Materials must first be located before they can be extracted from the earth through such processes as harvesting, drilling, and mining.
- Marketing a product involves informing the public about it as well as assisting in its sales and distribution.

Benchmarks for Grades 9–12

- Servicing keeps products in good operating condition.
- Materials have different qualities and may be classified as natural, synthetic, or mixed.
- Durable goods are designed to operate for a long period of time, while non-durable goods are designed to operate for a short period of time.
- Manufacturing systems may be classified into types, such as customized production, batch production, and continuous production.
- The interchangeability of parts increases the effectiveness of manufacturing processes.
- Chemical technologies provide a means for humans to alter or modify materials and to produce chemical products.
- Marketing involves establishing a product's identity, conducting research on its potential, advertising it, distributing it, and selling it.

Standard 20: Construction Technologies

Benchmarks for Grades K–2

- People live, work, and go to school in buildings, which are of different types: houses, apartments, office buildings, and schools.
- The type of structure determines how the parts are put together.

Benchmarks for Grades 3–5

- Modern communities are usually planned according to guidelines.
- Structures need to be maintained.
- Many systems are used in buildings.

Benchmarks for Grades 6–8

- The selection of designs for structures is based on factors such as building laws and codes, style, convenience, cost, climate, and function.
- Structures rest on a foundation.
- Some structures are temporary, while others are permanent.
- Buildings generally contain a variety of subsystems.

Benchmarks for Grades 9–12

- Infrastructure is the underlying base or basic framework of a system.
- Structures are constructed using a variety of processes and procedures.
- The design of structures includes a number of requirements.
- Structures require maintenance, alteration, or renovation periodically to improve them or to alter their intended use.
- Structures can include prefabricated materials.

APPENDIX C
Challenges and Opportunities for Assessing Technological Literacy in the United States

Workshop of the Committee on Assessing Technological Literacy

Lecture Room
National Academies Building
2100 C Street, NW
Washington, D.C.

September 28–29, 2004

September 28

6:30 p.m.–8:00 p.m.   **Pre-Workshop Informal Reception**
Rotunda of the National Academy of Sciences
2100 C Street, NW
(picture ID must be shown at door)

*   *   *   *

September 29

7:30 a.m.–8:00 a.m.   **Continental Breakfast**

8:00 a.m.–9:00 a.m.   **Plenary Session 1: The Project and Workshop in Context**
Topic 1: Project history and goals of the workshop
Elsa Garmire, Committee Chair

Topic 2: Overview of assessment instruments collected by the project
Greg Pearson, NAE
Topic 3: Challenges and opportunities for assessment of technological literacy
Committee Panel
Questions and Discussion

9:00 a.m–11:30 a.m.   **Concurrent Session I**

Panel 1 [LECTURE ROOM]: Federal and State Perspectives
Committee Moderator: Rodger Bybee
• Susan Brandon, Assistant Director, Social, Behavioral and Educational Sciences, White House Office of Science and Technology Policy
• Rep. Phyllis Heineman, Chair, House Education Committee, South Dakota State Legislature

Panel 2 [LECTURE ROOM]: District, School, and Classroom Perspectives
Committee Moderator: Martha Cyr
• Tony Bruno, Treasurer, Arizona School Board Association
• Ken Starkman, Technology and Engineering Consultant, Wisconsin Department of Public Instruction
• Arthur Linder, Principal, Oak Hill Academy, District of Columbia

Panel 3 [ROOM 250]: Business/Industry Perspectives
Committee Moderator: Marc deVries
• John Rauschenberger, Manager of Personnel Research and Development, Ford Motor Co.
• Ed Nicholson, Director, Media & Community Relations, Tyson Foods, Inc.

- Peter Joyce, Workforce Development Manager, Worldwide Education, Cisco Systems, Inc.

Panel 4 [ROOM 250]: Workforce and Employment Perspectives
Committee Moderator: Elsa Garmire
- Susan Sclafani, Counselor to the Secretary and Assistant Secretary for Vocational, Technical, Career Education, U.S. Department of Education
- Pamela Frugoli, Skill Assessment Team Lead, Office of Workforce Investment, Employment and Training Information, U.S. Department of Labor
- Thomas Carretta, Engineering Psychologist, Human Effectiveness Directorate, Air Force Research Laboratory

11:30 a.m.–12:30 p.m. **Plenary Session 2: Reporting Out from Concurrent Session I and Discussion [LECTURE ROOM]**
Committee Moderator: José Mestre

12:30 p.m.–1:30 p.m. **Lunch [LECTURE ROOM]**

1:30 p.m.–4:00 p.m. **Concurrent Session II**

Panel 1 [LECTURE ROOM]: International/Comparative Assessment Perspectives
Committee Moderator: Richard Kimbell
- Marian Lemke, National Program Manager for PISA (Programme for International Student Assessment), National Center for Education Statistics
- Christine O'Sullivan, Principal, K–12 Consulting

Panel 2 [LECTURE ROOM]: National Assessment Perspectives

Committee Moderator: Jon Miller

- Larry Suter, Statistician and Program Director, Division of Research, Evaluation, and Communication, National Science Foundation
- Dylan Wiliam, Senior Research Director, Learning and Teaching Research Center, Educational Testing Service

Panel 3 [ROOM 250]: Assessment Developers' Perspectives

Committee Moderator: Susanna Hornig Priest

- Stephen Lazer, Vice President for Assessment Development, Educational Testing Service
- Nancy Petersen, Distinguished Research Scientist, Measurement & Statistical Research, ACT
- Margaret Jorgensen, Senior Vice President for Product Research and Innovation, Harcourt Assessment

Panel 4 [ROOM 250]: Informal Education Perspectives

Committee Moderator: Sharif Shakrani

- Ray Vandiver, Vice President of Exhibits, Oregon Museum of Science and Industry
- Julie Benyo, Director of Education Initiatives, WGBH
- Regina A. Corso, Research Director, Public Policy, Harris Interactive

4:00 p.m.–5:00 p.m.   **Plenary Session 3: Reporting out from Concurrent Session II and Discussion [LECTURE ROOM]**

Committee Moderator: Rod Custer

5:00 p.m.–5:15 p.m.   **Closing Comments and Adjournment**
Elsa Garmire

APPENDIX **D**
Research on Learning in Technology and Engineering: A Selected Bibliography[1]

Technology

Angelides, D.C., A. Poulopoulos, I. Avgeris, and P. Haralampous. 2000. Case studies and information technology in civil engineering learning. Journal of Professional Issues in Engineering Education and Practice 126(3): 125–132.

Ankiewicz, P., and S. Van Rensburg. 2001. Assessing the attitudinal technology profile of South African learners: a pilot study. International Journal of Technology and Design Education 11(2): 93–109.

Autio, O. 2003. Decision-making process in technology education. Presented at the 66th International Technology Education Association Annual Conference: Teaching Decision Making in a Technological World, March 2003, Albquerque, New Mexico.

Barak, M., and Y. Doppelt. 1999. Integrating the Cognitive Research Trust (CoRT) Programme for creative thinking. Research in Science and Technological Education 17(2): 13–139.

Barak, M., and T. Maymon. 1998. Aspects of teamwork observed in a technological task in junior high schools. Journal of Technology Education 9(1): 4–18.

Barak, M., T. Maymon, and G. Harel. 1999. Teamwork in modern organizations: implications for technology education. International Journal of Technology and Design Education 9(1): 85–101.

Bhargava, A., A. Kirova-Petrova, and S. McNair. 1999. Computer, gender bias and young children. Information Technology in Childhood Education Annual 263–274.

Birol, G., A.F. McKenna, H.D. Smith, T.D. Giorgio, and S.P. Brophy. 2002. Integration of the "How People Learn" Framework into Educational Module Development and Implementation in Biotechnology. Pp. 2640–2641 in Proceedings of the Second Joint EMBS/BMES Conference. Houston, Tex: CD ROM Omnipress.

[1]The references in this bibliography were identified in research commissioned by the Committee on Assessing Technological Literacy. They are provided here for readers who may wish to do additional reading. Due to time and funding constraints, the committee was unable to verify the accuracy of the citations.

Boser, R. 1993. The development of problem solving capabilities in pre-service technology teacher education. Journal of Technology Education 4(2). Available online at: *http://scholar.lib.vt.edu/ejournals/JTE/v4n2/boser.jte-v4n2.html* (January 2004).

Bruer, J.T. 2003. Learning and Technology: A View from Cognitive Science. Pp. 159–172 in Technology Applications in Education: A Learning View, edited by H.F. O'Neil and R.S. Perez. Mahwah, N.J.: Lawrence Erlbaum Associates.

Bryson, M., S. Petrina, M. Braundy, and S. de Castell. 2003. Conditions for success?: gender in technology-intensive courses in British Columbia secondary schools. Canadian Journal of Science, Mathematics and Technology Education 3(2): 186–193.

Burnam, B., and Y. Kafai. 2001. Ethics and the computer: children's development of moral reasoning about computer and internet use. Journal of Educational Computing Research 25(2): 111–127.

Cajas, F. 2002. The role of research in improving learning technological concepts and skills: the context of technological literacy. International Journal of Technology and Design Education 12(3): 175–188.

Cash, J.R., M.B. Behrmann, R.W. Stadt, and H. McDaniels. 1996. Effectiveness of cognitive apprenticeship instructional methods in college automotive technology classrooms. Journal of Industrial Teacher Education 34(2): 29–49.

Childress, V.W. 1996. Do integrating technology, science, and mathematics improve technological problem solving?: a quasi-experiment. Journal of Technology Education 8(1): 16–26.

Cognition and Technology Group at Vanderbilt. 1997. The Jasper Project: Lessons in Curriculum, Instruction, Assessment, and Professional Development. Mahwah, N.J.: Lawrence Erlbaum Associates.

Conner, D.A. 2003. Comments on "Undergraduate Education" editorial appearing in November 2002 issue [and reply]. Transactions on Education 46(1): 207.

Coorden, L., and J. Vandenabeele. 2002. Public participation in decision-making on technology: a challenge for citizens and experts. Available online at: *http://extranet.ufsia.ac.be/MTT/STEM/docs/326.pdf&e=7418* (January 2004).

Cutler-Landsman, D. 1993. Bridging the Gender Gap with LEGO TC Logo. Pp. 91–99 in New Paradigms in Classroom Research on Logo Learning, edited by D. Watt and M. Watt. Eugene, Ore.: International Society for Technology in Education.

Davidovic, A., J. Warren, and E. Trichina. 2003. Learning benefits of structural example-based adaptive tutoring systems. IEEE Transactions on Education 46(2): 241–251.

Davis, R.S., I.S. Ginns, and C.J. McRobbie. 2002. Elementary school students' understandings of technology concepts. Journal of Technology Education 14(1). Available online at: *http://scholar.lib.vt.edu/ejournals/JTE/v14n1/davis.html* (January 2004).

Deal, W.F. 2001. Imagineering: designing robots imaginatively and creatively. The Technology Teacher 60(7): 17–25.

DeMiranda, M.A., and J.E. Folkestad. 2000. Linking cognitive science theory and technology education practice: a powerful connection not fully realized. Journal of Industrial Teacher Education 37(4): 5–23.

Driscoll, M.P. 2002. How People Learn (and What Technology Might Have to Do with It). Report No. RI89002001. Syracuse, N.Y.: ARC Professional Services Group (ERIC Document Reproduction Service No. ED470032).

Druin, A. 1999. The role of children in the design of new technology. Available online at: *http://citeseer.nj.nec.com/correct/232002* (January 2004).

Druin, A., and C. Fast. 2002. The child as learner, critic, inventor, and technology design partner: an analysis of three years of Swedish student journals. International Journal of Technology and Design Education 12(3): 189–213.

Druin, A., B. Bederson, A. Boltman, A. Miura, D. Knotts-Callahan, and M. Platt. 1999. Children as Our Technology Design Partners. Pp. 51–72 in The Design of Children's Technology, edited by A. Druin. San Francisco, Calif.: Morgan Kaufmann.

Duggan, A., B. Hess, D. Morgan, S. Kim, and K. Wilson. 2001. Measuring students' attitudes toward educational use of the Internet. Journal of Educational Computing Research 25(4): 267–281.

Eastman, C.M. 2001. New Directions in Design Cognition: Studies on Representation and Recall, in Design Knowing and Learning. Pp. 79–103 in Cognition in Design Education, edited by C.M. Eastman, W.M. McCracken, and W.C. Newstetter. Amsterdam: Elsevier Science Press.

Edelson, D.C. 2002. Design research: what we can learn when we engage in design. Journal of the Learning Science 11(1): 105–121.

Ferguson, D. 2001. Technology in a constructivist classroom. Information Technology in Childhood Education Annual 45–55.

Fleer, M. 2000. Working technologically: investigations into how young children design and make during technology education. International Journal of Technology and Design Education 10(1): 43–59.

Fowler, C.J.H., and J.T. Mayers. 1999. Learning relationships: from theory to design. Association for Learning Technology Journal 7(3): 6–16.

Frantom, C., K.E. Green, and E.R. Hoffman. 2002. Measure development: the Children's Attitudes Toward Technology Scale (CATS). Journal of Educational Computing Research 26(3): 249–263.

Ginns, I.S., S.J. Stein, and C.J. McRobbie. 2003. Female students' learning in design and technology projects. Canadian Journal of Science, Mathematics, and Technology 3(3): 304–321.

Gray, J., H. Groves, and J.L. Kolodner. 2000. A Survival Guide: The Student Success Handbook for Learners in Project Based Science Environments. International Conference of the Learning Sciences 2000 (ICLS). Mahwah, N.J.: Erlbaum and Associates.

Greene, P.J. 2000. Lego mindstorms: learning and leading with technology. Available online at: *http://www.ed.uiuc.edu/courses/edpsy490az-sp96/k12-technology/Resnick-Ocko/* (January 2004).

Gustafson, B.J., and P.M. Rowell. 1998. Elementary children's technological problem solving: selecting an initial course of action. Research in Science and Technological Education 16(2): 13–151.

Gustafson, B.J., and P.M. Rowell. 2001. Children's ideas about strengthening structures. Research in Science and Technological Education 19(1): 111–123.

Hennessy, S., and P. Murphy. 1999. The potential for collaborative problem solving in design and technology. International Journal of Technology and Design Education 9(1): 1–36.

Hill, A.M. 1998. Problem solving in real-life contexts: an alternative for design in technology education. International Journal of Technology and Design Education 8(2): 203–220.

Hill, A.M., and A. Anning. 2001. Comparisons and contrasts between elementary/primary "school situated design" and "workplace design" in Canada and England. International Journal of Technology and Design Education 11(2): 111–136.

Hill, R.B., and R.C. Wicklein. 1999. A factor analysis of primary mental processes for technological problem solving. Journal of Industrial Teacher Education 36(2): 83–100.

Institute of Electrical and Electronics Engineers. 1996. Special Issue on the Application of Information Technologies to Engineering and Science Education 39(3). Available on 1 computer laser optical disc. New York: Institute of Electrical and Electronics Engineers.

Jacobson, M., and A. Archodidou. 2000. The design of hypermedia tools for learning: fostering conceptual change and transfer of complex scientific knowledge. Journal of the Learning Science 9(2): 145–199.

Jarvinen, E. 1998. The Lego/Logo learning environment in technology education: an experiment in a Finnish context. Journal of Technology Education 9(2): 47–59.

Jarvis, T., and L.J. Rennie. 1998. Factors that influence children's developing perceptions of technology. International Journal of Technology and Design Education 8(3): 79–261.

Jonassen, D.H., K.L. Peck, and B.G. Wilson. 1999a. Learning by Reflecting with Technology: Mindtools for Critical Thinking. Pp. 151–191 in Learning with Technology: A Constructivist Perspective. Englewood Cliffs, N.J.: Prentice Hall.

Jonassen, D.H., K.L. Peck, and B.G. Wilson. 1999b. Learning by Visualizing with Technology. Pp. 51–84 in Learning with Technology: A Constructivist Perspective. Englewood Cliffs, N.J.: Prentice Hall.

Jones, A. 1997. Recent research in learning technological concepts and processes. International Journal of Technology and Design Education 7(1-2): 83–96.

Kadijevich, D. 2000. Gender differences in computer attitude among ninth-grade students. Journal of Educational Computing Research 22(2): 145–154.

Khazanchi, D. 1994. Does pedagogy make a difference?: an experimental study of unethical behavior information systems. Journal of Computer Information System 35(1): 54–63.

Koch, J., and M.D. Burghardt. 2002. Design technology in the elementary school: a study of teacher action research. Journal of Technology Education 13(2): 21–33.

Kolodner, J. 1997. Educational implications of analogy: a view from case-based reasoning. American Psychologist 52(1): 57–66.

Kolodner, J.L., and K. Nagel. 1999. The Design Discussion Area: A Collaborative Learning Tool in Support of Learning from Problem-Solving and Design Activities. Pp. 300–307 in Proceedings of CSCL '99. Palo Alto, Calif.: Stanford University.

Kolodner, J.L., D. Crismond, J. Gray, J. Holbrook, and S. Puntambekar. 1998. Learning by Design from Theory to Practice. Pp. 16–22 in Proceedings of International Conference of the Learning Sciences, edited by A. Bruckman, M. Guzdial, J. Kolodner, and A. Ram. Charlottesville, Va.: Association for the Advancement of Computing in Education.

Lee, J.S., H. Cho, G. Gay, B. Davidson, and A. Ingraffea. 2003. Technology acceptance and social networking in distance learning. Educational Technology and Society 6(2): 50–61. Available online at: *http://ifets.ieee.org/periodical/6-2/6.html* (January 2004).

Leung, C.F. 2000. Assessment for learning: using SOLO taxonomy to measure design performance of design and technology students. International Journal of Technology and Design Education 10(2): 149–161.

Liu, X. 2000. Elementary school students' logical reasoning on rolling. International Journal of Technology and Design Education 10(1): 3–20.

Martin, B.L., and W. Wager. 1998. Introduction to special issue on integrating the cognitive and affective domains of learning. Educational Technology 38(6): 5–6.

Matthews, D., and E. Geist. 2002. Technological applications to support children's development of spatial awareness. Information Technology in Childhood Education Annual 321–336.

Mbarika, V.W., C.S. Sankar, and P.K. Raju. 2003. Identification of factors that lead to perceived learning improvements for female students. IEEE Transactions on Education 46(1): 26–36.

McClelland, M.E. 2001. Closing the IT gap for race and gender. Journal of Educational Computing Research 25(1): 5–15.

McCormick, R. 2004. Issues of learning and knowledge in technology education. International Journal of Technology and Design Education 14(1): 21–44.

McCormick, R., P. Murphy, and S. Hennessy. 1994. Problem-solving processes in technology education: a pilot study. International Journal of Technology and Design Education 4(1): 5–34.

McLaren, S.V. 2003. Achieving education for technological capability in Scotland. Journal of Technology Studies 29(1): 33–41. Available online at: *http://scholar.lib.vt.edu/ejournals/JTS/Winter-Spring-2003/pdf/mclaren.pdf* (January 2004).

Mioduser, D. 1998. Framework for the study of cognitive and curricular issues of technological problem solving. International Journal of Technology and Design Education 8(2): 84–167.

Mioduser, D., and D. Kipperman. 2002. Evaluation/modification cycles in junior high students: technological problem solving. International Journal of Technology and Design Education 12(2): 123–138.

Mitra, A., S. Lenzmeier, R. Avon, and M. Hazen. 2000. Gender and computer use in an academic institution: report from a longitudinal study. Journal of Educational Computing Research 23(1): 67–84.

Mitra, A., B. Lafrance, and S. McCullough. 2001. Differences in attitudes between women and men toward computerization. Journal of Educational Computing Research 25(3): 227–244.

Moshe, B., and D. Yaron. 1999. Integrating the Cognitive Research Trust (CoRT) Programme for creative thinking. Research in Science and Technological Education 17(2): 123–139.

National Research Council. 2001. Theoretical Foundations for Decision Making in Engineering Design. Washington, D.C.: National Academy Press. Available online at: *http://www.nap.edu/books/NI000481/html/* (January 2004).

Nissenbaum, H., and D. Walker. 1998. A grounded approach to social and ethical concerns about technology and education. Journal of Computer Information Systems 19(4): 411–432.

Nuthall, G. 1997. Understanding Student Thinking and Learning in the Classroom. Pp. 618–678 in International Handbook of Teachers and Teaching, vol. 2, edited by B.J. Biddle, T.L. Good, and I.F. Goodson. Boston: Kluwer Academic Publishers.

Parkinson, E. 1999. Re-constructing the construction kit—re-constructing childhood: a synthesis of the influences which have helped to give shape and form to kit-based construction activities in the primary school classroom. International Journal of Technology and Design Education 9(2): 94–173.

Putnam, R.T., and H. Borko. 2000. What do new views of knowledge and thinking have to say about research on teacher learning? Educational Researcher 29(1): 4–15.

Resnick, M., and S. Ocko. 1988. LEGO, Logo, and Design, Children's Learning Environments. Available online at: *http://www.ed.uiuc.edu/courses/edpsy490az-sp96/k12-technology/Resnick-Ocko/* (January 2004).

Rieber, L.P., N. Luke, and J. Smith. 1998. Project KID DESIGNER: constructivism at work through play. Middle School Computer Technology Journal 1(1). Available online at: *http://www.ncsu.edu/meridian/jan98/index.html* (January 2004).

Rogers, G., and J. Wallace. 2000. The wheels of the bus: children design in an early years classroom. Research in Science and Technological Education 18(1): 127–136.

Roppel, T.A., J.Y. Hung, S.W. Wentworth, and A.S. Hodel. 2000. An interdisciplinary laboratory sequence in electrical and computer engineering: curriculum design and assessment results. IEEE Transactions on Education 43(2): 143–152.

Roth, W.M. 2001. Learning science through technological design. Journal of Research in Science Teaching 38(7): 768–790.

Rowell, P.M. 2002. Peer interactions in shared technological activity: a study of participation. International Journal of Technology and Design Education 12(1): 1–22.

Rowell, P.M. 2004. Developing technological stance: children's learning in technology education. International Journal of Technology and Design Education 14(1): 45–59.

Rowell, P., S. Guilbert, and B. Gufstafson. 1997. The Nature of Technological Problem Solving: Perceptions of Engineers. Pp. 199–203 in International Organization for Science and Technology Education, 8th Symposium Proceedings: vol. 1, edited by K. Calhoun, R. Panwar, and S. Schrum. Edmonton, Alberta: University of Alberta.

Rowell, P.M., B.J. Gustafson, and S.M. Guilbert. 1999. Engineers in elementary classrooms: perceptions of learning to solve technological problems. Research in science and technological education 17(1): 13–109.

Salomon, G. 1990. Cognitive effects with and of technology. Communication Research 17(1): 26–44.

Schallies, M., A. Wellensiek, and L. Anja. 2002. The development of mature capabilities for understanding and valuing in technology through school project work: individual and structural preconditions. International Journal of Technology and Design Education 12(1): 41–58.

Seels, B., S. Campbell, and V. Talsma. 2003. Supporting excellence in technology through communities of learners. Educational Technology Research and Development 51(1): 91–104.

Selwyn, N. 2001. Turned on/switched off: exploring children's engagement with computers in primary school. Journal of Educational Computing Research 25(3): 245–266.

Steffe, L.P., and J. Gale. 1995. Constructivism in Education. Hillsdale, N.J.: Lawrence Erlbaum Associates.

Stein, S.J., M. Docherty, and R. Hannam. 1997. Making the processes of designing explicit within an information technology environment. International Journal of Technology and Design Education 13(2): 145–170.

Stein, S.J., C.J. McRobbie, and J. Ginns. 2000. Recognising uniqueness in the technology key learning area: the search for meaning. International Journal of Technology and Design Education 10(2): 105–123.

Suomala, J., and J. Alajaasi. 2002. Pupils' problem-solving processes in a complex computerized learning environment. Journal of Educational Computing Research 26(2): 155–176.

Todd, R., and P. Hutchinson. 2000. The Transfer of Design and Technology to the United States: A Case Study. Pp. 215–223 in Proceedings of the Design and Technology International Millennium Conference. Edited by R. Kimbell. Wellesborne, England: Design and Technology Association.

Twyford, J., E.-M. Jarvinen. 2000. The formation of children's technological concepts: a study of what it means to do technology from a child's perspective. Journal of Technology Education 12(1): 32–48.

Venville, G., J. Wallace, L. Renie, and J. Malone. 2000. Bridging the boundaries of compartmentalised knowledge: student learning in an integrated environment. Research in Science and Technological Education 18(1): 23–35.

Volk, K.S., and Y.W. Ming. 1999. Gender and technology in Hong Kong: a study of pupils' attitudes toward technology. International Journal of Technology and Design Education 9(1): 57–71.

Wagner, S.P. 1998. Robotics and children: science achievement and problem solving. Journal of Computing in Childhood Education 9(2): 149–192.

Wai, K., and M. Siu. 2003. Nurturing all-round engineering and product designers. International Journal of Technology and Design Education 13(3): 243–254.

Waks, S., and M. Merdler. 2003. Creative thinking of practical engineering students during a design project. Research in Science and Technological Education 21(1): 101–121.

Walmsley, B. 2003. Student Decision-Making: The Teacher's Role. Presented at the 66th International Technology Education Association Annual Conference: Teaching Decision Making in a Technological World, Albuquerque, New Mexico.

Welch, M. 1998. Students' use of three-dimensional modeling while designing and making a solution to a technological problem. International Journal of Technology and Design Education 8(3): 60–241.

Welch, M. 1999. Analyzing the tacit strategies of novice designers. Research in Science and Technological Education 17(1): 19–34.

Welch, M. 2000. Sketching: friend or foe to the novice designer? International Journal of Technology and Design Education 10(2): 125–148.

Welch, M., D. Barlex, and H.S. Lim. 2000. The strategic thinking of novice designers: discontinuity between theory and practice. Journal of Technology Studies 25(2): 34–44.

Wilson, V., and M. Harris. 2003. Designing the best: a review of effective teaching and learning of design and technology. International Journal of Technology and Design Education 13(3): 223–241.

Wu, C. 1997. Using articulate virtual laboratories in teaching energy conversion at the U.S. Naval Academy. Journal of Educational Technology System 26(2): 127–136.

Wu, T., R.L. Custer, and M.J. Dyrenfurth. 1996. Technological and personal problem solving styles: is there a difference? Journal of Technology Education 7(2): 55–71.

Engineering

Adams, R.S., J. Turns, and C.J. Atman. 2003. Educating effective engineering designers: the role of reflective practice. Design Studies 24(3): 275–294.

Ahmed, S., K.M. Wallace, and L.T.M. Blessing. 2003. Understanding the differences between how novice and experienced designers approach design tasks. Research in Engineering Design 14(2003): 1–11.

Atman, C.J., and K.M. Bursic. 1996. Teaching engineering design: can reading a textbook make a difference? Research in Engineering Design 8: 240–250.

Atman, C.J., J.R. Chimka, K.M. Brusic, and H.L. Nachtmann. 1999. A comparison of freshman and senior engineering design processes. Design Studies 20(2): 131–152.

Borges, A.T., C. Tecnico, and J.K. Gilbert. 1998. Models of magnetism. International Journal of Science Education 20(3): 361–378.

Borges, A.T., C. Tecnico, and J.K. Gilbert. 1999. Mental models of electricity. International Journal of Science Education 21(1): 95–117.

Bursic, K.M., C.J. Atman. 1997. Information gathering: a critical step for quality in the design process. Quality Management Journal 4(4): 60–74.

Cardella, M.E., C.J. Atman, R.S. Adams, and J. Turns. 2002. Engineering Student Design Processes: Looking at Evaluation Practices across Problems. Paper in the Proceedings of the 2002 American Society for Engineering Education Annual Conference and Exposition, Montreal, Canada. Washington, D.C.: ASEE.

Chi, M.T.H., J.D. Slotta, and N. De Leeuw. 1994. From things to processes: a theory of conceptual change for learning science concepts. Learning and Instruction 4: 27–43.

Collin, K. 2000. Development of Engineers' Conceptions of Learning at Work. Studies in Continuing Education 24(2): 133–152.

Deek, F.P., S.R. Hiltz, H. Kimmel, and N. Rotter. 1999. Cognitive assessment of students' problem solving and program development skills. Journal of Engineering Education 88(3): 317–326.

Duit, R., W. Jung, and V.V. Rhoneck, eds. 1985. Aspects of Understanding Electricity. Kiel, Germany: IPN.

Eastman, C.M., W.M. McCracken, and W.C. Newstetter, eds. 2001. Design Knowing and Learning: Cognition in Design Education. Newsletter published by Elsevier.

Ebenezer, J.V., and G.L. Erickson. 1996. Chemistry students' conceptions of solubility: a phenomenography. Science Education 80(2): 181–201.

Elger, D., J. Beller, S. Beyerlein, and B. Williams. 2003. Performance Criteria for Quality in Problem Solving. Paper in the Proceedings of the 2003 American Society for Engineering Education Annual Conference and Exposition, Montreal, Canada. Washington, D.C.: ASEE.

Finegold, M., and P. Gorsky. 1991. Students' concepts of force as applied to related physical systems: a search for consistency. International Journal of Science Education 13(1): 97–113.

Herbeaux, J.-L., and R. Bannerot. 2003. Cultural Influences in Design. Paper in the Proceedings of the 2003 American Society for Engineering Education Annual Conference and Exposition, Montreal, Canada. Washington, D.C.: ASEE.

Maull, W.B., and J. Berry. 2000. A questionnaire to elicit the mathematical concept images of engineering students. International Journal of Mathematical Education in Science and Technology 31(6): 899–917.

McGown, A., G. Green, and P.A. Rodgers. 1998. Visible ideas: information patterns of conceptual sketch activity. Design Studies 19(4): 431–453.

Mullins, C.A., C.J. Atman, and L.J. Shuman. 1999. Freshman engineers' performance when solving design problems. IEEE Transactions on Education 42(4): 281–287.

Pahl, G., P. Badke-Schaub, and E. Frankenberger. 1999. Resume of 12 years interdisciplinary empirical studies of engineering design in Germany. Design Studies 20(5): 481–494.

Palmer, D.H., and R.B. Flanagan. 1997. Readiness to change the conception that "motion-implies-force": a comparison of 12-year-old and 16-year-old students. Science Education 81(3): 317–331.

Römer, A., S. Leinert, and P. Sachse. 2000. External support of problem analysis in design problem solving. Research in Engineering Design 12(2000): 144–151.

Rozer, S., and L. Viennot. 1991. Students' reasoning in thermodynamics. International Journal of Science Education 13(2): 159–170.

Schütze, M., P. Sachse, and A. Romer. 2003. Support value of sketching in the design process. Research in Engineering Design 14(2003): 89–97.

Sobek, D.K. II. 2002a. Use of Journals to Evaluate Student Design Processes. Paper published in the proceedings of the 2002 American Society for Engineering Education Annual Conference and Exposition, June 16–19, 2002, Montreal, Quebec. Washington, D.C.: ASEE.

Sobek, D.K. II. 2002b. Preliminary Findings from Coding Student Design Journals. Paper published in the proceedings of the 2002 American Society for Engineering Education Annual Conference and Exposition, June 16–19, 2002, Montreal, Quebec. Washington, D.C.: ASEE.

Sobek, D.K. II. 2002c. Representation in Design: Data from Engineering Journals. Paper presented at the American Society for Engineering Education and Institute for Electrical and Electronics Engineering Frontiers in Education Annual Conference, November 6–9, Boston, Massachusetts. Piscataway, N.J.: IEEE.

Taber, K.S. 2001. Shifting sands: a case study of conceptual development as competition between alternative conceptions. International Journal of Science Education 23(7): 731–753.

Tytler, R. 2000. A comparison of year 1 and year 6 students' conceptions of evaporation and condensation: dimensions of conceptual progression. International Journal of Science Education 22(5): 447–467.

Walker, J.M.T., and P.H. King. 2003. Concept mapping as a form of student assessment and instruction in the domain of bioengineering. Journal of Engineering Education 92(2): 167–179.

Watson, J.R., T. Prieto, and J.S. Dillon. 1997. Consistency of students' explanations about combustion. Science Education 81(4): 425–443.

APPENDIX E
Instrument Summaries

Contents

Armed Services Vocational Aptitude Battery

Background

Sponsor/Creator	U.S. Department of Defense
Purpose	Assess potential of military recruits for job specialties in the armed forces; provide a standard for enlistment
What is measured	Knowledge and reasoning skills in eight areas
Target population	Young Americans interested in military careers
Item format	Multiple choice
Sample size	More than 900,000 high school students annually
Frequency of administration	Ongoing in its present form since 1968
Availability	Sample items available from various test preparation books (e.g., Kaplan ASVAB 2004 edition, Simon and Schuster)

Scope

The U.S. Department of Defense maintains and administers the Armed Services Vocational Aptitude Battery (ASVAB)[1] to assess the potential of military recruits for enlistment and various specialties. ASVAB is currently administered in three forms. High school students, the most common test takers, can take the form 18/19 version of the ASVAB as early as 10th grade. Recruiters can also administer a paper version or computer-adapted exam to prospective recruits who are no longer in

---

[1]ASVAB is a registered trademark of the U.S. Department of Defense.

school. ASVAB includes eight sections: general science, arithmetic reasoning, word knowledge, paragraph comprehension, auto and shop information, mathematics, mechanical comprehension, and electronics information.

Scores are reported in each area, and a simple equation is used to calculate a raw score, which is converted into a percentile score. Test takers also receive composite scores in verbal ability, math ability, and academic ability. Minimum percentile scores are required for enlistment; combinations of scores from the eight areas are used to qualify test takers for specialties in each branch of the military.

Sample Items

Readers wishing to get a sense of the types of items on ASVAB are encouraged to look at an ASVAB test-preparation book, such as *ASVAB, The Armed Services Vocational Aptitude Battery, 2004 Edition* (Simon and Schuster).

Committee Observations

The ASVAB exam is an appropriate instrument for the military to assess a broad range of knowledge and abilities among high school students and young adults. The sections on spatial reasoning, mechanical comprehension, and auto and shop information seem relevant to technological literacy. Despite the emphasis on technological topics, however, most of the items are very narrow in scope and require only factual recall or low-level application of knowledge. The auto and shop questions favor males, who tend to have more exposure in these areas.

Assessment of Performance in Design and Technology

Background

Sponsor/Creator   Richard Kimbell, et al. at the Technology Education Research Unit, Goldsmiths College, University of London, with funding from the U.K. Department of Education and Science

Purpose	Curriculum development, research
What is measured	Design capabilities
Target population	15-year-old students in the United Kingdom
Item format	90-minute open-ended design tasks, half-day modeling tasks, and a long-term project
Sample size	Approximately 10,000 students from more than 700 schools in the United Kingdom
Frequency of administration	Once, in 1989
Availability	Kimbell, R., K. Stables, T. Wheeler, A. Wozniak, and V. Kelly. 1991. *The Assessment of Performance in Design and Technology: The Final Report of the APU Design and Technology Project.* London (D/010/B/91): Schools Examinations and Assessment Council/Central Office of Information. 285 pp.

Scope

The Assessment Performance Unit (APU) was established in 1975 to monitor student achievement in British schools. Over time, the focus of APU shifted from assessment to providing support for curriculum development. In 1985, APU commissioned an assessment of design and technology achievement to gauge how well students performed in design and technology activities. The assessment had three parts.

The first part, administered to approximately 9,000 students, was a 90-minute pencil-and-paper test on which students were asked to complete a structured activity. Twenty-one activities were created for the assessment each involving one of three contexts: people, environment, or industry. Each activity had a specific focus: starting point, early idea, development of a solution, evaluation of a product, or modeling. A "starting-point" activity might ask students to suggest new or improved products or systems that could be designed for the garden. A "developing-solutions" activity might ask students to design a self-watering plant pot that could be stacked and interlocked. The activities ranged from closed, well-defined questions to open, loosely defined tasks.

In the second part of the assessment, about 1,500 students who completed the paper-and-pencil test, took part in a half-day, team-based modeling activity in which they could use various soft and rigid modeling materials, such as rubber bands, beads, string, and fabric, to create a prototype design.

The final assessment component involved approximately 70 of the 1,500 students from the second test. The students participated in long-term (up to nine months) school projects. Students were regularly interviewed to develop a long-term history of individual performance.

In all three assessment components, researchers tried to determine how well students formed ideas, organized their time and resources, considered alternative solutions, and modeled solutions that could be evaluated against the user's needs. Activities were evaluated in three areas: the processes in design and development, the quality of communication, and conceptual understanding. Holistic marks indicating a student's overall capabilities were awarded based on pre-established characteristics of good and poor performance. Individual discriminators of capability, questions to ascertain if a student's responses included certain predetermined components, were also used to evaluate performance.

Sample Items

- Developing-solutions, concept-model activity for the 90-minute paper-and-pencil test. (Concept-model activities were presented to students in physical form. Ready-made ideas presented in half-developed form allowed students to proceed quickly into the design stage of the project.)

  When considering the needs of the elderly, a group of young people recognized the weakness of built-in cooker timers and decided to make one that was more suitable.

  A member of the team came up with the idea that a portable timer could be designed that was set by a twisting action.

  Design a timer for the elderly that:

a) is portable
b) is set with a twisting action
c) will sound an alarm when the time runs out
d) is a suitable size and shape

Your task today is to take this idea and develop it as far as you can in the time available.

(This activity included a drawing of a twist-type timer.)

- Modeling activity for the half-day, team-based assessment

The team has decided to make a bird scarer for use in gardens and allotments.

A member of the team came up with the idea that "spinning in the wind" advertising could be developed for scaring birds.

Design a bird scarer that:

a) Has sails or vanes that catch the slightest breeze
b) Makes "bird scaring" movements
c) Gives off "bird scaring" sounds from a sound box
d) Fits into the environment

Your task today is to take this idea and develop it as far as you can in the time available.

(This activity included two drawings. The first was of a wind-sail mounted on top of a sound box. The second depicted a garden and was accompanied by a number of thought-provoking questions, such as "what about high winds?", "what makes the sound?", and "is it safe?")

Committee Observations

This instrument reflects a curricular emphasis on "design and technology" in the U.K. educational system. Assessment activities seem to require higher order cognitive capabilities. The evaluation framework, which includes holistic, procedural, communication, and conceptual elements based on four domains (task clarification, investigation, solution generation, and appraisal), is conceptually robust.

This instrument is complex and would be difficult and expensive to administer, score, and report on a large scale. The task-centered approach to assessment offers real insights into design competency but does not address technological literacy in the broad sense defined by the committee.

Awareness Survey on Genetically Modified Foods

Background

Sponsor/Creator	Jane Macoubrie, Patrick Hamlett, and Carolyn Miller, North Carolina State University, with funding from the National Science Foundation
Purpose	Research on public involvement in decision making on science and technology issues
What is measured	Knowledge and attitudes toward genetically modified foods
Target population	American adults
Item format	Multiple choice
Sample size	45 adults in North Carolina
Frequency of administration	Once, in 2001
Availability	Jane Macoubrie, Department of Communication, North Carolina State University

Scope

This project was inspired by the Danish practice of providing opportunities for citizens to participate in "consensus conferences" to discuss science and technology issues and make policy recommendations to the government. Conference participants are non-experts who are provided with extensive background information on a subject and then convened to discuss the issue. Researchers at North Carolina State University conducted a Danish-style consensus conference in 2001 to assess the feasibility of consensus conferences in the United States. This survey, which was administered to participants prior to the conference, included 20 multiple-choice questions addressing ethical and scientific issues, as well as current practices in the farming of genetically modified crops.

Sample Items[2]

- Can genes escape from genetically modified crops and jump to other plants?

  A. Yes and they often do
  B. Only to some crops, but those crops aren't genetically modified
  C. Only during rare climatic conditions
  D. No, genes cannot move from species to species without human intervention
  E. I don't know

  (Suggested correct answer: A)

- To keep genetically modified crops separate from traditional crops, farmers are currently required to do which of the following?

  A. Use different machines to harvest each field
  B. Use different storage bins and silos
  C. Transport separately to the production facility
  D. None of the above
  E. I don't know

  (Suggested correct answer: D)

- Ethical arguments against the genetic modification of food products include:

  A. Genetically modified crops violate species integrity
  B. Biotechnology changes too fast to effectively understand and regulate it
  C. The belief that scientists should not "play God"
  D. All of the above
  E. I don't know

  (Suggested correct answer: D)

---

[2]Reprinted with permission of the North Carolina Citizens' Forum Project Team

Committee Observations

This content-specific survey does not require higher order thinking skills. In addition, the level of factual knowledge required to perform well is likely to be beyond the capability of most individuals in the target population. It would be interesting to administer a survey like this before and after participation in a consensus-type conference to determine what, if any, learning has taken place.

Design-Based Science

Background

Sponsor/Creator	David Fortus, University of Michigan
Purpose	Curriculum development, research
What is measured	Science and technology knowledge and transfer of design skills to new situations
Target population	9th- and 10th-grade students in the United States
Item format	Multiple-choice and open-ended questions and design skills projects
Sample size	92 students in 9th and 10th grade in one Michigan public high school
Frequency of administration	Once, in 2001–2002
Availability	Dissertation held at University of Michigan and an article describing the instrument (Journal of Research in Science Training 41(10): 1081–1110).

Scope

David Fortus developed the design-based science (DBS) curriculum as part of the dissertation for his Ph.D. The DBS curriculum has three units: structures for extreme environments, environmentally safe batteries, and safer cell phones. The course instructor (not Fortus) started each unit by administering a pre-instruction content-knowledge test. The test was followed by a number of weeks of classroom teaching on the science and technology related to the unit, as well as instruction in the design process. At the end of each unit, students were given an exam that included 13–15 multiple-choice questions and 2–5 open-ended questions. Multiple-choice questions required low, medium, and high cognitive skills; open-ended questions required medium and high cognitive skills (as determined by Fortus).

To test the transfer of design skills, students in groups of four were asked to apply knowledge from each unit to a new situation. The structures for extreme environments unit was followed by a design project requiring the design of a kite that could fly a mile high. The environmentally safe batteries unit was followed by a project requiring the design of a battery for an artificial heart. The unit on safer cell phones was followed by a project requiring the design of a hearing protector for rock musicians. Groups were evaluated in five categories: design variables; gathering of information; comparison of options; model, drawing, or diagram; and design evaluation. All four students in each group earned the same grade on the project.

Sample Items[3]

• Safer cell phones unit multiple-choice question

A cell phone is similar to a microwave oven because:

A. Both have been proven to be dangerous to your health
B. They both emit microwaves
C. They operate on the same voltage

---

[3]From Fortus, D., R.C. Dershimer, J.S. Krajcik, R.W. Marx, and R. Mamlok-Naaman. 2004. Design-based science (DBS) and student learning. Journal of Research in Science Teaching 41(10): 1081–1110.

D. They both operate on the same frequency

• Environmentally safe batteries unit open-ended question

A group of students builds a battery from two strips of aluminum metal immersed in a beaker of distilled water. They connect the battery to the voltmeter and are surprised that the voltmeter shows no reading. Explain what's wrong with their battery and what they should change in order to measure a voltage reading. Assume that the voltmeter and connecting wires are not broken, and that you can add or change materials to the setup if necessary.

• Structures for extreme environments unit assessment of design skills

Can you design a kite that will fly one mile high?

Students were evaluated based on their analysis in the following areas (criteria were given to students with the assignment):

1) Why won't a standard kite you can buy at any toy store be able to fly one mile high? If you understand this, you then will know what will have to be the special characteristics of your kite.
2) Where did you gather the information you needed (encyclopedias, books in the library, the web, hobby shops, family and friends, magazines, and so on)? What was the information you gathered and what was its relevance to the kite you designed?
3) Did you identify all the factors that needed to be considered in designing the kite?
4) Did your group come up with a range of design options? What were they?
5) Did you select a single option from this range? Did you justify your decision based on functional, scientific, aesthetic or other considerations?
6) How did you describe your solution? Did you use technical and concept drawings? Did you build models?
7) Did you develop a plan for testing the kite and its components?

Committee Observations

The knowledge-transfer aspect of this instrument is intriguing. Knowledge transfer in the context of design seems to require higher order thinking, and requiring both written answers and an evaluation of the processes used to come to those answers further suggests a focus on higher order thinking. The curriculum and the assessment could be improved by placing more emphasis on technological capabilities.

Design Team Assessments for Engineering Students

Background

Sponsor/Creator	Transferable Integrated Design Engineering Education (TIDEE), a consortium of schools under the direction of Denny C. Davis, Washington State University
Purpose	Assess students' knowledge, performance, and evaluation of the design process; evaluate student teamwork and communication skills
What is measured	Student knowledge and skills in engineering design
Target population	Baccalaureate engineering students
Item format	Constructed-response, team design exercise, reflective essay
Sample size	Unknown
Frequency of administration	Unknown
Availability	*http://www.tidee.cea.wsu.edu/assessment-tools/*

Scope

This three-part assessment was developed in 2002. The first component, intended for early-stage baccalaureate engineering students, is a formative assessment of students' knowledge of the engineering design process, teamwork, and design communication. It includes three constructed-response questions and requires 15 to 20 minutes to administer. A detailed evaluation rubric identifies seven criteria for scoring each question.

The second component addresses students' ability to perform crucial engineering design processes and is intended for pre-capstone design-project students. The assessment is administered to teams of four students who are allowed 35 minutes for the design activity and 7 minutes to complete the associated worksheets. A three-part evaluation rubric focuses on the steps of the design process rather than on the final project.

The final component, which builds on the second, requires a reflective essay in which students are asked to explain and improve upon the design process, as well as to consider the role of teamwork and communication in their design effort. The essay rubric evaluates how well students reflect on their team design experience.

Sample Items[4]

- Component 1: Knowledge of engineering design process, teamwork, and design communication

  > In general, a process is an ordered set of activities to accomplish a goal. In the space below, describe and/or diagram your understanding of the **engineering design process**.

  > > (Suggested correct answer mentions gathering information, defining requirements, generating ideas, evaluating ideas, making decisions, implementing ideas, and developing a process.)

- Component 2: Ability to perform engineering design processes (in groups of four)

[4]From Davis, D., S. Beyerlein, K. Gentili, L. McKenzie, M. Trevisan, C. Atman, R. Adams, J. McCauley, P. Thompson, P. Daniels, R. Christianson, T. Rutar, and D. McLean. 2002. Design Team Knowledge Assessment, Part 1 of the Design Team Readiness Assessment developed by the Transferable Integrated Design Engineering Education (TIDEE) Consortium. Available online at: *http://www.tidee.wsu.edu*.

Your group is charged with developing **a testing procedure** to convincingly show how well an assigned hand tool (or other device) **satisfies one key customer expectation**. Your testing procedure should be described such that another engineer could independently implement your procedure and obtain the same results.

A. Describe your team organization and member responsibilities assigned to ensure that your team can complete this activity effectively and in the 35 minutes allotted.

B. Identify customer expectations of the tool (list and give brief explanation of each).

C. What source or sources of information did you use to aid in identifying customer expectations?

D. Identify the most essential customer expectation. Justify your selection.

E. Describe a complete testing procedure for your **one selected** feature. Itemize steps. As appropriate, include sketches or specifics about data collection and analysis.

(Suggested correct answer: (A) Credit is awarded for leadership assignment, explanation of time/task management, and details of roles and responsibilities of team members. (B) Credit is awarded for identifying at least five customer needs and explaining three of them. (C) Credit is awarded for identifying at least two sources of information. (D) Credit is awarded for selecting only one customer expectation as the most important and providing a reasonable explanation of its importance. (E) Points are awarded for listing relevant ideas for testing, defining detailed steps of testing procedures, considering variability and replication of the results, defining a means of quantifying test results, and providing criteria for the tool to pass the test.)

- Component 3: Understanding of the engineering design process and analysis of team design performance

Prepare a 2-page essay, double-spaced in 12-point font, demonstrating your understanding of team-based engineering design processes focused on meeting a customer's needs. Reflecting on your recent team design experience

(Component 2), explain what you did as a team, why it worked or didn't work, and how you could improve your team's performance. Specifically address these issues with respect to (1) the engineering design process; (2) teamwork; and (3) design communication.

(Suggested correct answer: A correct answer will include a discussion of actions and occurrences in the group, explain why things were effective or not, and propose improvements in the team design process in six areas: customer focus, management of the design process, assignment of roles/responsibilities, management of task/time, oral/team dynamics, and writing the team log.)

Committee Observations

The multiple forms of assessment and open format provide a broad exploration of what students know about the design process. Although intended for a highly focused audience of baccalaureate engineering students, this assessment could also be used for teachers, high school students, and perhaps even middle school students. The reflective essay may be the most valuable part of the assessment, because it encourages metacognition but does not require specific jargon for a positive evaluation. However, this instrument does not require knowledge transfer, which seems to disconnect it from a real-world design situation. Students could perform well on this assessment without believing in any of the lessons of teamwork or the design process. That is, by memorizing jargon and the school-learned steps of the design process, a student could do well without demonstrating higher order thinking skills.

Design Technology (Higher Level)

Background

Sponsor/Creator   International Baccalaureate Organization, Geneva, Switzerland

Purpose   Student achievement (part of qualification for diploma)

What is measured	Knowledge and capability in technological design
Target population	Students in IB programs, ages 16 to 19
Item format	Multiple-choice, data-based, short-answer, and extended-response items
Sample size	IB students throughout the world following an "experimental sciences" curriculum
Frequency of administration	Regularly since 2003
Availability	IB North America, *ibna@ibo.org*

Scope

The International Baccalaureate (IB) Organization oversees the IB Diploma Program, which offers intensive pre-university courses and exams. Students in the program choose the focus of their intensive study while still pursuing a broad education in the sciences and humanities. The IB Diploma Program offers courses in six academic subjects: language A1, a second language, individuals and societies, experimental sciences, mathematics and computer sciences, and the arts. Students must take at least one course in each area. Diploma candidates must pursue at least three, but not more than four, subjects at the higher level (at least 240 teaching hours). All other courses are taken at the standard level (150 teaching hours).

Students who choose to focus their studies on the experimental sciences take courses in biology, chemistry, environmental systems, physics, and design technology. The syllabus for the standard-level design technology course stipulates that the curriculum must cover six areas of design technology: designers and the design cycle; the responsibility of the designer; materials, manufacturing processes, and techniques; production systems; and clean technology and green design. The curriculum for higher level courses covers these additional topics: raw material to final product; microstructures and macrostructures; and appropriate technologies.

Items in the three-part assessment—called Papers 1, 2, and 3—

are grouped into three increasingly challenging objectives. At the Objective 1 level, students are required to define, list, or measure, among other tasks. At the Objective 2 level, students are required to compare, calculate, estimate, and outline. At the highest level, Objective 3, students are asked to deduce, predict, evaluate, and design. Student performance is also evaluated by a teacher-directed "internal assessment," which includes a design project. The rubric for the internal assessment includes student planning, data collection, data processing and presentation, and manipulative and personal skills.

Sample Items[5]

• Paper 1, higher level, multiple-choice (November 2004)

Which technique fuses solid particles with heat and pressure without completely liquefying them?

    A. Injection molding
    B. Casting
    C. Sintering
    D. Lamination

(Suggested correct answer: C)

• Paper 2, higher level, data-based (November 2004)

Figure 1 shows the London Eye, which was designed as a landmark project for the millennium. It is like a giant bicycle wheel (circumference 424 m) with a central hub and spindle (330 tonnes) connected to outer and inner rims by a total of 64 cable spokes, each 75 m long. 32 passenger capsules are mounted around the rim with a maximum capacity of 25 people per capsule. The entire structure stands 135 m high and is supported from one side only (see Figure 2). The wheel turns continuously anti-clockwise, during operating hours, at 0.26 m/s, even when people are getting on and off. As passengers travel from X to Y in fine weather they can see over 40 km in each direction (see Figure 3).

(Figure 1 is an aerial photograph of the London Eye on the Thames River in London. Figure 2 is an engineering drawing of the London

---

[5]Reprinted with permission of International Baccalaureate Organization.

Eye that depicts the A-frame design and how the structure is supported. Figure 3 shows a circle representing the London Eye and demonstrates the height at which optimum views are possible. When radii are drawn to points X and Y, they form a right angle. The exam question has 10 parts; 3 are reproduced below.)

(a) Calculate how long to the nearest minute passengers enjoy the optimum views as the capsule they are inside is rotated from X to Y, as shown in Figure 3.
(b) List two dominant considerations in the design of the London Eye.
(c) State the importance of tensile forces in relation to the design of the wheel.

- Paper 2, higher level, extended response (November 2004)

Figure 6 shows the Tizio lamp, a steel desk lamp using a low voltage/ low wattage light bulb designed by Richard Sapper in 1972. In this design there are two hollow beams connecting the electric cables which can be moved to adjust the angle and height of a light source over a working surface. Each beam has a counterbalanced weight at the end to keep the whole lamp in equilibrium.

(Figure 6 is a schematic drawing of the Tizio lamp, with diagrams showing the characteristics described in the question. There are 7 parts to this question; 2 are reproduced below.)

(a) Outline one suitable treatment or finish for the steel lamp.
(b) Suggest three ways in which the designer has balanced form with function in the design of the lamp.

- Paper 3, higher level, extended response (November 2004)

Explain three problems associated with existing agricultural practices that have led to increased interest in organic agriculture.

Committee Observations

This instrument does a very good job of assessing knowledge related to the IB curriculum. Paper 1 tests basic knowledge at the application level. Papers 2 and 3 require in-depth, higher order processing skills. The assessment seems particularly effective at teasing out knowledge of the design process. All three papers require technical knowledge beyond what might be considered basic technological literacy. Many of the items are difficult and may be appropriate only for 12th-grade or post-secondary students who have completed the appropriate coursework.

Engineering K–12 Center Teacher Survey

Background

Sponsor/Creator	American Society for Engineering Education (ASEE)
Purpose	Inform outreach efforts to K–12 teachers
What is measured	Attitudes, knowledge, and interest about engineering
Target population	K–12 teachers
Item format	Survey
Sample size	Approximately 400 teachers
Frequency of administration	Continuously available
Availability	*http://www.engineeringk12.org/educators/ taking_a_closer_look/survey1.cfm*

Scope

ASEE uses this instrument to help shape communications, products, and services for the K–12 community. The instrument's 44-question survey probes teachers' perceptions of the accessibility of various careers, including engineering, to women and minorities. It also addresses teachers' attitudes toward engineers as well as the efficacy of using engineering to help teach other subjects. In addition to tapping attitudes, the survey collects demographic data, including gender, ethnicity, age, type of school, years of teaching experience, and family and friendship connections to an engineer.

Sample Items

- Indicate whether you strongly disagree, disagree, are neutral, agree, or strongly agree with the following statement:

  Engineering can be a way to help teach students language arts.

  > (Strongly disagree: 1.4 percent, disagree: 8.1 percent, neutral: 28.7 percent, agree: 47.2 percent, strongly agree: 14.6 percent)

- Indicate whether you strongly disagree, disagree, are neutral, agree, or strongly agree with the following statement:

  Majoring in engineering is harder than majoring in English.

  > (Strongly disagree: 2.1 percent, disagree: 9.4 percent, neutral: 25.0 percent, agree: 30.9 percent, strongly agree: 32.5 percent)

- For which of the following careers would an engineering degree prepare you? Please select all that apply.
  ___ NASCAR crew chief
  ___ Sneaker designer
  ___ Business consultant
  ___ Pop music producer
  ___ Perfume maker
  ___ None of the above

  > (NASCAR crew chief: 89.9 percent; sneaker designer: 96.3 percent; business consultant: 75.5 percent; pop music producer: 57.9 percent; perfume maker: 72.4 percent; none of the above: 2.4 percent)

Committee Observations

This instrument does not, nor is it intended to, assess higher order thinking. However, by assessing teachers' attitudes about engineering, the survey does convey a general sense of how effective teachers might be at encouraging student technological literacy. If teachers' attitudes indicate inaccurate perceptions of engineering, it is unlikely they will be able to teach effectively technology-related concepts and skills or provide sound advice to students about opportunities for technology-related careers.

Eurobarometer: Europeans, Science and Technology

Background

Sponsor/Creator	European Union (EU) Directorate-General for Press and Communication
Purpose	Monitor changes in public views of science and technology to assist decision making by policy makers
What is measured	Opinions about science and technology
Target population	People 15 years and older in the EU
Item format	Survey
Sample size	16,029 people in all 14 EU member states
Frequency of administration	Surveys on various topics conducted regularly since 1973; this poll was taken in May/June of 2001
Availability	*http://europa.eu.int/comm/research/press/2001/pr0612en-report.pdf*

Scope

Participants (approximately 1,000 from each country) were asked to give their opinions on questions related to seven areas of science and technology: (1) information, interest, knowledge; (2) values, science, technology; (3) responsibilities and accountability of scientists; (4) genetically modified food; (5) levels of confidence; (6) young people and the scientific vocation crisis; and (7) European scientific research. Although some questions in the "information, interest, knowledge" section included questions testing knowledge of general science and technology, most questions asked only for opinions. The option of "don't know" was always available.

Sample Items

- Information, interest, and knowledge question related to how people get scientific information

Participants were asked if they tended to agree or disagree with the following statement.

> **I prefer to watch television programs on science and technology rather than read articles on this subject.**

>> (66 percent of participants agreed with this statement, 24 percent disagreed, and 10 percent said they did not know.)

- Information, interest, and knowledge question related to knowledge and perception of topical scientific subjects

Participants were asked to indicate whether the following statement is true or false.

> **Mad cow disease (bovine spongiform encephalopathy) is due to the addition of hormones in cattle feed.**

>> (Suggested correct answer: false. 49 percent of participants thought the statement was true, 32 percent thought it was false, and 19 percent did not know.)

- Values, science, and technology question on optimism regarding science

Participants were asked whether or not they agreed with the following statement.

Thanks to scientific and technological progress, the earth's natural resources will be inexhaustible.

(21 percent agreed with the statement, 61 percent disagreed, and 17 percent did not know.)

Committee Observations

This is predominantly an opinion survey. Thus, it does not provide a meaningful assessment of technological literacy. However, it does demonstrate the importance of measuring public perceptions of science and technology. Most questions are straightforward and focus on current issues, but a few questions in the "perceptions of scientific methods" section appear to require some higher order thinking. In addition, the poll has a much stronger emphasis on environmental and biorelated science and technology issues (e.g., mad cow disease and genetically modified food) than might be expected in a similar American survey.

European Commission Candidate Countries Eurobarometer: Science and Technology

Background

Sponsor/Creator   Gallup Organization of Hungary, with funding from the European Commission

Purpose   Monitor public opinion on science and technology issues of concern to policy makers

What is measured   Opinions about various science and technology issues

Target population	People 15 years and older
Item format	Survey
Sample size	12,247 adults in 13 EU candidate countries
Frequency of administration	Periodically since 1973; this survey was administered in November 2002
Availability	*http://www.europa.eu.int/comm/ public_opinion/archives/cceb/2002/ 2002.3_science_technology.pdf*

Scope

The European Union (EU) regularly monitors the opinions of citizens of member states about issues of concern to policy makers. This poll extends that model to a group of countries seeking membership in the EU. Poll questions primarily solicit opinions about science and technology, but a few questions attempt to assess general knowledge of these subjects. The accompanying report presents findings in eight areas: (1) information, interest, knowledge; (2) values, science, and technology; (3) the morality of science; (4) the bovine spongiform encephalopathy (BSE) epidemic; (5) food based on genetically modified organisms; (6) the scientific profession; (7) the scientific vocational situation; and (8) European scientific research. Survey results are weighted by age, sex, region, profession, religion, size of locality, educational level, and marital status. The results of this survey were compared to those of a poll in 2001, Eurobarometer 55.2, Europeans, Science and Technology (also reviewed by the committee), that asked similar questions.

Sample Items

• Information, interest, knowledge related to fundamental scientific facts

Here is a little quiz. For each of the following statements, please tell me if you think it is true or false. If you don't know, say so, and we will go on to the next one.

Antibiotics kill viruses as well as bacteria.

> (Suggested correct answer: False. 23 percent in candidate countries and 40 percent in member countries answered correctly.)

- Values, science, and technology question on superstition, ignorance about science and pre-modern nostalgia

  I will now read out some statements about science, technology, or the environment. For each statement, please tell me if you tend to agree or tend to disagree.

  In my daily life, it is not important to know about science.

  > (In candidate countries, 37 percent tended to agree and 52 percent tended to disagree. In member countries, 42 percent tended to agree and 49 percent tended to disagree.)

- Lessons from the BSE epidemic

  There has been much discussion about responsibilities for the "mad cow disease" problem. Could you please tell me if you tend to agree or disagree with the following statements?

  The food industry carried a major part of the responsibility.

  > (51 percent of those polled in candidate countries tended to agree with this statement. 74 percent of those polled in EU member countries tended to agree.)

Committee Observations

Although this instrument mostly reflects opinions rather than knowledge or capabilities, some aspects of these polls are worth examining more closely. For example, correlating opinions and knowledge with religion and educational level, among other factors, may be useful for this type of assessment. In terms of technological literacy, however, the poll does not assess design or technology skills of any kind. Nor does it require higher order thinking.

Future City Competition—Judges Manual

Background

Sponsor/Creator	Engineers Week Committee, a consortium of professional and technical societies and U.S. corporations
Purpose	To help rate and rank design projects and essays submitted to the Future City Competition
What is measured	Design, writing, and presentation skills
Target population	7th- and 8th-grade American students
Item format	Scoring sheets with numerical scales (e.g., 0–5 and 0–10) to indicate performance on various parameters
Sample size	Approximately 30,000 students each year
Frequency of administration	Yearly since 1992
Availability	*http://www.futurecity.org/docs/ 2004JudgesManual.pdf*

Scope

In the Future City Competition, teams composed of three students, a teacher, and an engineer-mentor create a computer city design with SimCity software and a physical, scale model of part of the city. At the competition, students deliver a short, oral presentation to the judges in which they describe their model and computer simulation. The students also write an essay that describes how technology can meet an important social need. In 2005, the essay topic was "How can futuristic transportation systems effectively use aggregate materials—crushed stone, sand, and gravel—as a basic construction product?" Winners of regional competitions are invited to a national competition in Washington, D.C. The instrument is part of the manual judges use to evaluate student submissions. It includes specific criteria for awarding points in five areas: computer evaluation of city (standard set of questions about the group's SimCity model), computer city design, city model, presentation, and essay/abstract.

Sample Items

(The following are some of the criteria that the judges use to evaluate the students' designs.)

- Computer city design—transportation criteria (graded on a scale of 0 to 5 points)

    1) Does the public transportation system provide full mobility for the people? (rail, subway, and buses)
    2) Is there adequate mobility for the transport of goods and services? (rail and roads)
    3) Is there a seaport and an airport in the city?

- City model—creativity criteria (graded on a scale of 0 to 10 points)

    1) Does the city illustrate futuristic concepts?
    2) Are there different sizes and shapes of buildings?
    3) Are different types of building materials used?
    4) Did any of the building components incorporate recycled materials?

- Team presentation of city design and model—cooperation criteria (graded on a scale of 0 to 10 points)

    1) How well do the students work as a team during their presentation?
    2) How well do the students work as a team during the Question and Answer session by the judges?
    3) Are all the students able to answer questions about their city, or does only one student know all the answers?

Committee Observations

The Future City Competition allows students to combine an open-ended, engineering design task with communication skills, use of technology, teamwork and an innovative, out-of-the-box thinking exercise. These activities foster higher-order thinking and allow students to be assessed in areas that have historically been extremely difficult to gauge with standard paper-and-pencil exams. This type of assessment can be very expensive to administer, although Future City relies on volunteer judges local to the competition venue. The instrument does not allow for individual assessment, which may present accountability problems. Despite the detailed judge's manual, it may be extremely difficult to grade such projects consistently.

Gallup Poll on What Americans Think About Technology (2001, 2004)

Background

Sponsor/Creator	International Technology Education Association (ITEA), with funding from the National Science Foundation and National Aeronautics and Space Administration
Purpose	Determine public knowledge and perceptions of technology to inform efforts to change and shape public views
What is measured	Public understanding, opinions, and attitudes about technology and technological literacy
Target population	American adults
Item format	Survey
Sample size	1,000 people in 2001; 800 in 2004
Frequency of administration	Twice, in 2001 and 2004
Availability	Contact ITEA, which commissioned the poll, at *http://www.iteawww.org*

Scope

In 2001, ITEA contracted with the Gallup organization to conduct a survey of Americans' understanding, attitudes, and beliefs about technology and technological literacy. ITEA was particularly interested in measuring public opinion about the importance of technological literacy. The 17-question telephone poll of 1,000 randomly selected Americans resulted in three major conclusions: (1) Americans believe technological literacy is important for everyone; (2) technology is understood very narrowly as being computers and the Internet; and (3) most people believe that schools should include the study of technology in their curricula.

Three years later, ITEA and Gallup conducted a follow-up poll, in which they repeated 5 questions from the first poll and introduced 11 new ones to build on and extend the findings of the first poll. The 2004 poll examined seven areas: (1) public concepts of technology; (2) the importance of being knowledgeable about technology; (3) the impact of technology on daily life and the world; (4) what people want to know and what they do know about technology: (5) decision making regarding technology and technological literacy; (6) differences based on gender: (7) and technology and education. For both polls, demographic information was collected, including age, gender, race, grade/educational level, and geographic location.

Sample Items

• Public understanding of technology (2001 and 2004)

When you hear the word "technology," what first comes to mind?

(In the 2001 survey, 67 percent of respondents answered computers; 4 percent electronics; 2 percent education; 2 percent new inventions; 1 percent or less all other answers. In the 2004 survey, 68 percent answered computers; 5 percent electronics; 2 percent advancement; 2 percent Internet; 1 percent or less all other answers.)

• Knowledge of technology (2001)

Tell me if each of the following statements is true or false. How about:

1. Using a portable phone while in the bathtub creates the possibility of being electrocuted.
2. FM radios operate free of static.
3. A car operates through a series of explosions.
4. A microwave heats food from the outside to the inside.

> (1. Correct answer is False. 46 percent of respondents thought this statement was true; 51 percent said it was false. 2. Correct answer is true. 26 percent answered true; 72 percent false. 3. Correct answer is true. 82 percent said true; 15 percent false. 4. Correct answer is false. 37 percent said true; 62 percent false.)

• Influence on technology-related decision making (2004)

How much influence do you think people like yourself have on decisions about such things as the fuel efficiency of cars, the construction of roads in your community, and genetically modified foods? Would you say a great deal, some, very little, or no influence?

> (9 percent of respondents said a great deal; 32 percent said some; 40 percent said very little; and 19 percent said no influence.)

Committee Observations

Both polls addressed aspects of the ITEA Standards of Technological Literacy related to the nature of technology, technology and society, and abilities for a technological world. Although the polls did not explicitly assess higher order thinking, some of the questions may have prompted participants to think deeply about certain issues, for example how technology is defined. On the whole, the polls were well designed, and the questions were clear and unbiased. However, opinion polls do not always yield valid information. Responses may represent confidence rather than competence. That is, a self-assessment of a person's knowledge or capability may not reflect reality.

ICT Literacy Assessment

Background

Sponsor/Creator	Educational Testing Service (ETS)
Purpose	Proficiency testing
What is measured	Ability to use digital technology, communication tools, and/or networks to solve information-related problems
Target population	High school students, community college students, and freshmen and sophomores in four-year colleges (core assessment); rising juniors at four-year colleges (advanced assessment)
Item format	14 4-minute and one 15-minute simulated, scenario-based tasks delivered via the Web
Sample size	Approximately 4,500 examinees at 31 campuses (January through April 2005 administration of advanced assessment)
Frequency of administration	Advanced assessment launched in January 2005 (2006 test window was January 23–April 3; continuous testing to begin in August 2006). Pilot testing of the core assessment was January 23–February 17 (2006 test window was April 5–May 5; continuous testing to begin in August 2006.)
Availability	Test details and sample items available at *http://www.ets.org/ictliteracy*

Scope

The ICT Literacy Assessment was developed by ETS in collaboration with a consortium of seven institutions of higher education. The work of the consortium was guided by an International ICT Literacy Panel that published a framework document, "Digital Transformation: A Framework for ICT Literacy," in 2002.[6] The ETS proficiency model has seven elements:

Define—Use ICT tools to identify and appropriately represent an information need.

Access—Collect and/or retrieve information in digital environments.

Manage—Use ICT tools to apply an existing organizational or classification scheme for information.

Integrate—Interpret and represent information, such as by using ICT tools to synthesize, summarize, compare, and contrast information from multiple sources.

Evaluate—Judge the degree to which information satisfies the needs of the task in ICT environments (including determining authority, bias, and timeliness of materials).

Create—Adapt, apply, design, or invent information in ICT environments.

Communicate—Communicate information properly in its context (audience, media) in ICT environments.

According to ETS, academic institutions can use test results to decide about new course offerings, determine which courses need additional resources, and provide data for accreditation purposes. Students can use assessment results to help select courses and majors or determine readiness for the workforce or graduate school. Tests cost $35 each, and initial orders must include a minimum of 100 tests.

Sample Items

Actual test items are not publicly available. The ETS website contains a demo with three sample tasks.

Display and Interpret Data. Examinees create a visual representation of data to answer two research questions.

---

[6]Available online at: *http://www.ets.org/Media/Tests/Information_and_ Communication_Technology_Literacy/ictreport.pdf.*

Scenario: As part of a project for a cultural studies class, examine trends in the public's taste in books and use a graph creator to show how the popularity of different types of books has varied since the advent of television.

Advanced Search. Examinees construct an advanced search based on a complex information need. Scenario: Search a university library database for information about plans that various California state or municipal governing bodies (excluding San Francisco) have made to protect the public in the event of an earthquake. The search strategy must include Boolean logic, quotation marks, and asterisks.

Comparing Information. Examinees summarize information from a variety of courses and draw conclusions from their summary. Scenario: Collect information from several sources about office products intended for use by left-handed persons, and rank the desirability of these products based on a set of features desired by the office manager of an architectural firm.

Committee Observations

The strength of this assessment instrument is the measurement of practical skills in narrow, but important, information-technology applications. Questions are posed in a real-world context, which gives meaning to the scenario-based tasks. Successful performance requires more than information recall and rote memorization. Because examinees can improve their responses based on feedback, the assessment might be used to ascertain not only *what* examinees know, but also *how* they go about learning. It is not evident, however, that the test is designed to capture data on the how of learning.

Although the committee examined only a handful of sample tasks, it was apparent that examinees who do not have regular access to the Internet, e-mail, electronic card catalogs, graphing software, and other technologies featured in the assessment would be at a disadvantage. Given the target population for the assessment, this may not be a significant worry. The assessment was not designed with the ITEA Standards for Technological Literacy in mind, but it addresses some of the benchmarks in ITEA Standard 17: Information and Communication Technology. The assessment would be more challenging and perhaps more revealing of test takers' capabilities if some of the tasks included open-ended elements.

Illinois Standards Achievement Test—Science

Background

Sponsor/Creator	Illinois State Board of Education
Purpose	Measure student achievement in five areas and monitor school performance
What is measured	Science-related knowledge and capability
Target population	4th- and 7th-grade students in Illinois
Item format	Multiple choice
Sample size	All eligible public school students in 4th and 7th grade in Illinois
Frequency of administration	Annually in April since 2000
Availability	*http://www.isbe.net/assessment/PDF/2003ScienceSample.pdf*

Scope

This assessment is aligned with the *Illinois Learning Standards*, which were adopted in 1997. Standards 11B and 13B are related to technology. Standard 11B requires that students "know and apply the concepts, principles, and processes of technological design." Standard 13B requires that students "know and apply concepts that describe the interaction between science, technology, and society." Four questions for 4th-grade students and five questions for 7th-grade students in the 2003 sample assessment address Standard 11B. Seven questions on the 4th-grade exam and six questions on the 7th-grade exam address standard 13B. The 70-question exam is administered in 80 minutes and covers science inquiry, life sciences, physical sciences, earth and space sciences, and science, technology and society. The committee reviewed only sample test items because the Illinois Board of Education does not release actual test items.

Sample Items

• 4th grade, Standard 11B

Which color of roofing material would be best to help keep a house cool?

   A. White
   B. Black
   C. Gray
   D. Green

(Suggested correct answer: A)

• 7th grade standard 11B

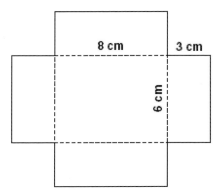

What is the volume of this box when folded together?

   A. 17 cubic centimeters
   B. 42 cubic centimeters
   C. 66 cubic centimeters
   D. 144 cubic centimeters

(Suggested correct answer: D)

• 7th grade, Standard 13B

One of the principal causes of acid rain is

   A. acid from chemical laboratories leaking into ground-water.
   B. gases from burning coal and oil released into the air.

C. gases from air conditioners and refrigerators escaping into the atmosphere.
D. waste acid from chemical factories pumped into rivers.

(Suggested correct answer: B)

Committee Observations

In general, the questions in this assessment address everyday topics that average citizens might be expected to encounter. However, although the educators who designed the assessment claim that it tests higher order thinking skills, many test items require only low-level cognitive skills, mostly at the knowledge level, and occasionally at the application level. The 4th-grade exam includes questions that assess student awareness of how common technological devices function in their environment; these questions do not require recall of specific technical knowledge or jargon. Many items on the 7th-grade exam, however, either require factual recall or rely on logical reasoning. On the whole, a number of questions could be answered with little or no technological knowledge or understanding.

Industrial Technology Literacy Test

Background

Sponsor/Creator	Michael Hayden, Iowa State University
Purpose	Assess the level of industrial-technology literacy among high school students
What is measured	Knowledge in systems, applications, and interpretations of industrial technology
Target population	American high school students
Item format	Multiple choice
Sample size	806 high school and 265 college students

Frequency of administration   Once in 1988 or 1990

Availability   Dissertation by Michael Allen Hayden held at Iowa State University

Scope

Michael Hayden, a Ph.D. candidate in industrial education and technology at Iowa State University, created the Industrial Technology Literacy Test as part of his dissertation. The questions in the instrument, which were generated by students in an advanced industrial education and technology course in the spring of 1988, were modified and evaluated to create the present exam. The 45-question exam was administered to a group of high school students in Iowa in 1988 or 1989. The questions are intended to show students' knowledge of industrial systems, applications, and interpretation. The results of Hayden's study were correlated with several factors, such as grade level, gender, mother/father's contact with tools or machines, and previous courses in industry/technology.

Sample Items

- Multiple choice

   The space shuttle and the Alaskan pipeline have as their most common characteristic the fact that:

   A. they were both the center of accidents
   B. they were both invented in the USA
   C. they are both made of metal
   D. USA workers made both of them
   E. they are both transportation systems

   (Suggested correct answer: E)

- Multiple choice

   A superconductor is:

   A. a material that has very little electrical resistance at a certain temperature
   B. a type of elevated train

C. a machine that accelerates nuclear material

D. the electronic component that makes compact discs possible

E. a type of metal used in cookware

(Suggested correct answer: A)

- Multiple choice

One of the fastest growing "high tech" firms is RBI Incorporated. During each of the past 5 years it has added another 50 R&D specialists to its staff. These and other technologists have consistently kept RBI at the leading edge of computer innovation. On the average, the speed and capacity of RBIs CPUs has doubled every year. Their X1000 micro computer can perform a calculation in a nano-second. The chip that allows this speed stores a megabyte of information.

How many calculations can an X1000 computer perform in 1 second?

A. 10^3

B. 10^5

C. 10^9

D. 10^{12}

E. 10^{15}

(Suggested correct answer: C)

Committee Observations

Considering the broad range of questions about industrial technology in this instrument, it may be appropriate for measuring industrial-technology literacy for high school students who have taken courses in the field. A few of the questions require higher order thinking, such as interpreting a graph; however, the majority of questions require factual recall. The exam is also gender biased, as was recognized by its author. In addition, the choices of answers for some questions (e.g., Sample Question 1) appear to be "incomparable alternatives" (i.e., some questions either have no clear answer or have more than one correct answer).

Infinity Project Pretest and Final Test

Background

Sponsor/Creator	Geoffrey Orsak, Southern Methodist University, with sponsorship from Texas Instruments and the Institute for Engineering Education
Purpose	Basic aptitude (pre-test) and student performance (end-of-year test)
What is measured	Cognitive skills and curriculum-related knowledge
Target population	American high school students
Item format	Open-ended and multiple-choice questions
Sample size	Thousands of students in 20 states
Frequency of administration	Ongoing since 1999
Availability	Samples are available at *ftp://ftp.prenhall.com/pub/esm/sample_chapters/engineering_computer_science/orsak/index.html*

Scope

Geoffrey Orsak, dean of the School of Engineering at Southern Methodist University, founded the Infinity Project in 1999 to interest more high school students in pursuing careers in engineering. The Infinity Project is a one-year high school curriculum designed for students who have taken algebra II and at least one course in a laboratory science. The curriculum, which focuses on information technology, includes textbooks, an Infinity Technology Kit for use in the classroom, and training for educators. The textbook, *Engineering Our Digital Future* (Prentice Hall, 2002), covers a variety of subjects in engineering and technology: the world of modern engineering, creating digital music, making digital images, math you can see, digitizing the world, coding information for storage and security, communicating with ones and zeros, networks from the telegraph to the Internet, and the big picture of engineering. According to the Infinity Project website, more than 65 percent of students who complete the course plan to study engineering in college.

The problem-solving pre-test has 10 questions to measure cognitive skills, such as recognition of discrete patterns from continuous patterns, proportional reasoning, and reverse implication. All questions are open ended and include at least one figure. The end-of-year basic test (from May 2003) consists of 12 multiple-choice knowledge-based questions that cover course content.

Sample Items[7]

• Coding information—problem-solving pre-test

Compressing information without information loss:

Engineers compress information. In critical situations, they can retrieve all the information.

(continued on next page)

---

[7]The Infinity Project™, Institute for Engineering Education, School of Engineering, Southern Methodist University.

On the grid below, each row has a pattern representing the number of alternating white and black squares. For example, the first row has 9 white squares. The second row has 1 white, 1 black, 4 white, 1 black, and 2 white squares. If the # sign represents a new row then this image can be represented by the sequence

9#11412#12312#1111212#1121112#11322#11412#9

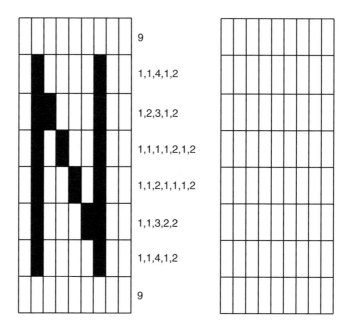

9

1,1,4,1,2

1,2,3,1,2

1,1,1,1,2,1,2

1,1,2,1,1,1,2

1,1,3,2,2

1,1,4,1,2

9

Using the blank grid above determine the image for the following sequence.

9#333#21312#1151#21312#333#9

(Suggested correct answer: The letter "O")

• Signal analysis—end-of-year basic test (May 2003)

If the period of a sinusoidal signal is 0.4ms, what is the frequency?

A. 2500 Hz
B. 2500 MHz
C. 2.5×10^4 Hz
D. 2.5×10^5 Hz

(Suggested correct answer: A)

- Communication technology—end-of-year basic test (May 2003)

  For a touchtone telephone which uses two tones per character, how many tones are used to make the signals for the twelve buttons?

  A. 2
  B. 7
  C. 12
  D. 27

  (Suggested correct answer: B)

Committee Observations

The pre-test, with its open-ended format, tests higher order thinking skills at the applications, analysis, and evaluation levels. It also assesses students' common sense, intelligence, and creativity, but these are not closely related to knowledge of specific technological systems. The end-of-year basic test is fact oriented and specific to course content and, therefore, not appropriate for assessing technological literacy in a general sense. A list of 36 cognitive specifications that were used to formulate the pre-test could be used to design an assessment of technological literacy.

Information Technology in a Global Society

Background

Sponsor/Creator	International Baccalaureate Organization (IBO), Geneva, Switzerland
Purpose	Student evaluation
What is measured	Students' knowledge of information technology terminology, concepts, developments, trends, social significance, and ethical issues
Target population	16–19-year-old high school students who have taken the Information Technology in a Global Society course

Item format	Multiple-choice and extended-answer questions, portfolio, and project
Sample size	The IB program is active in 1,468 schools in 119 countries; 56,284 diploma candidates took a total of 186,661 exams (in all subjects) in May of 2004
Frequency of administration	Semiannually at the standard level since 2002; higher level exams will be available in 2006
Availability	IBO in North America at *http://www.ibna@ibo.org*

Scope

The International Baccalaureate Organization (IBO) oversees the IB Diploma Program, which offers intensive pre-university courses and exams. Students in the IB program choose their focus of concentrated study, and at the same time pursue a broad education in the sciences and humanities. The purpose of the ITGS course is to give students a broad knowledge of information technology, skills to understand and explore new technologies, and an appreciation of the ethical and social effects of technology on the world.

The student assessment includes components designed by IBO (external), taken by every student enrolled in the course, and by the school (internal), taken only by the students in that school. The assessment requires that students demonstrate an ability to understand, apply, use, discuss, evaluate, explore, and construct information technology in four areas: terminology and concepts, developments and trends, social significance, and ethical considerations. The external review has two parts: a 40-question multiple-choice exam focused on tools and applications of information technology; and five extended-response questions that emphasize social and ethical considerations related to information technology. Extended-answer questions are graded according to a detailed rubric that awards points based on the mention of correct topics/concepts.

The internal assessment includes a portfolio with at least four pieces of written work and a project. The works in the portfolio, which focus on "the social significance of, and ethical considerations arising from, the widespread use of information technology in society," are drawn from the following categories: abuse/security/crime; global society; the workplace; privacy; leisure, home, and travel; education; and networks/communication. The project involves solving a problem that requires extensive use of information technology hardware and software and the integration of technology tools.

Sample Items[8]

- Multiple-choice question

  What feature of a spreadsheet makes it ideally suited to the construction of financial models?

  A. Video clips can be incorporated into some cells.
  B. Data can be validated easily by the use of a custom-ized macro.
  C. Formulae allow the effect of a change of variable to be seen easily.
  D. Three-dimensional images can be created from the model.

  (Suggested correct answer: C)

- Extended-response question

  Some schools issue identification cards to each student. These cards are similar to a credit card and contain the student's identification number and other personal infor-mation. When a student arrives at school in the morning, the student swipes the identification card through a card reader which records the date and time of arrival at the school. In the afternoon the card is again used to record when the student has left the school.

  Students may also use their identification card to purchase small stationary items in the school store, and lunches in the cafeteria. These purchases will be billed at the end of the month to the parents. This student's identification card is also used to sign out books in the school library. As an added benefit, some local stores give a 5% discount to

---

[8]Information Technology in a Global Society, Standard Level Paper 1, November 2002 © International Baccalaureate Organization 2002. The assessment model for the subject was changed in May 2004, and this style of question is no longer used.

students who show their identification cards when making a purchase.

(a) State **two** pieces of student information, other than identification number, which could be contained in the card.
(b) State **two** methods for indicating the identification number on the card so that it could be read by the identification card reader.
(c) Describe how **two** items of information are obtained by the school about a student without the student knowing it.
(d) Discuss **three** social **and/or** ethical concerns which students may have about owning and using the identification card and weigh up the importance of your arguments.

(Suggested correct answers: (a) photograph of the student, name of the student, signature of the student, address, telephone number, etc.; (b) printed as letters and numbers and read by using OCR software, printed as a bar code, on a magnetic strip, on a chip; (c) pattern of attendance, accumulated number of absences and latenesses, eating habits and food preferences, type of library products signed out, etc.; (d) ease of duplication for misuse, access by the student to the data collected, number and identity of people with access, access of data to other organizations or institutions, etc.).

Committee Observations

This instrument assesses students' knowledge of information technology in considerable depth. The format allows for a thorough analysis of student achievement using a variety of assessment tools. In the external assessment, most of the multiple-choice questions rely on recall of information. The open-ended questions require higher order thinking in cognitive and affective dimensions. It was not possible to judge the capabilities portion of the assessment because the external assessment did not include skills tasks. Although this instrument has a number of strong points, it assesses only knowledge of information technology specifically, as opposed to knowledge of technology in general.

Massachusetts Comprehensive Assessment System—Science and Technology/ Engineering

Background

Sponsor/Creator	Massachusetts Department of Education
Purpose	Monitor individual student achievement, gauge school and district performance, satisfy requirements of No Child Left Behind Act
What is measured	Knowledge of technology and engineering
Target population	5th-, 8th-, and 10th-grade students in Massachusetts
Item format	Multiple-choice and open-response items
Sample size	74,605 5th-grade and 78,686 8th-grade students in Massachusetts
Frequency of administration	Annually since 1998
Availability	*http://www.doe.mass.edu/mcas/ testitems.html*

Scope

The 5th- and 8th-grade assessment is part of a combined Science and Technology/Engineering Test that all students must take. Ten of the 39 questions are devoted to technology and engineering. The 10th-grade Technology/Engineering Test is one of four subject-area assessments (the others are biology, chemistry, and introductory physics) designed for students who have taken courses in these areas. The 10th-grade

Technology/Engineering Test includes 20 multiple-choice questions and two open-response questions.

The questions become increasingly sophisticated and difficult through the grades. Fifth-grade students are tested on their knowledge of materials and tools and their understanding of the design process. The 8th-grade test requires deeper knowledge of the nature of technology, as well as specific domains of technology, such as construction, communication, manufacturing, transportation, and biotechnologies. The 10th-grade test is even more specific, with topics such as power and energy technologies in fluid, thermal, and electrical systems.

Sample Items

- 5th-grade multiple-choice question (2003)

  Which of the following tools would be most useful in determining the length and width of a school cafeteria?

  A. scale
  B. centimeter ruler
  C. tape measure
  D. thermometer

  (Suggested correct answer: C)

- 5th-grade open-ended question (2003)

  The lever, pulley, inclined plane, wedge, wheel-and-axle, and the screw are simple machines.

  a. Identify and sketch four of these simple machines
  b. For each of the four machines that you sketch, describe an example of how it is used.

- 8th-grade multiple-choice question (2004)

  Several students are entering a bridge-building contest that requires using ice cream sticks and glue to construct the strongest bridge possible. The bridges must by 5 in. wide and span the length of 18 in.

  Which of the following tests is the most accurate way to determine the strongest span design for these bridges?

  A. roll toy cars across each bridge until it collapses

B. place concrete construction blocks on top of each bridge until it collapses

C. stack coins on both ends of each bridge until it collapses

D. place D-cell batteries at the center of each bridge until it collapses

(Suggested correct answer: D)

- 10th-grade multiple-choice question (2004)

    In the first step of making some ceramic cups, the following manufacturing process is used. Liquid clay is poured into a mold, allowed to solidify, then removed from the mold.

    What is the name of this manufacturing process?

    A. casting
    B. milling
    C. finishing
    D. refining

(Suggested correct answer: A)

Committee Observations

This instrument is well matched to the Massachusetts standards in science, technology, and engineering at the 5th-, 8th-, and 10th-grade levels. Most of the questions are multiple choice and focus on knowledge of course content, identification of terms, and rote memorization. A few open-ended questions require higher order thinking or design thinking to solve problems. For some questions, the distracters seemed just as plausible as the suggested correct answers.

Multiple-Choice Instrument for Monitoring Views on Science-Technology-Society Topics

Background

Sponsor/Creator   Glen Aikenhead and Alan Ryan, University of Saskatchewan, with funding from the Canadian Social Sciences and Humanities Research Council

Purpose	Curriculum evaluation, research
What is measured	Student attitudes and understanding of science, technology, and society (STS)
Target population	12th-grade high school students in Canada
Item format	Multiple choice
Sample size	5,250 English-speaking and 1,732 French-speaking students
Frequency of administration	Once, September 1987–August 1989
Availability	G.S. Aikenhead and A.G. Ryan, University of Saskatchewan

Scope

This instrument was developed in the late 1980s in response to changes in the science curriculum in secondary schools in Ontario that placed new emphasis on the social context of science and technology. Questions were derived from an eight-part conceptual scheme: science and technology, influence of society on science/technology, influence of science/technology on society, influence of social science on society, characteristics of scientists, social construction of scientific knowledge, social construction of technology, and nature of scientific knowledge. During the development of the instrument, high school seniors were asked to provide written responses to statements about science/technology/society (STS) topics; their views were then used to create answers for multiple-choice questions. The answers not only reflect students' stated opinions but are written in their own words.

Sample Items

• Science and technology, defining technology

Defining what technology is can cause difficulties because technology does many things in Canada. But MAINLY technology is:

Your position, basically: (please read from A to J, and then choose one.)

   A. very similar to science.
   B. the application of science.
   C. new processes, instruments, tools, machinery, appliances, gadgets, computers, or practical devices for everyday use.
   D. robotics, electronics, computers, communications systems, automation, etc.
   E. a technique for doing things, or a way of solving practical problems.
   F. inventing, designing, and testing things (for example, artificial hearts, computers, space vehicles).
   G. ideas and techniques for designing and manufacturing things, for organizing workers, business people and consumers, for the progress of society.
   H. I don't understand.
   I. I don't know enough about this subject to make a choice.
   J. None of these choices fits my basic viewpoint.

- Influence of society on science/technology government

Science would advance more efficiently in Canada if it were more clearly controlled by the government.

Your position, basically: (Please read from A to H, and then choose one.)

   A. Government should control science and make it more efficient by coordinating research work and by providing the money.
   B. The government's control should depend on how useful the particular scientific research will be for Canadian society. Useful research should be more closely controlled and money should be provided.
   C. Government should NOT control science, but should give it money and leave the conduct of the science up to the scientists.
   D. Government should NOT control science but should leave the scientific research to private agencies or corporations; though government should provide the money for the scientific research.
   E. Government cannot make science more efficient because government is inefficient and cannot always be trusted.
   F. I don't understand.

G. I don't know enough about this subject to make a choice.

H. None of these choices fits my basic viewpoint.

- Social construction of scientific knowledge, professional communication among scientists

When a research team makes a discovery, it is all right for them to announce it to the press before other scientists have discussed it.

Your position, basically: (Please read from A to H, and then choose one.)

The research team should announce it directly to the public:

A. to *get the credit* for the discovery and prevent other scientists from stealing the idea.

B. because the public has the *right to know* about a discovery as soon as it is made. Other scientists can discuss it later.

C. the research team should be free to decide who hears about it first.

The research team should first present it to other scientists for discussion:

D. to *test and verify* the discovery and prevent inaccurate stories from being published. This would ensure that harmful or embarrassing errors are worked out before it was made public.

E. to improve the discovery before it is made public.

F. I don't understand.

G. I don't know enough about this subject to make a choice.

H. None of these choices fits my basic viewpoint.

Committee Observations

Because the answer choices are generated by students, they provide a genuine reflection of how students feel about STS topics. By design, no attempt is made to gauge capabilities or knowledge of technology concepts, per se. Therefore, it would be difficult to assess technological literacy based on the results. In addition, because the authors make no judgments about the relative value of the answer choices, it is very difficult to determine students' understanding of STS issues. A high level of reading competency is required to complete the test. Thus, students with reading problems may have difficulty with this format.

New York State Intermediate Assessment in Technology

Background

Sponsor/Creator	New York State Education Department and University of the State of New York (USNY)
Purpose	Student evaluation; curriculum improvement
What is measured	Students' knowledge and skills in seven areas
Target population	7th- and 8th-grade students in New York who have taken a technology education course
Item format	Multiple choice and extended response
Sample size	Unknown
Frequency of administration	Unknown
Availability	*http://www.emsc.nysed.gov/ciai/mst/pub/tqsample.pdf*

Scope

In 1986, New York schools began offering an Introduction to Technology course for 7th- and 8th-grade students. The State Department of Education developed this instrument in 2001 to test their knowledge. The exam is administered in one 90-minute session and contains

40 multiple-choice and 10 extended-answer questions in order of difficulty. The sample assessment reviewed by the committee included just 14 multiple-choice and four extended-answer questions. The sample questions covered engineering design; tools, resources, and technological processes; computer technology; technological systems; history and evolution of technology; impacts of technology; and management of technology. The state of New York does not require that schools administer this test or report the results.

Sample Items

- History, evolution of technology multiple choice

     Eli Whitney's invention of the cotton gin changed the production of cotton by

     1. creating lighter cotton
     2. saving labor costs at harvest time
     3. enabling the production of cloth
     4. proving that some processes could never be automated

     (Suggested correct answer: 2)

- Technological systems multiple choice

     Which type of system is operated by liquid under pressure?

     1. mechanical
     2. steam
     3. pneumatic
     4. hydraulic

     (Suggested correct answer: 4)

- Tools, resources, and technological processes multiple choice

     Which device produces power by means of a chemical reaction?

     1. generator
     2. alternator
     3. battery
     4. engine

     (Suggested correct answer: 3)

• Tools, resources and technological processes extended response

Your class has been studying skyscraper design and the tremendous influence of skyscrapers on the landscape of cities. You are part of a group that has been assigned to build a model of the Empire State Building. You will be using balsa wood, construction paper, and acrylic plastic for your model.

Describe how each tool would be used:

- Backsaw
- Hot-melt glue and glue gun
- Tape measure
- Scissors or x-acto knife
- Abrasive paper
- Computer

> (Students are awarded three points for identifying an appropriate use for at least five tools; two points for identifying an appropriate use for three or four tools; one point for one or two appropriate uses; and no points for no response or no identification of appropriate uses of tools.)

Committee Observations

This assessment includes a balance of multiple-choice questions on technological concepts and open-ended questions that require a reasonable level of higher order thinking. Although this is a paper-and-pencil assessment, some of the open-ended questions touch on the capabilities and ways of thinking and acting dimension of technological literacy. A few multiple-choice questions do not have clear answers (e.g., Sample Question 1), and some of the knowledge-based questions require only recall of definitions.

Praxis Specialty Area Test: Technology Education

Background

Sponsor/Creator	Educational Testing Service (ETS)
Purpose	Teacher licensing
What is measured	Pedagogical practices and knowledge in four areas of technology
Target population	College education majors who wish to teach technology education at the middle or high school level
Item format	Multiple choice
Sample size	Unknown
Frequency of administration	Regularly
Availability	*http://ftp.ets.org/pub/tandl/0050.pdf*

Scope

ETS offers a series of three tests, administered by the Praxis Service, to assess beginning teachers. Praxis I measures basic academic skills of students entering teacher-education programs. Praxis II tests mastery of particular subjects and is designed primarily to assist in licensing teachers. Praxis III assesses the classroom performance of first-year teachers and is also used in licensing decisions.

Of more than 100 Praxis II tests, the only one focused on technology education is designed for prospective technology education teachers at the middle and high school levels. In recent years, ETS has modified the test to bring it into alignment with the ITEA Standards for Technological Literacy. The test has 120 multiple-choice questions divided into five categories: pedagogical and professional studies, information and communication technologies, construction technologies, manufacturing technologies, and energy/power/transportation technologies. The committee reviewed a 12-question sample test, provided by ETS on the Web. Thirty percent of Praxis II is devoted to pedagogical issues, including program development, implementation, and evaluation. Questions covering the four types of technologies focused on design, systems, processes, outputs, resources, and managerial processes.

Sample Items[9]

• Pedagogical and professional studies

A student in the process of solving a fabrication problem in the manufacturing laboratory asks the teacher what assembly procedures should be used. The teacher's best response would be to

A. give an opinion as to the best assembly procedure for the particular problem
B. suggest two or three possible assembly procedures and have the student select one
C. place the responsibility completely on the student for making the judgment
D. use leading questions to help the student review and analyze the relative merits of several assembly procedures
E. refer the student to a reference on assembly procedures

(Suggested correct answer: D)

• Information and communications technologies

The most important consideration in designing successful messages to be transmitted through graphic communications is knowledge and understanding of

A. current technologies
B. the capabilities of the designer
C. the estimated cost of the project
D. the limitations of the printer
E. the nature of the audience

(Suggested correct answer: E)

---

[9]Materials were selected from Tests at a Glance, Educational Testing Service. Reprinted by permission of Educational Testing Service, the copyright owner, for limited use by the National Academy of Engineering.

- Construction technologies

Which two of the following composite materials used in manufacturing would generally be classified as laminar composites in the United States?

I. Particle board
II. Plywood
III. Fiberglass
IV. Bimetal coins
V. Concrete

A. I and II
B. I and III
C. II and IV
D. III and V
E. IV and V

(Suggested correct answer: C)

Committee Observations

Although the items in the assessment are aligned with the ITEA Standards on Technological Literacy, they do not probe higher order thinking. Most questions focus on terminology, recall of definitions, and the identification of basic concepts. The test does not address the question of whether a teacher could put any of his or her knowledge related to technology into practice.

Provincial Learning Assessment in Technology Literacy

Background

Sponsor/Creator	Saskatchewan Education
Purpose	Analyze students' technological literacy to improve their understanding of the relationship between technology and society
What is measured	Capabilities, knowledge, attitudes, and practices related to technological literacy

Target population	5th-, 8th-, and 11th-grade students in Saskatchewan, Canada
Item format	Multiple-choice, open-response, and hands-on computer and technology skills items
Sample size	Approximately 3,500 students from 182 schools
Frequency of administration	Dozens of times in many countries since 1988
Availability	*http://www.sasked.gov.sk.ca/branches/ cap_building_acct/afl/docs/plap/techlit/ 1999techlit.pdf*

Scope

Saskatchewan Education created the Provincial Learning Assessment in Technology Literacy in 1999 to assess student skills, knowledge, attitudes, and practices in technological literacy and collect information on their home and school environments. The instrument focuses on four domains: (1) understanding, describing, and adapting technology; (2) accessing, processing, and communicating information; (3) responsible citizenship and technology; and (4) using technology, including computers.

Two different exams were administered. The performance exam consisted of five stations at which students carried out hands-on activities, such as word processing; using the Internet; using technology; and design, planning, and building models of technology. Student performance was assessed on a scale of 1 to 5 with a well defined rubric for each task (see sample question). The paper-and-pencil exam included open-format and multiple-choice items. Students were also required to submit a research project completed at school. Performance-related aspects of the exam were scored on a scale of 1 to 5 using a rubric for achievement in each domain.

Saskatchewan Education has not repeated this assessment and has no plans to do so in the future.

Sample Items

- 5th-, 8th- and 11th-grade multiple-choice question

    The *main* reason special effects are used in a number of commercials is

    A. To entertain the television audience
    B. To allow producers to show their creativity
    C. To show how technology has advanced
    D. To sell more product
    E. None of the above

    (Suggested correct answer: D)

- 8th -grade performance-station activity

    Hint the best SEARCH ENGINE for item #5 is *YAHOO*

    Item #5 Use the internet to find an INTERNET address or INTERNET site name on the *Saskatchewan Roughriders*

    Item #6 Use the INTERNET to find the population of *New Zealand*

- 8th-grade open-response question

    Technology means different things to different people. When you read the word "**technology**" what comes into your mind? Tell what technology means to you by drawing pictures and writing about it in the space below.

    Please write your definition of technology:

    (Suggested best answer: A level-5 answer includes a sophisticated definition that encompasses a full range of technologies and provides four or more examples, with two strong contrasts, such as simple vs. complex. A level 3 answer provides a general definition that includes *one criterion of product, process, and reason*, and three or more examples, with one contrast. A level 1 answer includes one or two examples of similar technologies.)

Committee Observations

Many of the questions and skill assessments require that students engage in higher order thinking, as opposed to rote memorization. The rubrics seem flexible enough for educators to gauge multiple levels of student accomplishment. The assessment is computer intensive both in the performance-skills and knowledge sections.

Pupils' Attitudes Toward Technology (PATT-USA)

Background

Sponsor/Creator	E. Allen Bame, Marc de Vries, and William E. Dugger, with funding from Virginia Polytechnic Institute and State University, the state of New Jersey, and the International Technology Education Association
Purpose	Assess student attitudes toward and knowledge of technology
What is measured	How gender, age, parents' professions, technology in the home, and courses in technology influence students' conceptions of and attitudes toward technology
Target population	American middle school students
Item format	Multiple-choice and open-ended questions
Sample size	10,349 students in seven states
Frequency of administration	Once in 1988
Availability	*http://www.iteawww.org* (under Conference Proceedings)

Scope

Pupils' Attitudes Toward Technology (PATT), developed in the Netherlands in 1984 by Marc de Vries and colleagues, has been adapted and used in more than 20 countries around the world, making it particularly useful for cross-country comparisons. Nearly 77 percent of the students who took the PATT-USA survey were enrolled in or had previously taken a technology education or industrial arts class. The open-ended question asked student to describe what technology is. The 100 multiple-choice questions were divided into three sections. In one section, 11 questions asked for demographic information. In a second section, 58 questions were related to attitudes toward technology and used a Likert-scale response format (agree, tend to agree, neutral, tend to disagree, disagree). The questions in this section addressed interest in technology, beliefs about the consequences of technology, perceptions of the difficulty of technology, ideas about technological professions, gender stereotypes, and student ideas about technology as a subject in school. The final section included 31 questions that tested understanding and conceptions of technology. In this section, students were given three choices: agree, disagree, and don't know. The questions concerned the relationship between technology and society, the relationship between technology and science, skills in technology, and the raw materials (or "pillars") of technology.

Sample Items

- Gender stereotypes

   Boys know more about technology than girls do

   > (On the 5-point Likert scale, girls were more likely to consider technology an activity for both boys and girls [mean for girls = 1.66; mean for boys = 2.28]).

- Consequences of technology

   Because technology causes pollution, we should use less of it

   > (Students whose parents' professions had "nothing" to do with technology had significantly more negative views

toward the consequences of technology than students whose parents' professions had at least "a little" to do with technology. If technical toys or a personal computer was present in the home, attitudes toward the consequences of technology were more positive. Students who had taken a technology course or were interested in a technical profession also had more positive attitudes toward the consequences of technology.)

- Knowledge about the relationship between science and technology

  In my opinion, I think technology is not very old

  (35 percent of students agreed with this statement, 27 percent did not know if it was true or not, and 38 percent disagreed.)

Committee Observations

The PATT-USA focuses on assessing attitudes of students toward technology. The questions that test students' understanding of technological concepts do not require higher order thinking. Nevertheless, questions eliciting student views about technology yields some interesting results, especially with regard to gender differences. The survey is long and so might be be difficult for younger students to complete.

Science and Technology: Public Attitudes and Public Understanding

Background

Sponsor/Creator	National Science Board
Purpose	Monitor public attitudes, knowledge, and interest in science and technology issues
What is measured	Attitudes, opinions, and knowledge of science and technology

Target population	U.S. residents 18 and older
Item format	Survey
Sample size	Approximately 2,000 adults
Frequency of administration	Biennially from 1979 to 2001
Availability	*http://www.nsf.gov/sbe/srs/seind02/c7/ c7h.htm*

Scope

The National Science Board (NSB), an independent body that oversees the National Science Foundation and provides policy advice to the president and Congress, has conducted biennial telephone surveys to assess public knowledge, attitudes, and opinions about science and technology since 1979. The 2001 survey questions were organized into the following categories: public interest and knowledge of science and technology (S&T); public attitudes toward S&T; public image of the science community; where Americans get information about S&T; science fiction and pseudoscience; and demographic questions (age, computer access, educational level, occupation, geographic location in the United States, race/ethnicity, sex). Based on this information, NSB reports on trends in public knowledge and interest in science correlated with the demographic data. NSB also compares American attitudes with attitudes on similar surveys in the European Union, Canada, and Japan.

The 2001 survey was the last in the series. Since 2004, the NSB report has relied on the 2001 survey, new Eurobarometer surveys on S&T, a number of Gallup polls, and other sources. Currently, NSB has no plans to resume the telephone surveys, and the 2006 survey will also rely on data from other sources. A major conclusion of both the 2001 and 2004 surveys was that, although Americans are interested in scientific discoveries and new technologies, they do not feel well informed or know a lot about technology-related issues.

Sample Items

(From the 2001 survey)

- Where Americans get information about S&T

  Now, I'd like to read you a short list of television shows and ask you to tell me whether you watch each show regularly, that is, most of the time, occasionally, or not at all.

  Do you watch Nova regularly, occasionally, or not at all?

  > (8 percent answered regularly, 29 percent occasionally, and 63 percent not at all.)

- Public interest and knowledge of S&T

  Lasers work by focusing sound waves, true or false?

  > (45 percent of respondents knew that this statement was false. 61 percent of men, but only 30 percent of women, answered this question correctly.)

- Public attitudes toward S&T

  I'm going to name three types of biotechnology applications. I'd like you to tell me if you strongly support, moderately support, moderately oppose, or strongly oppose these uses of biotechnology.

  Using genetic testing to detect diseases we might have inherited from our parents, such as cystic fibrosis. Overall would you say you strongly support, moderately support, moderately oppose, or strongly oppose this use of biotechnology?

  > (89 percent of survey participants answered either strongly support or moderately support genetic testing for inherited diseases. 9 percent were opposed.)

Committee Observations

(2001 survey only)

The *NSF Indicators, Public Understanding of Science and Technology* reports provide the only long-term data on trends in U.S. adult knowledge and attitudes toward science and, to a lesser extent, technology. Most of the questions focused on attitudes, and the knowledge-related questions did not require higher order thinking. Respondents with college degrees fared better on the limited number of knowledge questions than respondents who did not have college degrees. This may be attributable simply to exposure to more scientific information, or it may indicate a bias in the poll. As an assessment of technological literacy, the survey had limited value because very few questions focused on or emphasized technology. Science is related to technology, of course, but the connection is indirect. Therefore, this survey is not very useful for assessing many domains of technological literacy.

Student Individualized Performance Inventory

Background

Sponsor/Creator	Rodney L. Custer, Brigitte G. Valesey, and Barry N. Burke, with funding from the Council on Technology Teacher Education, International Technology Education Association, and the Technical Foundation of America
Purpose	Develop a model to assess the problem-solving capabilities of students engaged in design activities
What is measured	Student achievement in 12 areas of design and problem solving
Target population	American high school students
Item format	Rubric
Sample size	Two small high school classes of 12 and 15 students
Frequency of administration	Several times for research purposes
Availability	Rodney Custer, Department of Technology, Illinois State University

Scope

The Student Individualized Performance Inventory, developed by education researchers at three different institutions, is a model for assessing students' problem-solving skills on a design activity. The model divides the design process into four dimensions: problem and design clarification; development of a plan; development of a model/prototype; and evaluation of the design solution. Each dimension is further categorized into three "strands." Students are evaluated on each strand of the four dimensions by matching their performance with descriptions in a detailed rubric. A score of 1 indicates the novice level of proficiency, 2 beginner, 3 competent, 4 proficient, and 5 expert.

The authors tested their model with two small groups of high school students. The students were asked to design the "school locker of the future" and given eight hours over a period of two days to complete the task. Student achievement was correlated with a number of factors, including geographic location, technology education experience, grade level, mathematics and science achievement score, personality type, problem-solving style, and gender.

Sample Items

(Because this instrument is a rubric, rather than an exam, there are no sample questions. The following examples illustrate the detailed descriptions of student performance in various dimensions and strands spelled out in the rubric.)

- Dimension: Problem solving and design clarification

  Strand: Examine content and define problem

  - (5) Expert: Poses pertinent questions for clarification; identifies and prioritizes sub-problems (within the larger problem); explores context.
  - (4) Proficient: Poses questions; identifies sub-problems but does not prioritize. Ignores context.
  - (3) Competent: Identifies key content; defines problem adequately. Asks some pertinent questions. Ignores context.
  - (2) Beginner: Expresses limited knowledge of context of problem area; problem is defined but needs clarification. Asks questions but not pertinent and too few.

Ignores context. Exhibits some indifference or frustration.

(1) Novice: Tends to home in on wrong problem, isolated subset, or easiest part to solve. Begins to solve without clarification or questions. Doesn't see context. Exhibits considerable indifference or frustration.

- Dimension: Model/prototype

    Strand: Produce model/prototype

    (5) Expert: Is adept with tools and resources, making continual adjustments to "tweak" the model/prototype. Demonstrates persistence with minor problems. Enjoys the challenge of refinements.
    (4) Proficient: Uses tools and resources without guidance. Refines model to enhance appearance and capabilities.
    (3) Uses tools and resources with little or no guidance. May redo model/prototype parts to improve quality.
    (2) Uses tools and resources with some guidance. May have difficulty selecting the appropriate resource. Refines work, but may prefer to leave model as first produced.
    (1) Novice: Needs guidance in order to use resources safely and appropriately. Model/prototype is crude, with little or no refinements made.

Committee Observations

The Student Individualized Performance Activity is a well considered tool for assessing design skills, and the rubric adheres to the ITEA Standards for Technological Literacy. Acceptable performance for particular scores in each dimension or strand is well defined. The most attractive feature of this instrument is that it is based on authentic responses of learners. The instrument genuinely provides data based on the processes students use in design, as well as the outcomes that result from their work. The expert-to-novice scoring scale, as opposed to an A-to-F scale, is another positive feature. Like all rubrics, this one raises questions about the reliability of the rater. Normative words, such as "pertinent" and "limited" may contribute to these questions. The underlying assumption that successful, effective designers are always associated with the same qualities may not be correct.

Survey of Technological Literacy of Elementary and Junior High School Students

Background

Sponsor/Creator	Ta Wei Lee, Wei Lin, Kuo-Hung Tseng, and Kuang-Chao Yu at National Taiwan Normal University
Purpose	Curriculum development and planning
What is measured	Knowledge in 10 areas of technological literacy and 6 technology systems
Target population	Elementary and junior high school students in Taiwan
Item format	Multiple choice
Sample size	3,066 9th-grade and 3,420 6th-grade students
Frequency of administration	Once in March 1995
Availability	Not available in English. An article describing the assessment is available online at: *http://nr.stic.gov.tw/ejournal/Proceeding D/v8n2/68-76.pdf*

Scope

The Survey of Technological Literacy among Junior High School and Elementary Students was created for educators to provide a reference point for planning a new curriculum emphasizing the study of technology. According to the test developers, the 80-question exam includes questions in 10 areas of abilities in technological literacy and six technology systems.

Abilities in Technological Literacy:
1. understand the definition and content of technology
2. understand the major domains of technology
3. understand the evolution of technology
4. understand and predict future trends of technological development
5. understand the basic principles of technology
6. understand and use effectively the tools, machines, materials, products, and operational procedures of technology systems
7. use technological literacy in the cognitive, affective, and psychomotor domains for problem solving
8. make proper judgments of technology and its products through data gathering, analysis, and induction
9. understand the impacts of technology on the individual, society, culture, and environment
10. adopt measures to adapt to changes brought on by technology

Technology Systems:
1. construction technology
2. manufacturing technology
3. transportation technology
4. communication technology
5. energy and power technology
6. biotechnology

This instrument was intended for both elementary and junior high students. The first 40 questions were considered "fundamental" and appropriate for both groups. The next 40 questions were considered "advanced" and were only administered to junior high students. In addition to the exam questions, students were asked to provide their gender and grade level, which were used to demonstrate correlations in the final analysis of the assessment. Between 1995 and 2000, this assessment was used in several local studies and a number of master's theses. However, it is not used regularly or widely to assess technological literacy.

Sample Items

(This instrument was written in Chinese and translated into English by one of the authors for the committee's review.)

- Fundamental section

In general, which of the following is not the function of a reservoir?

A. Flood prevention
B. Water supply for farm fields
C. Water power supply
D. Ecological conservation

(Suggested correct answer: D)

- Fundamental section

Place the following air transportation in order of their invention

A. Hot air balloon → glider → airplane
B. Glider → hot air balloon → airplane
C. Hot air balloon → airplane → glider
D. Airplane → hot air balloon → glider

(Suggested correct answer: A)

- Advanced section

How is the method of laser incision on hard materials different from traditional method?

A. The tool does not contact the item
B. The tool requires electricity
C. The size of incision is uncontrollable
D. The tool has multiple shapes

(Suggested correct answer: A)

Committee Observations

For the most part, the items in this assessment appear to be appropriate for the target populations. With the multiple-choice format, knowledge of technology can be assessed, but not students' capabilities. Many of the test questions require higher order thinking, but problems with the translation to English seem to reveal cultural bias in some items.

Test of Technological Literacy

Background

Sponsor/Creator	Abdul Hameed, Ohio State University
Purpose	Research
What is measured	Knowledge in four areas: construction, manufacturing, communication, and transportation technologies
Target population	7th- and 8th-grade American students
Item format	Multiple choice
Sample size	1,350 students from 20 schools
Frequency of administration	Once in April 1988
Availability	Dissertation by Abdul Hameed held at Ohio State University

Scope

This test was developed by Abdul Hameed in the late 1980s as part of his Ph.D. dissertation in technical education (industrial arts) at Ohio State University. The 64-question exam, which is intended to be completed in a single class period, tests students' understanding of using, making, and controlling technology.

Sample Items

• A manufacturing control question

Which of the following items needs the highest design safety factor?

A. Airplane
B. Gasoline Engine

C. Radio
D. Bicycle

(Suggested correct answer: A)

• A construction making question

Steel reinforcement is placed in concrete in order to

A. Help keep the concrete from breaking and separating
B. Improve the appearance
C. Provide holes for ventilation
D. Increase the weight

(Suggested correct answer: A)

• An understanding transportation question

The first manned rocket to enter space was launched in the

A. late 1930s and early 1940s
B. late 1940s and early 1950s
C. late 1950s and early 1960s
D. late 1960s and early 1970s

(Suggested correct answer: C)

Committee Observations

This assessment covers a broad range of general knowledge about technology, but few questions require that students do anything other than recall information. The test does not require problem-solving, decision-making, or technology-related skills. A number of test items refer to specific technologies that were state of the art in the early 1980s but would not be familiar to many students today.

TL50: Technological Literacy Instrument

Background

Sponsor/Creator   Michael Dyrenfurth, Purdue University

Purpose   Gauge technological literacy

What is measured	General knowledge of technology in eight areas
Target population	High school students, university students, and adults
Item format	Multiple choice
Sample size	Unknown
Frequency of administration	Unknown
Availability	Michael J. Dyrenfurth, College of Technology, Purdue University

Scope

This 50-question, multiple-choice instrument is designed to assess technological literacy in eight areas: (1) working with technology; (2) technological procedures; (3) overview of technology; (4) overview of industrial technology; (5) fundamentals of communications technology; (6) applications of energy and power technologies; (7) fundamentals of materials and processing technologies; and (8) impact of technologies on society. Slightly more than half of the items address technological procedures.

Sample Items

• Technological procedures: systems analysis and synthesis questions

Consider a typical factory's automated spray paint station that uses a robot to paint parts passing on a conveyor. Which of the answers contains the best list of subsystems of such a work station?

A. Controlling computer, transfer robot, auto-conveyor, cell perimeter
B. Instrumentation unit, auto-conveyor, warehouse unit, read-out and input unit

C. Auto-conveyor, controlling computer, spray robot, read-out and input unit
D. Vision system, auto-conveyor, light system, transfer robot

(Suggested correct answer: C)

- Fundamentals of materials and processing technologies: materials technology basics question

The process of tempering material:

A. Softens the metal and removes internal stresses
B. Increases the metal's resistance to scratching and abrasion
C. Toughens the material
D. Is not described

(Suggested correct answer: C)

- Technological procedures: technology assessment/evaluation (impacts) question

To properly judge the effects of a technological innovation, one should:

A. Measure the dollar effects resulting from it
B. Estimate the impacts of it on our society
C. Identify its impact on the people using it
D. All of the above

(Suggested correct answer: D)

Committee Observations

Although this instrument includes questions that require interpretations of simple graphs and analog scales, the majority of questions rely heavily on memorization and knowledge of terminology that may become outdated or may not transfer well among population groups. The instrument may not be appropriate for university students in most science or technology fields because much of the content is basic and does not require a higher education.

WorkKeys—Applied Technology

Background

Sponsor/Creator	ACT
Purpose	Determine workforce readiness; identify skills gaps in current and potential employees.
What is measured	Practical reasoning and problem-solving skills related to four applied-technology domains: electricity, mechanics, fluid dynamics, and thermodynamics
Target population	High school and community college students, adults transitioning to the workforce, current workers in technology-dependent businesses
Item format	32 items at four levels of difficulty administered over 55 minutes (online) or 45 minutes (paper and pencil)
Sample size	Since 1992, when ACT introduced the WorkKeys Program, some 9 million individuals have taken one or more of the program's 10 assessments (M.J. Klemme, WorkKeys consultant, personal communication, December 20, 2005).
Frequency of administration	There is no fixed schedule of test administration. Assessments may be taken either through an employer licensed by ACT or a licensed WorkKeys site, typically an educational institution.
Availability	Test details, sample items, and information about ordering a practice test are available at *http://www.act.org/workkeys*

Scope

The Applied Technology Assessment is one of 10 assessments offered by WorkKeys. The others are Reading for Information, Applied Mathematics, Business Writing, Writing, Locating Information, Teamwork, Observation, Listening, and Readiness. Although the assessments can be given individually, they were originally designed to be part of a larger ACT job-skills program. The program includes a component to help employers identify the skills necessary for specific jobs and a training element to close skill gaps revealed by the assessment. Test items are grouped into four difficulty levels, 3–6, based on the number and complexity of the skills required to answer each item correctly. A Level 3 item, for instance, describes a simple system with three to five components, portrays a problem with one variable, and includes all the information necessary to solve it. A Level 6 item describes a complex system with 10 or more components, presents a variety of possible problem sources, and includes considerable extraneous information. Assessment results can be presented as a level score, which ACT says should be used for employee selection, promotion, or other high-stakes purposes, or a scale score, which can show individual improvement over time, provide for group comparisons, or show a likelihood of benefit from educational opportunity. ACT charges $4 per test for educational and government institutions that use the assessment with their own students. The rate is higher for businesses.

Sample Items[10]

Level 3

You are building a greenhouse like the one shown in Figure 1 for a local nursery. The owners specified that the greenhouse should have automatic vents, controlled by a thermostat, which will open when the temperature in the greenhouse gets too high for the plants. Figure 2 shows the floor plan of the greenhouse.

---

[10]These sample items appear on the WorkKeys website at *http://www.act.org/workkeys/assess/tech* and are reprinted with permission.

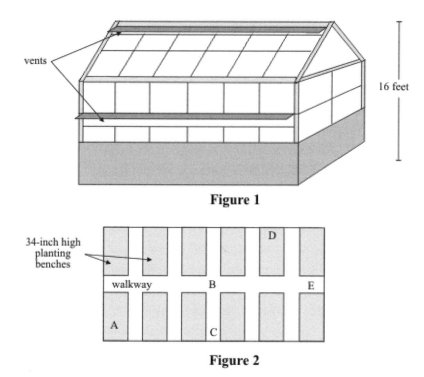

Figure 1

vents

16 feet

34-inch high planting benches

walkway   B   D   E

A   C

Figure 2

A thermostat will control the opening and closing of the automatic vents. It is a temperature-sensitive device that can be set to activate when the air around it reaches a certain temperature. The owners of the greenhouse want to have the vents open when the air around the majority of the plants reaches 90°F. At what height and location in Figure 2 should you install the thermostat so it gives the desired results?

A. About 4 feet from the floor at location A
B. About 4 feet from the floor at location B (suggested correct answer)
C. About 8 feet from the floor at location C
D. About 8 feet from the floor at location D
E. Near the peak of the roof at location E

Level 4

Your industrial services company has been hired to deliver a small but heavy gearbox. The container is too small to justify renting a large truck and too heavy for the company's pickup truck. You decide to rent a heavy-duty utility trailer

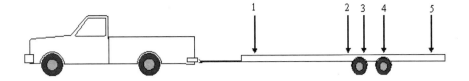

and pull it with the pickup truck.

At which spot, labeled 1–5, on the trailer shown should you place the container to pull the load most easily and safely?

A. 1
B. 2
C. 3 (suggested correct answer)
D. 4
E. 5

Level 5

The band saw where you work will not start. This saw uses 240 volts, draws 25 amps, and has 30-amp cartridge fuses. These fuses (see diagram shown) are designed to protect an electrical circuit. Their main component is a fuse wire made of a low-resistance, low-melting-point alloy. When a higher than tolerable current goes through such a fuse, this fuse wire melts. Your supervisor has told you to check the fuses in the band saw. By looking at the fuses, you cannot tell if they are good or bad.

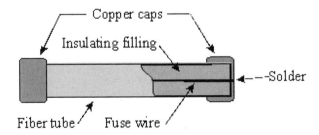

You have turned off the power to the saw and removed one of the fuses. You check this fuse with a *volt-ohmmeter* (a device that measures resistance to the flow of electrical current). If the fuse is good, the resistance (measured in ohms) for the fuse will be:

A. 0 ohms (suggested correct answer)
B. 10 ohms
C. 50 ohms
D. 100 ohms
E. infinite

Level 6

The garage where you work is equipped with a hydraulic
lift, like the one shown, that you use to raise cars off the
floor so it is easier to service them. An air compressor
capable of generating pressures of 120 pounds per square
inch (psi) powers the lift. The air regulator releases a steady
amount of air pressure (usually 30 to 40 psi), and the control
valve directs the flow of that air through the lines. Pushing
the control valve forward (as shown in the figure) allows air
into the lines, raising the lift. Moving the valve to the middle
position seals the line so no air can escape, and pulling the
valve back releases air from the line, lowering the lift. The
air from the compressor exerts a force on a tank of hydraulic fluid, which, in turn, transmits this force to the bottom of
the lifting piston.

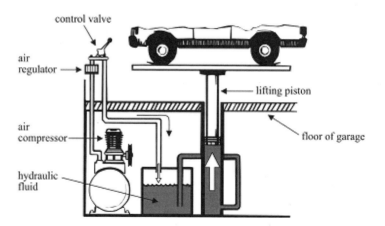

*Figure adapted from *Principles of Technology Teacher's Guide*, Year 1,
Unit 7, *Force Transformers* (Waco, TX: Center for Occupational Research
and Development, 1991), 94. Used with permission.

You have been working on a car up on the lift for about an
hour. When you raised the car, the lift worked normally, but
now the lifting piston has begun to creep down. You check
the control valve and it is fine. Also, there is no hydraulic

fluid on the garage floor or in the lift pit below the garage floor. The next thing you should check to determine the problem is the:

A. air compressor
B. air regulator
C. air line between the compressor and the control valve
D. air line between the control valve and the hydraulic fluid reservoir (suggested correct answer)
E. line between the hydraulic fluid reservoir and the lifting piston

Committee Observations

This assessment is notable for its focus on problem solving and reasoning in technological systems. Although not designed with the ITEA Standards for Technological Literacy in mind, the sample items are consistent with benchmarks described in the ITEA standards related to energy and power (Standard 16), using and maintaining technological products and systems (Standard 12), and problem solving and trouble-shooting (part of Standard 10). The sample items suggest that the assessment requires that examinees have basic knowledge of fundamental scientific concepts and cause-and-effect relationships in technological systems. The items also require a fairly high degree of reading skill, which may pose challenges for examinees learning English. The scenarios presented

Index

Computer-based assessment methods, 161–174
　computer-based adaptive assessments, 162–164
　computer-based and web-based games, 168–169
　electronic portfolios, 170–171
　electronic questionnaires, 171–172
　simulations, 164–168
Computer-based games, 168–169
Computer literacy, 169
Concept inventories, 85
Conceptual change, 78–80
Conceptual ecology, 79
Conceptual framework for identifying design criteria, 51–56
　assessment matrix for technological literacy, 53
　cognitive dimensions of assessment frameworks, 55
Conceptual frameworks, 51–56
　developing, 5–6
Conceptual understanding, 84
Consensus, 272–273
Constraints, identifying, 45–48
Constructed-response formats, 70
Construction technologies, 31, 250
　benchmarks for grades 3–5, 250
　benchmarks for grades 6–8, 250
　benchmarks for grades 9–12, 250
　benchmarks for grades K–2, 250
Content knowledge, 100
Content standards, reflecting appropriate, 50
Core concepts of technology, 230–231
　benchmarks for grades 3–5, 230
　benchmarks for grades 6–8, 230–231
　benchmarks for grades 9–12, 231
　benchmarks for grades K–2, 230
Criterion-referenced interpretations, 72
Critical thinking, 112
　and the decision-making dimension, 111–112
　by a technologically literate person, 34
Cultural, social, economic, and political effects of technology, 232–233
　benchmarks for grades 3–5, 232
　benchmarks for grades 6–8, 233
　benchmarks for grades 9–12, 233
　benchmarks for grades K–2, 232
Currency, reviewing items for, 50

D

Data from the NAEP long-term science assessment, 101
DBS. *See* Design-Based Science
Decision making, 112
　by a technologically literate person, 34
Defining technological literacy, 29–40
　assessing technological literacy, 38–39
　attitudes and the assessment of technological literacy, 36
　attitudes toward technology, 36–37
　the designed world, 30–31
　dimensions of technological literacy, 37–38
Design and systems, 214–215
　benchmarks for grades 3–5, 214
　benchmarks for grades 6–8, 214–215
　benchmarks for grades 9–12, 215
　benchmarks for grades K–2, 214
Design attributes, 236–237
　benchmarks for grades 3–5, 237
　benchmarks for grades 6–8, 237
　benchmarks for grades 9–12, 237
　benchmarks for grades K–2, 236
Design-Based Science (DBS), 95, 274–277
　background, 274
　committee observations, 276–277
　sample items, 275–276
　scope, 275
Design criteria, 48–56
　avoiding bias and accommodating disabilities, 50
　conceptual framework, 51–56
　encouraging higher-order thinking, 50, 280, 335
　gathering data useful to the purpose, 49
　general criteria, 48–50
　identifying, 48–56
　meeting a specific purpose, 48–49
　possible purposes for assessments, 49
　reflecting appropriate content standards, 50
　reviewing items for currency, 50
　using insights from cognitive science about how people learn, 49–50
Design process, 41–59
　applying, 239–241
　interative, 43
　linear steps in, 43–59
　standards related to, 236–239
　and technology, 271

Mental models, assessing, 84
Metacognition, 77–78
Mid-Continent Research for Education
    and Learning (MCREL), 142
MMOGs. *See* Massive, multiplayer, on-
    line games
Modified Angoff standards-setting, 72
"Monkey Wrench Conspiracy," 168
Multiple-Choice Instrument for
    Monitoring Views on Science-
    Technology-Society Topics,
    96, 313–317
  background, 313–314
  committee observations, 316–317
  sample items, 314–316
  scope, 314

N

NAEP. *See* National Assessment of
    Educational Progress
NAGB. *See* National Assessment
    Governing Board
National Academies Press (NAP), 17
National Academy of Engineering, 15,
    25, 192–193
National Adult Literacy Survey, 185
National Assessment Governing Board
    (NAGB), 8, 13–14, 51, 180–
    181, 183, 191
National Assessment of Educational
    Progress (NAEP), 5, 8, 20,
    51–54, 71, 101, 136–138,
    178–181
National Center for Education
    Statistics, 146n, 185
National Center for Technological
    Literacy, 114
National Council for Excellence in
    Critical Thinking, 112
National Education Association, 24
National Household Education Survey
    (NHES), 10, 185–186
National Institute of Standards and
    Technology, 13, 189
National Institutes of Health, 10, 186
National Opinion Research Center, 185
National Research Council (NRC), 15,
    25, 38, 66, 131, 192–193
National-sample assessment of teachers,
    140–145
  administration and logistics, 143
  content, 142–143

  description and rationale, 140–141
  obstacles to implementation, 144
  performance levels, 143
  performance rubric for sample task, 141
  purpose, 142
  sample assessment items, 144–145
National Science Board (NSB), 105,
    148, 327–328
National Science Education Standards, 30,
    131, 137, 142, 207–212
  abilities to distinguish between
    natural objects and objects
    made by humans, 212
  standards related to "science and
    technology," 207–209
  understanding about science and
    technology, 210–211
National Science Foundation (NSF), 1,
    8–14, 19, 25, 41, 180–181,
    184–188, 191
"The nature of technology," standards
    related to, 212–218
NCLB. *See* No Child Left Behind Act
New York Hall of Science, 156
New York State Intermediate
    Assessment in Technology,
    96, 317–319
  background, 317
  committee observations, 319
  sample items, 318–319
  scope, 317–318
NHES. *See* National Household
    Education Survey
No Child Left Behind Act (NCLB), 9,
    14, 24, 45, 60, 72, 129, 133–
    134, 143, 179, 183
Norm-referenced interpretations, 71
North Carolina State University, 105, 273
NRC. *See* National Research Council
NSB. *See* National Science Board
NSF. *See* National Science Foundation
Numeracy, 33

O

Obstacles to assessing technological
    literacy, 24–25
Online surveys, 171
Opportunities for assessment, 7–10,
    176–186
  findings and recommendations for
    K–12 students, 8–9, 95–96,
    178–181

norm-referenced interpretations, 71
standards-based interpretation, 72
Research
conducting relevant, 56
on learning, 11–12
Research on technological learning, 80–86
concept inventories, 85
learning related to engineering, 83–86
learning related to technology, 80–83
Resource constraints, 144
Review, of instruments, 93–126

S

Sample cases, from theory to practice, 127–160
Science and Engineering Indicators, 20, 105, 113, 184
"Science and technology"
standards related to, 207–209
understanding about, 210–211
Science and Technology—Public Attitudes and Public Understanding, 97, 327–330
background, 327–328
committee observations, 329–330
sample items, 328–329
scope, 328
Science for All Americans, 35, 190
Science/technology/society (STS) topics, 314
Scientific literacy, 33
Scope of technology, 229
benchmark for grades 3–5, 229
benchmark for grades 6–8, 229
benchmark for grades 9–12, 229
benchmark for grades K–2, 229
Selected-response formats, 69
Shen, Benjamin, 147
Sim City™ software, 111, 292
Simulations, 164–168
SIPI. *See* Student Individualized Performance Inventory
Society, technology-dependent, 195
Society's role in the development and use of technology, 234–235
benchmarks for grades 3–5, 234
benchmarks for grades 6–8, 235
benchmarks for grades 9–12, 235
benchmarks for grades K–2, 234
Software piracy, 83
Solutions, identifying potential, 57–58

Stakeholders, input from, 47
Stand-alone testing, 60
Standards-based interpretation, 72
Standards for Educational and Psychological Testing, 162
Standards for technological literacy, 229–250
Standards for Technological Literacy: Content for the Study of Technology, 22, 26, 29, 36, 42, 51, 54, 65, 93, 104, 106, 131, 137, 142, 185, 193
Standards related to abilities for a technological world, 239–243
applying the design process, 239–241
assessing the impact of products and systems, 242–243
using and maintaining technological products and systems, 241–242
Standards related to design, 236–239
the attributes of design, 236–237
engineering design, 237–238
role of troubleshooting, research and development, invention and innovation, and experimentation in problem solving, 238–239
Standards related to "science and technology," 207–209
abilities of technological design, 207–209
Standards related to technology and society, 232–236
the cultural, social, economic, and political effects of technology, 232–233
the effects of technology on the environment, 233–234
influence of technology on history, 235–236
the role of society in the development and use of technology, 234–235
Standards related to the design world, 243–250
agricultural and related biotechnologies, 244–245
construction technologies, 250
energy and power technologies, 245–246
information and communication technologies, 246–247
manufacturing technologies, 248–249
medical technologies, 243–244
transportation technologies, 247–248

National Science Education
Standards, 207–212
standards for technological literacy,
229–250
Test of Technological Literacy, 96, 336–
337
background, 336
committee observations, 337
sample items, 336–337
scope, 336
Test-taking skills, 69
Testing, defined, 64
Testing and measurement, 64–72
avoiding bias, 68
basic vocabulary, 64–65
central themes, 66–69
ensuring fairness, 68–69
measurement issues, 69–71
purpose defined, 66–67
reporting of results, 71–72
selecting content, 67
*Thinking Through Technology: The Path
Between Engineering and
Philosophy,* 54
TIDEE. *See* Transferable Integrated
Design Engineering
Education Consortium
TIMSS. *See* Trends in Mathematics and
Science Study
TL50—Technological Literacy
Instrument, 96, 337–339
background, 337–338
committee observations, 339
sample items, 338–339
scope, 338
"Trading off," 57–58
Training, in administering tests, 135
Transferable Integrated Design
Engineering Education
(TIDEE) Consortium, 103,
277
Transportation technologies, 31, 247–248
benchmarks for grades 3–5, 247–248
benchmarks for grades 6–8, 248
benchmarks for grades 9–12, 248
benchmarks for grades K–2, 247
Trends in Mathematics and Science
Study (TIMSS), 8, 71, 179–
180

U

Understanding about science and
technology, 210–211
benchmarks for grades 5–8, 210–211
benchmarks for grades 9–12, 211
benchmarks for grades K–4, 210
University of Michigan, 185–186
University of Southern California, 166
U.S. Census Bureau, 146n
U.S. Department of Defense, 10, 163,
186
U.S. Department of Education, 8–15,
72, 180, 183–188, 191–193

V

Validity, defined, 65
Verbal protocol analysis, 83
Views on Science, Technology, and
Society (VOSTS), 114–115
Visualization, development of, 82
Vocabulary of testing and measurement,
64–65
assessment defined, 64
errors of measurement defined, 65
measurement defined, 64
reliability defined, 64–65
testing defined, 64
validity defined, 65
VOSTS. *See* Views on Science,
Technology, and Society

W

Web-based games, 168–169
WestEd, 179, 185
WorkKeys—Applied Technology, 96,
106, 111, 340–345
background, 340
committee observations, 345
sample items, 341–345
scope, 341
World of design, standards related to,
243–250